Mometrix
TEST PREPARATION

STAAR

Test Prep Guide
Grade 6
Math

I0892939

DEAR FUTURE EXAM SUCCESS STORY

First of all, **THANK YOU** for purchasing Mometrix study materials!

Second, congratulations! You are one of the few determined test-takers who are committed to doing whatever it takes to excel on your exam. **You have come to the right place.** We developed these study materials with one goal in mind: to deliver you the information you need in a format that's concise and easy to use.

In addition to optimizing your guide for the content of the test, we've outlined our recommended steps for breaking down the preparation process into small, attainable goals so you can make sure you stay on track.

We've also analyzed the entire test-taking process, identifying the most common pitfalls and showing how you can overcome them and be ready for any curveball the test throws you.

Standardized testing is one of the biggest obstacles on your road to success, which only increases the importance of doing well in the high-pressure, high-stakes environment of test day. Your results on this test could have a significant impact on your future, and this guide provides the information and practical advice to help you achieve your full potential on test day.

Your success is our success

We would love to hear from you! If you would like to share the story of your exam success or if you have any questions or comments in regard to our products, please contact us at **800-673-8175** or **support@mometrix.com**.

Thanks again for your business and we wish you continued success!

Sincerely,
The Mometrix Test Preparation Team

Written and edited by the Mometrix Exam Secrets Test Prep Team
Printed in the United States of America

TABLE OF CONTENTS

Introduction

Thank you for purchasing this resource! You have made the choice to prepare yourself for a test that could have a huge impact on your future, and this guide is designed to help you be fully ready for test day. Obviously, it's important to have a solid understanding of the test material, but you also need to be prepared for the unique environment and stressors of the test, so that you can perform to the best of your abilities.

For this purpose, the first section that appears in this guide is the **Success Strategies**. We've devoted countless hours to meticulously researching what works and what doesn't, and we've boiled down our findings to the four most impactful steps you can take to improve your performance on the test. We start at the beginning with study planning and move through the preparation process, all the way to the testing strategies that will help you get the most out of what you know when you're finally sitting in front of the test.

We recommend that you start preparing for your test as far in advance as possible. However, if you've bought this guide as a last-minute study resource and only have a few days before your test, we recommend that you skip over the first two Success Strategies since they address a long-term study plan.

If you struggle with **test anxiety**, we strongly encourage you to check out our recommendations for how you can overcome it. Test anxiety is a formidable foe, but it can be beaten, and we want to make sure you have the tools you need to defeat it.

Strategy #1 – Plan Big, Study Small

There's a lot riding on your performance. If you want to ace this test, you're going to need to keep your skills sharp and the material fresh in your mind. You need a plan that lets you review everything you need to know while still fitting in your schedule. We'll break this strategy down into three categories.

Information Organization

Start with the information you already have: the official test outline. From this, you can make a complete list of all the concepts you need to cover before the test. Organize these concepts into groups that can be studied together, and create a list of any related vocabulary you need to learn so you can brush up on any difficult terms. You'll want to keep this vocabulary list handy once you actually start studying since you may need to add to it along the way.

Time Management

Once you have your set of study concepts, decide how to spread them out over the time you have left before the test. Break your study plan into small, clear goals so you have a manageable task for each day and know exactly what you're doing. Then just focus on one small step at a time. When you manage your time this way, you don't need to spend hours at a time studying. Studying a small block of content for a short period each day helps you retain information better and avoid stressing over how much you have left to do. You can relax knowing that you have a plan to cover everything in time. In order for this strategy to be effective though, you have to start studying early and stick to your schedule. Avoid the exhaustion and futility that comes from last-minute cramming!

Study Environment

The environment you study in has a big impact on your learning. Studying in a coffee shop, while probably more enjoyable, is not likely to be as fruitful as studying in a quiet room. It's important to keep distractions to a minimum. You're only planning to study for a short block of time, so make the most of it. Don't pause to check your phone or get up to find a snack. It's also important to **avoid multitasking**. Research has consistently shown that multitasking will make your studying dramatically less effective. Your study area should also be comfortable and well-lit so you don't have the distraction of straining your eyes or sitting on an uncomfortable chair.

The time of day you study is also important. You want to be rested and alert. Don't wait until just before bedtime. Study when you'll be most likely to comprehend and remember. Even better, if you know what time of day your test will be, set that time aside for study. That way your brain will be used to working on that subject at that specific time and you'll have a better chance of recalling information.

Finally, it can be helpful to team up with others who are studying for the same test. Your actual studying should be done in as isolated an environment as possible, but the work of organizing the information and setting up the study plan can be divided up. In between study sessions, you can discuss with your teammates the concepts that you're all studying and quiz each other on the details. Just be sure that your teammates are as serious about the test as you are. If you find that your study time is being replaced with social time, you might need to find a new team.

Strategy #2 – Make Your Studying Count

You're devoting a lot of time and effort to preparing for this test, so you want to be absolutely certain it will pay off. This means doing more than just reading the content and hoping you can remember it on test day. It's important to make every minute of study count. There are two main areas you can focus on to make your studying count.

Retention

It doesn't matter how much time you study if you can't remember the material. You need to make sure you are retaining the concepts. To check your retention of the information you're learning, try recalling it at later times with minimal prompting. Try carrying around flashcards and glance at one or two from time to time or ask a friend who's also studying for the test to quiz you.

To enhance your retention, look for ways to put the information into practice so that you can apply it rather than simply recalling it. If you're using the information in practical ways, it will be much easier to remember. Similarly, it helps to solidify a concept in your mind if you're not only reading it to yourself but also explaining it to someone else. Ask a friend to let you teach them about a concept you're a little shaky on (or speak aloud to an imaginary audience if necessary). As you try to summarize, define, give examples, and answer your friend's questions, you'll understand the concepts better and they will stay with you longer. Finally, step back for a big picture view and ask yourself how each piece of information fits with the whole subject. When you link the different concepts together and see them working together as a whole, it's easier to remember the individual components.

Finally, practice showing your work on any multi-step problems, even if you're just studying. Writing out each step you take to solve a problem will help solidify the process in your mind, and you'll be more likely to remember it during the test.

Modality

Modality simply refers to the means or method by which you study. Choosing a study modality that fits your own individual learning style is crucial. No two people learn best in exactly the same way, so it's important to know your strengths and use them to your advantage.

For example, if you learn best by visualization, focus on visualizing a concept in your mind and draw an image or a diagram. Try color-coding your notes, illustrating them, or creating symbols that will trigger your mind to recall a learned concept. If you learn best by hearing or discussing information, find a study partner who learns the same way or read aloud to yourself. Think about how to put the information in your own words. Imagine that you are giving a lecture on the topic and record yourself so you can listen to it later.

For any learning style, flashcards can be helpful. Organize the information so you can take advantage of spare moments to review. Underline key words or phrases. Use different colors for different categories. Mnemonic devices (such as creating a short list in which every item starts with the same letter) can also help with retention. Find what works best for you and use it to store the information in your mind most effectively and easily.

Strategy #3 – Practice the Right Way

Your success on test day depends not only on how many hours you put into preparing, but also on whether you prepared the right way. It's good to check along the way to see if your studying is paying off. One of the most effective ways to do this is by taking practice tests to evaluate your progress. Practice tests are useful because they show exactly where you need to improve. Every time you take a practice test, pay special attention to these three groups of questions:

- The questions you got wrong
- The questions you had to guess on, even if you guessed right
- The questions you found difficult or slow to work through

This will show you exactly what your weak areas are, and where you need to devote more study time. Ask yourself why each of these questions gave you trouble. Was it because you didn't understand the material? Was it because you didn't remember the vocabulary? Do you need more repetitions on this type of question to build speed and confidence? Dig into those questions and figure out how you can strengthen your weak areas as you go back to review the material.

Additionally, many practice tests have a section explaining the answer choices. It can be tempting to read the explanation and think that you now have a good understanding of the concept. However, an explanation likely only covers part of the question's broader context. Even if the explanation makes perfect sense, **go back and investigate** every concept related to the question until you're positive you have a thorough understanding.

As you go along, keep in mind that the practice test is just that: practice. Memorizing these questions and answers will not be very helpful on the actual test because it is unlikely to have any of the same exact questions. If you only know the right answers to the sample questions, you won't be prepared for the real thing. **Study the concepts** until you understand them fully, and then you'll be able to answer any question that shows up on the test.

It's important to wait on the practice tests until you're ready. If you take a test on your first day of study, you may be overwhelmed by the amount of material covered and how much you need to learn. Work up to it gradually.

On test day, you'll need to be prepared for answering questions, managing your time, and using the test-taking strategies you've learned. It's a lot to balance, like a mental marathon that will have a big impact on your future. Like training for a marathon, you'll need to start slowly and work your way up. When test day arrives, you'll be ready.

Start with the strategies you've read in the first two Success Strategies—plan your course and study in the way that works best for you. If you have time, consider using multiple study resources to get different approaches to the same concepts. It can be helpful to see difficult concepts from more than one angle. Then find a good source for practice tests. Many times, the test website will suggest potential study resources or provide sample tests.

Test-Taking Strategies

This section contains a list of test-taking strategies that you may find helpful as you work through the test. By taking what you know and applying logical thought, you can maximize your chances of answering any question correctly!

It is very important to realize that every question is different and every person is different: no single strategy will work on every question, and no single strategy will work for every person. That's why we've included all of them here, so you can try them out and determine which ones work best for different types of questions and which ones work best for you.

Question Strategies

✓ Read Carefully

Read the question and the answer choices carefully. Don't miss the question because you misread the terms. You have plenty of time to read each question thoroughly and make sure you understand what is being asked. Yet a happy medium must be attained, so don't waste too much time. You must read carefully and efficiently.

✓ Contextual Clues

Look for contextual clues. If the question includes a word you are not familiar with, look at the immediate context for some indication of what the word might mean. Contextual clues can often give you all the information you need to decipher the meaning of an unfamiliar word. Even if you can't determine the meaning, you may be able to narrow down the possibilities enough to make a solid guess at the answer to the question.

✓ Prefixes

If you're having trouble with a word in the question or answer choices, try dissecting it. Take advantage of every clue that the word might include. Prefixes can be a huge help. Usually, they allow you to determine a basic meaning. *Pre-* means before, *post-* means after, *pro-* is positive, *de-* is negative. From prefixes, you can get an idea of the general meaning of the word and try to put it into context.

✓ Hedge Words

Watch out for critical hedge words, such as *likely, may, can, often, almost, mostly, usually, generally, rarely*, and *sometimes*. Question writers insert these hedge phrases to cover every possibility. Often an answer choice will be wrong simply because it leaves no room for exception. Be on guard for answer choices that have definitive words such as *exactly* and *always*.

✓ Switchback Words

Stay alert for *switchbacks*. These are the words and phrases frequently used to alert you to shifts in thought. The most common switchback words are *but, although*, and *however*. Others include *nevertheless, on the other hand, even though, while, in spite of, despite*, and *regardless of*. Switchback words are important to catch because they can change the direction of the question or an answer choice.

☑ Face Value

When in doubt, use common sense. Accept the situation in the problem at face value. Don't read too much into it. These problems will not require you to make wild assumptions. If you have to go beyond creativity and warp time or space in order to have an answer choice fit the question, then you should move on and consider the other answer choices. These are normal problems rooted in reality. The applicable relationship or explanation may not be readily apparent, but it is there for you to figure out. Use your common sense to interpret anything that isn't clear.

Answer Choice Strategies

☑ Answer Selection

The most thorough way to pick an answer choice is to identify and eliminate wrong answers until only one is left, then confirm it is the correct answer. Sometimes an answer choice may immediately seem right, but be careful. The test writers will usually put more than one reasonable answer choice on each question, so take a second to read all of them and make sure that the other choices are not equally obvious. As long as you have time left, it is better to read every answer choice than to pick the first one that looks right without checking the others.

☑ Answer Choice Families

An answer choice family consists of two (in rare cases, three) answer choices that are very similar in construction and cannot all be true at the same time. If you see two answer choices that are direct opposites or parallels, one of them is usually the correct answer. For instance, if one answer choice says that quantity *x* increases and another either says that quantity *x* decreases (opposite) or says that quantity *y* increases (parallel), then those answer choices would fall into the same family. An answer choice that doesn't match the construction of the answer choice family is more likely to be incorrect. Most questions will not have answer choice families, but when they do appear, you should be prepared to recognize them.

☑ Eliminate Answers

Eliminate answer choices as soon as you realize they are wrong, but make sure you consider all possibilities. If you are eliminating answer choices and realize that the last one you are left with is also wrong, don't panic. Start over and consider each choice again. There may be something you missed the first time that you will realize on the second pass.

☑ Avoid Fact Traps

Don't be distracted by an answer choice that is factually true but doesn't answer the question. You are looking for the choice that answers the question. Stay focused on what the question is asking for so you don't accidentally pick an answer that is true but incorrect. Always go back to the question and make sure the answer choice you've selected actually answers the question and is not merely a true statement.

☑ Extreme Statements

In general, you should avoid answers that put forth extreme actions as standard practice or proclaim controversial ideas as established fact. An answer choice that states the "process should be used in certain situations, if..." is much more likely to be correct than one that states the "process should be discontinued completely." The first is a calm rational statement and doesn't even make a definitive, uncompromising stance, using a hedge word *if* to provide wiggle room, whereas the second choice is far more extreme.

⊘ BENCHMARK

As you read through the answer choices and you come across one that seems to answer the question well, mentally select that answer choice. This is not your final answer, but it's the one that will help you evaluate the other answer choices. The one that you selected is your benchmark or standard for judging each of the other answer choices. Every other answer choice must be compared to your benchmark. That choice is correct until proven otherwise by another answer choice beating it. If you find a better answer, then that one becomes your new benchmark. Once you've decided that no other choice answers the question as well as your benchmark, you have your final answer.

⊘ PREDICT THE ANSWER

Before you even start looking at the answer choices, it is often best to try to predict the answer. When you come up with the answer on your own, it is easier to avoid distractions and traps because you will know exactly what to look for. The right answer choice is unlikely to be word-for-word what you came up with, but it should be a close match. Even if you are confident that you have the right answer, you should still take the time to read each option before moving on.

General Strategies

⊘ TOUGH QUESTIONS

If you are stumped on a problem or it appears too hard or too difficult, don't waste time. Move on! Remember though, if you can quickly check for obviously incorrect answer choices, your chances of guessing correctly are greatly improved. Before you completely give up, at least try to knock out a couple of possible answers. Eliminate what you can and then guess at the remaining answer choices before moving on.

⊘ CHECK YOUR WORK

Since you will probably not know every term listed and the answer to every question, it is important that you get credit for the ones that you do know. Don't miss any questions through careless mistakes. If at all possible, try to take a second to look back over your answer selection and make sure you've selected the correct answer choice and haven't made a costly careless mistake (such as marking an answer choice that you didn't mean to mark). This quick double check should more than pay for itself in caught mistakes for the time it costs.

⊘ DON'T RUSH

It is very easy to make errors when you are in a hurry. Maintaining a fast pace in answering questions is pointless if it makes you miss questions that you would have gotten right otherwise. Test writers like to include distracting information and wrong answers that seem right. Taking a little extra time to avoid careless mistakes can make all the difference in your test score. Find a pace that allows you to be confident in the answers that you select.

⊘ KEEP MOVING

Panicking will not help you pass the test, so do your best to stay calm and keep moving. Taking deep breaths and going through the answer elimination steps you practiced can help to break through a stress barrier and keep your pace.

Final Notes

The combination of a solid foundation of content knowledge and the confidence that comes from practicing your plan for applying that knowledge is the key to maximizing your performance on test day. As your foundation of content knowledge is built up and strengthened, you'll find that the strategies included in this chapter become more and more effective in helping you quickly sift through the distractions and traps of the test to isolate the correct answer.

Now that you're preparing to move forward into the test content chapters of this book, be sure to keep your goal in mind. As you read, think about how you will be able to apply this information on the test. If you've already seen sample questions for the test and you have an idea of the question format and style, try to come up with questions of your own that you can answer based on what you're reading. This will give you valuable practice applying your knowledge in the same ways you can expect to on test day.

Good luck and good studying!

Number and Operations

Classifying Numbers

Whole numbers, **integers**, and **rational numbers** are three categories used to classify numbers. Let's explore these categories from broad to specific. The broadest category is rational numbers.

Rational Numbers

Rational numbers are all numbers that can be written as a fraction. **Rational numbers** can be positive or negative and include fractions, improper fractions, terminating decimals, and some repeating decimals. If it can be written as a fraction, it is rational. Some examples include 6, which can be written as $\frac{6}{1}$; -23, which can be written as $\frac{-23}{1}$; $\frac{1}{4}$, which is already written as a fraction, as is $\frac{-7}{2}$; 0.46, which can be written as $\frac{46}{100}$ or $\frac{23}{50}$; $0.3\overline{3}$, which can be written as $\frac{1}{3}$; and $\sqrt{64}$, which can be written as 8, or $\frac{8}{1}$. The number π, or 3.14159265... is not a rational number because it is a decimal that continues infinitely without repeating and cannot be written as a fraction. It is an **irrational number**.

Review Video: Rational and Irrational Numbers
Visit mometrix.com/academy and enter code: 280645

Integers

Integers are numbers that can be written without a fraction or a decimal. They can be positive, negative, or zero. Some examples include 7; -56; $\frac{8}{4}$, which can be written as 2; and $-\sqrt{81}$, which can be written as -9. If it can be written as a number without a fraction or decimal component, it is an integer. All integers are rational numbers, because they can be written as a fraction, but not all rational numbers are integers, because not all of them can be written *without* a fraction.

Whole Numbers

Whole numbers include the positive integers and zero. 0, 1, 2, 3... and so on, are all whole numbers. Some whole numbers can be written as fractions, like $\frac{7}{1}$, or $\frac{9}{3}$, but because they can be written without the fraction component and they are not negative, they are whole numbers. So, rational numbers are the largest category including fractions, integers, and whole numbers. Integers are the next largest category including negative numbers and whole numbers. Whole numbers are the smallest category, including only zero and positive numbers that are not fractions.

Review Video: Classification of Numbers
Visit mometrix.com/academy and enter code: 461071

Opposites and Absolute Value

A number's **opposite** is the number that is opposite to it on a number line or has an opposite sign. The opposite of -53 is 53. The opposite of 187 is -187. The opposite of a number can be found by multiplying the number by -1. They both have the same distance from zero on a number line, just in different directions. Opposite numbers have the same **absolute value**.

The **absolute value** of a number is its distance from zero. Absolute value is notated by placing a vertical line on each side of a number. For instance, $|-46|$ means the absolute value of -46. We know the names of numbers based on their distance from zero. Numbers and their opposite have the same distance from zero. -2 and 2 have a distance of 2 from zero. So, the absolute value of -2 is 2, or $|-2| = 2$. Also, the absolute value of 2 is 2, or $|2| = 2$. This may be noted by words, or with symbols. You may see something like "$| - 89| = 89$," or "the absolute value of $|543|$ is 543," or "find the absolute value of $-\frac{1}{3}$ on a number line." In the last case, you would select $\frac{1}{3}$ on a number line.

Zero is its own opposite. The absolute value of zero is zero.

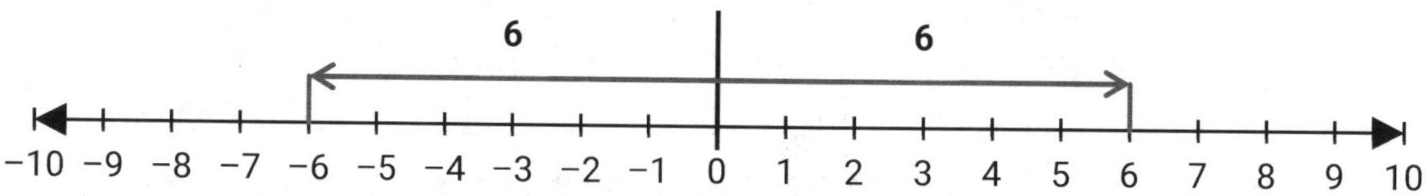

Review Video: Absolute Value
Visit mometrix.com/academy and enter code: 314669

Rational Numbers

Locating Rational Numbers on a Number Line

When locating the placement of integers and rational numbers on a number line, we use whole numbers and negative numbers as a guide. We can easily locate, compare, and order whole numbers like 0, 1, 2, 5, 9, and 258 on a number line. They lie in ascending order to the right of zero. Negative numbers lie on the number line to the left of zero in ascending order. An integer that is in the form of an improper fraction or square root, such as $\frac{12}{3}$ or $-\sqrt{49}$, should be converted into its whole number or negative number counterpart, so $\frac{12}{3}$ simplifies to 4, and $-\sqrt{49}$ simplifies to -7, and can now be placed appropriately on a number line.

Rational numbers can be slightly more complicated. When you are given a rational number, a number that can be written as a fraction, it is best to convert it to a number that is easy for you to use. Are you more familiar with the values of fractions or decimals? That is a decision only you can make. Regardless of which you choose, convert the rational number to a number that is easier to work with, and find its place on the number line.

Example

Place $-\frac{8}{3}$ on the number line.

There are three strategies to approach this task:

Strategy 1: Convert to a decimal using division.

$$\begin{array}{r} 2.6\overline{6} \\ 3\,\overline{)\,8.00} \\ \underline{6} \\ 2\,0 \end{array}$$

$$\begin{array}{r} \underline{18} \\ 20 \\ \underline{18} \\ 2 \end{array}$$

$$-\frac{8}{3} = -2.\overline{6}$$

Given this value, we can determine that this number belongs to the left of the number line because it is less than zero. It is between −3 and −2. And we can divide the section between −3 and −2 into tenths, and estimate that this value is slightly to the right of −2.7.

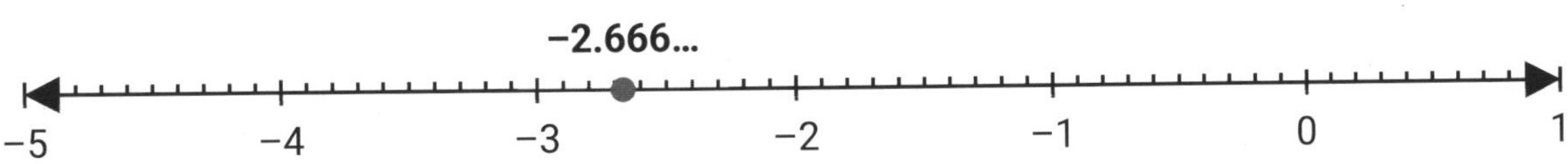

Strategy 2: Convert to a mixed number.

Ask yourself, how many times will 3 go into 8 evenly, or how many $\frac{3}{3}$ are in $\frac{8}{3}$?

3 goes into 8 two times and has a remainder of 2.

In other words, there are two $\frac{3}{3}$ in $\frac{8}{3}$ with $\frac{2}{3}$ left over.

$$-\frac{8}{3} = -2\frac{2}{3}$$

Given this value, we can determine that this number is between −3 and −2. We can divide this section further into thirds, and count two to the left to place this value at $-2\frac{2}{3}$.

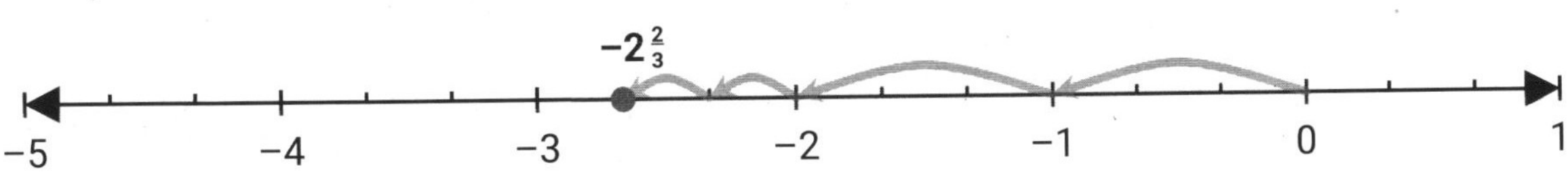

Strategy 3:

Place $-\frac{8}{3}$ on the number line using thirds.

Given this value, we can determine that this value is less than one and will be to the left of 0. We can also determine that each section between whole numbers should be divided into 3 sections to represent thirds.

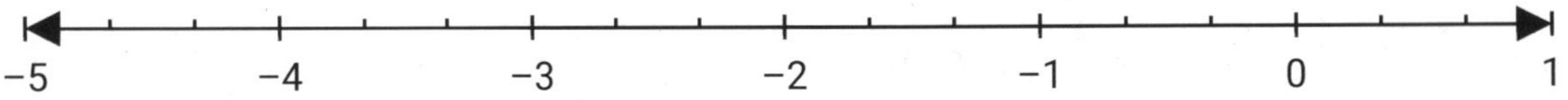

We can now count 8 thirds to the left because we are dealing with a negative fraction.

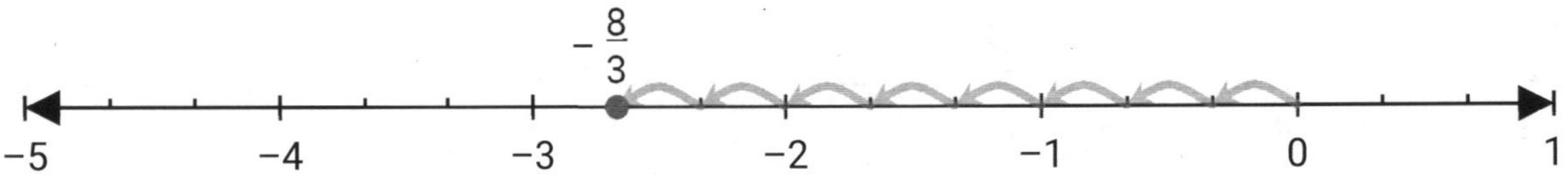

Each strategy will give you the same approximate placement on the number line. The strategy that is chosen is dependent on which type of value is the simplest for you. Each person has number preferences. Choose the best strategy for you based on your preferences. Which strategy was easier for you to follow? Which version of the same value (decimal, mixed number, or improper fraction) was simpler for you to estimate? You may choose more than one strategy!

Comparing and Ordering Rational Numbers

Comparing numbers involves making decisions about whether one number is greater than, less than, or equal to another. Ordering numbers involves making comparisons between more than two numbers to order them from least to greatest, or greatest to least. When you compare and order a set of rational numbers, it is important to first identify where you can make simple judgments. Can you identify the negative and positive numbers? That can help narrow down which numbers are greater and less than others. Can you identify a number that is much larger or much smaller than the rest of the set of numbers? Great! Use your knowledge of numbers to make some judgments and narrow down the set from there. Each set of numbers is different, and you will have to make observations and judgments based on the values given.

Once you have made preliminary judgments, next it is time to rewrite the remaining values as a representation that is easy to work with and convert them appropriately. The goal is to have forms that are easy to visualize so you may make comparisons between numbers. When you are given a list of fractions, it is often helpful to find a common denominator. When working with a mix of decimals and fractions, it is often helpful to convert the values to a common format: all fractions or all decimals. When you are given a rational number using an exponent or a square root, express these numbers in their integer form. Remember, place value is very important when comparing and ordering numbers, specifically integers and decimals.

Do not make the mistake of comparing numbers correctly but not ordering them the way the question is asked. Pay attention and double check if the question is asking for numbers to be ordered from greatest to least, or least to greatest.

Review Video: Ordering Rational Numbers
Visit mometrix.com/academy and enter code: 419578

EXAMPLE

Order the values from greatest to least.

$$-3.48, -\frac{3}{5}, 4, \frac{17}{4}, -3\frac{1}{2}$$

Step 1: Start by making some judgments about the numbers in this list. We can see that there are some negative values and some positive values. Using this judgment, we can determine that 4 and $\frac{17}{4}$ are greater than the other values just by their signs alone. These two values will be first in our list because they are the greatest. Let's compare these values first to create the beginning of our list.

4 is a value that is easy to work with, but $\frac{17}{4}$ is a little tougher. This should be converted to a number that is easier to work with. You may choose to perform the division problem, $17 \div 4$, to find this value as a decimal. Or, you may choose to find the mixed number form of this improper fraction. Let's find both.

Converting to decimal:

$$
\begin{array}{r}
4.25 \\
4\,\overline{)\,17.00} \\
\underline{16} \\
1\,0 \\
\underline{8} \\
20 \\
\underline{20} \\
0
\end{array}
$$

So, $\frac{17}{4} = 4.25$.

Converting to mixed number:

To find the whole number, we can ask ourselves, how many times does 4 go into 17 evenly, or how many times does $\frac{4}{4}$ go into $\frac{17}{4}$? 4 times, so 4 is our whole number.

Now, to find the fractional part of this number, we can ask, what is left over. Since $\frac{4}{4} \times 4 = \frac{16}{4}$, we can subtract and find that $\frac{17}{4} - \frac{16}{4} = \frac{1}{4}$. So, 4 is our whole number, and $\frac{1}{4}$ is our fraction.

This means that $\frac{17}{4} = 4\frac{1}{4}$.

Step 2: Now that we have a decimal or mixed number, we can compare this value to 4. We make the judgment that $4 < \frac{17}{4}$.

Now we have our first two values. We are ordering numbers from greatest to least, so the greatest value is $\frac{17}{4}$ and the next greatest value is 4.

Step 3: Continue to make judgments about the remaining values. We can see that there are two values that include −3 as a whole number and then a negative proper fraction. Without doing any conversions, we can determine that the numbers that have −3 as a whole number are smaller than the negative proper fraction. This tells us that $-\frac{3}{5} > -3.47$ and $-\frac{3}{5} > 3\frac{1}{2}$.

We can now include this value to our list from greatest to least. So far, we know:

$$\frac{17}{4} > 4 > -\frac{3}{5}$$

Step 4: Compare the remaining values. We only have two values left, –3.48 and $-3\frac{1}{2}$. We can now make judgments on these values. To compare these numbers, we can convert them both to decimals, convert them both to fractions, or use our number sense. You may be able to look at these values and make an automatic judgment. Let's convert our values to decimals to make sure. I know that $\frac{1}{2}$ is equivalent to 0.5, so I can say that $-3\frac{1}{2} = -3.5$.

Now that our values are in similar forms, we can compare.

When dealing with negative numbers, remember the "larger" the number, the smaller the value. Given -3.48 and -3.5, we will start with the largest place value and compare. We can say that they each have a 3 in the ones place, so we will move to the tenths. The tenths are different. –3.48 has a 4 in the tenths place and –3.5 has a 5 in the tenths place. Because these are negative numbers, we can determine that $-3.48 > -3.5$, or $-3.5 < -3.48$.

Step 5: Review the order and rewrite the values.

We are asked to order this list from greatest to least and we have all the information needed to do this. We have found that $\frac{17}{4} > 4 > -\frac{3}{5} > -3.48 > -3.5$. We can now order these values from greatest to least.

$$\frac{17}{4}, 4, -\frac{3}{5}, -3.48, -3\frac{1}{2}$$

The Four Operations

It is very important to be able to **add**, **subtract**, **multiply**, and **divide** integers quickly and easily. This includes operations with positive and negative numbers. Addition, subtraction, multiplication, and division with positive numbers should be automatic. Now you will use what you know about whole number operations to help you with integer operations involving negative numbers. When you are solving operations with integers, the most common way to get a question wrong is by mixing up your signs. There are a few rules that you can use to remember and practice frequently so the process is solid and automatic.

Addition

When you add two positive numbers, your answer will be positive.

$$7 + 32 = 39$$

When you add two negative numbers, your answer will be negative.

$$-7 + (-32) = -39$$

When you add a negative number to a positive number, the total value will be less than the positive number. Adding a negative number is the same as subtracting the positive version of that negative number.

$$= 25 + (-5)$$
$$= 25 - 5$$

$$= 20$$

When you add a positive number to a negative number, the total value will be greater than the negative number. When adding a positive number to a negative number, use subtraction.

$$\begin{aligned} &= -6 + 36 \\ &= 36 + -6 \\ &= 36 - 6 \\ &= 30 \end{aligned}$$

SUBTRACTION

When you subtract two positive numbers, and the first number is larger, your answer will be positive.

$$24 - 3 = 21$$

When you subtract two positive numbers, and the first number is smaller, your answer will be negative.

$$3 - 24 = -21$$

When you subtract two negative numbers, your answer will be greater than the starting value. Subtracting a negative number is equivalent to adding the number.

$$-16 - (-4) = -16 + 4 = -12$$
$$-4 - (-16) = -4 + 16 = 12$$

MULTIPLICATION AND DIVISION

When multiplying and dividing positive and negative rational numbers, it is important to remember the rules for integer multiplication and division. Whether the answer is positive or negative depends on the number of negative numbers in your problem. If the total number of negative signs is even, your answer will be positive. If you have an odd number of negative numbers, your answer will be negative.

When multiplying or dividing two positive numbers, the answer will be positive.

$$5 \cdot 6 = 30$$
$$72 \div 9 = 8$$

When multiplying or dividing two negative numbers, the answer will be positive.

$$-7 \cdot (-3) = 21$$
$$-16 \div (-4) = 4$$

When multiplying or dividing a negative number and a positive number, the answer will be negative.

$$-2 \cdot 8 = -16$$
$$24 \div -6 = -4$$

REPRESENTING DIVISION

Division can be represented in many ways. A scenario for division is typically expressed as a group of items being divided among multiple groups with a certain number of items per group. Perhaps a group of flowers are divided among multiple vases, or a collection of pictures is being put in a photo album with multiple pages. Whatever the scenario, there are many ways to express it numerically. Let's say Terrance has 24 photos and can put 4 photos on each page. What are some ways to express this division problem?

- We could write it out: 24 divided by 4
- We could use the division symbol: $24 \div 4$
- We could write it using the long division symbol:
- We could write it as a fraction: $\frac{24}{4}$

Every division problem can be represented in these four ways.

> **Review Video: Mathematical Operations**
> Visit mometrix.com/academy and enter code: 208095

EXAMPLE

Simplify the expression $4(-3) + (-25 \times -4)$.

When approaching this expression, we will simplify in multiple steps using the order of operations, PEMDAS, as a guide. The first step is to simplify the items in parentheses.

$$4(-3) + (-25 \times -4)$$
$$4(-3) + (100)$$

-25×-4 is 100 because 25×4 is 100, and both signs are negative. There are an even number of negative signs, so the answer is positive.

Now we can continue simplifying by solving the multiplication problem.

$$4(-3) + 100$$
$$-12 + 100$$

$4(-3)$ is -12 because 4×3 is 12 and there is 1 negative number. There is an odd number of negative signs, so the answer is negative.

Now we can use addition to simplify further.

$$-12 + 100 = 100 - 12 = 88$$

The simplified expression is 88.

Using Multiplication and Division to Identify Equivalent Values

Division is commonly represented using language, symbols, and fractions, but division can also be represented by using the multiplication operation. Sometimes it makes sense to use different methods of division, and reciprocal multiplication is one of those ways. Division can be considered backwards multiplication. We find this when we are looking at fact families, such as the set of equations involving the numbers 3, 2, and 6. We know that $2 \times 3 = 6$, $3 \times 2 = 6$, $6 \div 2 = 3$, and $6 \div 3 = 2$. If multiplication is the inverse operation of division, we can use that fact to deal with reciprocals in multiplication and division.

A **reciprocal number** is a number's multiplicative inverse. This is directly related to the inverse property of multiplication. When reciprocal numbers are multiplied, their product is always 1. Reciprocal numbers have their numerators and denominators flipped. They are like mirror images of each other.

2 and $\frac{1}{2}$ are reciprocal numbers. Their numerators and denominators are in switched positions, and when they are multiplied, the product is 1.

$$2 = \frac{2}{1}$$
$$\frac{2}{1} \times \frac{1}{2} = \frac{2}{2} = 1$$

When a number is divided by another number, we can get an equivalent value when that same number is multiplied by its reciprocal. Let's look at the known fact $6 \div 2 = 3$, and test the theory that dividing by a number and multiplying by its reciprocal are equivalent. That would mean that $6 \div 2$ and $6 \cdot \frac{1}{2}$ are equivalent.

$$6 \div 2 = \frac{6}{2} = 6 \times \left(\frac{1}{2}\right) = \left(\frac{1}{2}\right) \times 6$$

If we complete the computation, we can see that these are equivalent.

$$6 \times \frac{1}{2} = \frac{6}{1} \times \frac{1}{2} = \frac{6 \times 1}{1 \times 2} = \frac{6}{2} = 6 \div 2 = 3$$

This works for all rational numbers: whole numbers and fractions.

Multiplying and Dividing Large Numbers, Decimals, and Fractions

Multiplying Large Numbers

Multiplying large numbers takes practice. When you set up a multiplication problem with large numbers, it is very important to line up place values and understand the concept of **partial products**. Partial products are the pieces of a larger multiplication problem that, when added together, give the whole product. When multiplying these numbers, you can approach the problem using the distributive property. This allows the values in the problem to be broken into small pieces based on place value.

Consider the following scenario: The soccer league is holding a bake sale. Each team made $1,542, and there are 12 teams in the league. How much money did the league raise?

This problem gives two values, 1,542 and 12, and this is a multiplication problem. We can set up this problem using expanded form and the distributive property.

One way to represent $1{,}542 \times 12$ is to break 12 into $10 + 2$ and distribute.

$$(1{,}542 \times 10) + (1{,}542 \times 2)$$

$$15{,}420 + 3{,}084$$

$$18{,}504$$

We can also use this strategy the other way, where 1,542 is written in expanded form and the 12 is distributed.

$$(12 \times 1{,}000) + (12 \times 500) + (12 \times 40) + (12 \times 2)$$

$$12{,}000 + 6{,}000 + 480 + 24$$

$$18{,}504$$

We can also set up a problem using the standard algorithm.

$$\begin{array}{r} {}^{1} \\ 1{,}542 \\ \times \quad 12 \\ \hline 3\ 084 \end{array}$$

$$\begin{array}{r} 1{,}542 \\ \times \quad 1\not{2} \\ \hline 3{,}084 \\ 15{,}420 \end{array}$$

$$\begin{array}{r} {}^{1} \\ 3{,}084 \\ +15{,}420 \\ \hline 18{,}504 \end{array}$$

EXAMPLE

You are making an art project that includes beading 35 strands of beads. Each strand holds 1,254 beads. How many beads will you need to complete the project?

We can set up our problem in a few ways.

Using the distributive property and expanded notation:

$$(1{,}254 \times 30) + (1{,}254 \times 5)$$

or

$$(1{,}000 \times 35) + (200 \times 35) + (50 \times 35) + (4 \times 35)$$

We can expand each of these expressions further to find easier numbers to work with.

$$(1{,}000 \times 30) + (1{,}000 \times 5) + (200 \times 30) + (200 \times 5) + (50 \times 30) + (50 \times 5) + (4 \times 30) + (4 \times 5)$$
$$30{,}000 + 5{,}000 + 6{,}000 + 1{,}000 + 1{,}500 + 250 + 120 + 20$$

Once at this step, add all your partial products. You can add them in any order. In this example, we added two at a time until the answer was simplified completely.

$$35{,}000 + 7{,}000 + 1{,}750 + 140$$
$$42{,}000 + 1{,}890$$
$$43{,}890$$

We can also set this problem up traditionally and get the same product.

To solve traditionally, line up your factors based on place value where the ones, tens, hundreds, etc. line up. Then, you will begin with the ones place and multiply each digit. This is the same process as the expanded notation, just a shorthand version.

$$\begin{array}{r} {}^{1\,2\,2} \\ 1{,}254 \\ \times \quad 35 \\ \hline 6{,}270 \end{array}$$

Multiplying the ones gives us the first partial product. This is the product of 1,254 times 5.

Now, we need to multiply the tens. When we multiply the tens, we write our product starting in the tens place. You can put a zero in the ones place or use a placeholder. θ will be our placeholder.

$$\begin{array}{r} {}^{1\,1} \\ 1{,}254 \\ \times \quad 35 \\ \hline 6{,}270 \\ 37{,}62\theta \end{array}$$

Now we have our second partial product. This is the product of 1,254 times 30.

Now we can add our partial products.

$$\begin{array}{r} 6{,}270 \\ +37{,}620 \\ \hline 43{,}890 \end{array}$$

The answer is 43,890, which means that we need 43,890 beads.

Multiplying Decimals

When multiplying decimals, you use the same strategy as multiplying whole numbers. The difference is that you have digits to the right of the decimal. Using the traditional strategy of multiplication is the most common way to solve problems with decimals, because the distributive property and expanded form would be extremely tedious. When using the traditional method, you will solve the multiplication with no decimals, and add a decimal to your solution at the end of the problem.

When you are setting up a multiplication problem, the number with more digits will be on the top, and the number with fewer digits will be on the bottom.

For example, find the value of 23.142 times 0.045.

We will set up this problem traditionally, with no decimal places. The number 23,142 has more digits than 45, so 23,142 will be at the top of our problem, and 45 will be at the bottom.

$$\begin{array}{r} 23{,}142 \\ \times \quad 45 \\ \hline \end{array}$$

When using this strategy, you add the decimal at the end. To figure out how many decimal places the answer will have, you count the number of digits behind the decimal point in each factor to find the decimal in the product. In this example, there are 3 decimal places in the first number (23.142) and 3 in the second number (0.045), so the answer will have 6 decimal places. Once the product is found, you would count back 6 digits and place the decimal in the appropriate place.

```
   1   1
   1   2 1
    23,142
×       45
   115,710
+  925,680
 1,041,390
```

So, 23.142 times 0.045 is 1.04139, which can be rounded to the nearest thousandth to get 1.041.

Review Video: How to Multiply Decimals
Visit mometrix.com/academy and enter code: 731574

Example

You are making a blanket for a friend, and you cut 244 squares. Each square is 2.125 inches across. If you laid the squares out in a line, how long would the line be?

In this problem, we are multiplying 244 and 2.125.

2.125 has more digits than 244, so place 2,125 on top when multiplying.

```
 2,125
×  244
```

We can multiply each place value to find the partial products.

```
        1
      1 2
      1 2
    2,125
×     244
    8,500
   85,000
  425,000
```

Then we will add the partial products.

```
   1 1
     8,500
    85,000
+  425,000
   518,500
```

And finally, add our decimal point. The original problem was $244 \cdot 2.125$. Here, the first factor has zero decimal places and the second factor has 3, so this answer has 3 decimal places.

So, if we lined all 244 squares in a line, it would be 518.5 inches long.

Multiplying Fractions

When you multiply fractions, you must convert each factor to a fraction, and multiply across the denominators and numerators.

If you are multiplying 3 by $\frac{2}{3}$, you convert each factor to a fraction, and multiply across.

$$3 = \frac{3}{1}$$
$$\frac{3}{1} \times \frac{2}{3} = \frac{3 \times 2}{1 \times 3} = \frac{6}{3}$$

We should convert $\frac{6}{3}$ to a simplified fraction or whole number.

$$\frac{6}{3} = \frac{6 \div 3}{3 \div 3} = \frac{2}{1} = 2$$

Follow the same process to find the value of 3 times $\frac{5}{5}$.

$$3 = \frac{3}{1}$$
$$\frac{3}{1} \times \frac{5}{5} = \frac{3 \times 5}{1 \times 5} = \frac{15}{5} = \frac{3}{1} = 3$$

And for $3 \times \frac{5}{2}$.

$$3 = \frac{3}{1}$$
$$\frac{3}{1} \times \frac{5}{2} = \frac{3 \times 5}{1 \times 2} = \frac{15}{2}$$

$\frac{15}{2}$ is in simplest form.

Review Video: Multiplying and Dividing Fractions
Visit mometrix.com/academy and enter code: 473632

Example

Solve $7 \cdot \frac{4}{5}$.

In this problem, we are multiplying 7 and $\frac{4}{5}$, a fraction that is less than 1. This tells us that our answer will be less than 7.

We will start by writing 7 as a fraction.

$$7 = \frac{7}{1}$$

Now, we can set up our multiplication problem.

$$\frac{7}{1} \times \frac{4}{5}$$

Now, we can multiply each numerator and each denominator to find our answer.

$$\frac{7 \times 4}{1 \times 5} = \frac{28}{5}$$

Estimating the Value of a Number Multiplied by a Fraction

Fractions Less Than 1

A fraction is less than 1 when the numerator is smaller than the denominator. The fractions $\frac{1}{8}, \frac{1}{2}, \frac{2}{3}, \frac{7}{8}$, and $\frac{23}{50}$ are all examples of fractions less than one. When we multiply a number by a fraction less than one, we get a smaller value than what we started with. Think about what happens when we multiply by a number that is greater than one. When we multiply 5 by a number greater than 1, we get a number larger than 5, like $5 \cdot 10 = 50$. When we multiply 5 by 1, we get 5. But when we multiply 5 by a number less than 1, we get a number that is smaller than 5. This is true for all multiplication by a fraction whose value is less than 1. You may be asked to estimate the value of a number multiplied by a fraction less than 1, or asked what may be true about a value when multiplied by a fraction less than 1. Remember, if you are multiplying by a value that is less than 1, you are going to get a smaller value.

Fractions Greater Than 1

When you review a problem where a number is being multiplied by a fraction that is greater than 1, it is important to be able to estimate its value. Fractions are greater than 1 when the numerator is greater than the denominator. Some examples are $\frac{2}{1}, \frac{4}{3}, \frac{9}{7}$, and $\frac{100}{25}$. When a number is being multiplied by a given factor, it follows a general rule: if the factor is less than one, the value will be smaller, if the factor is equal to 1, the value will be the same, and if the factor is greater than 1, the value will be greater. If we are multiplying 5 by a number, we know a few things about it. If 5 is being multiplied by a number greater than 1, the product will be greater than 5, like $5 \times \frac{3}{2} = \frac{15}{2}$ or 7.5. If 5 is multiplied by 1, the product is 5. If 5 is being multiplied by a number less than 1, the product will be less than 5, like $5 \times \frac{1}{10} = \frac{1}{2}$. Knowing this, if a number is being multiplied by a fraction that is greater than 1, we can determine that the product will be greater than the original number.

Dividing Large Numbers

Dividing large numbers takes practice. The most common strategy for large-digit division is using long division. Long division is a shorthand way to divide large numbers by place value. There are a couple of ways to complete long division problems. Let's look at the problem 6,585 divided by 25.

When using long division, we set up our problems like this:

$$25\overline{)6{,}585}$$

The first step in this problem is to ask how many times 25 goes into 6. 25 is larger than 6, so the answer would be zero. We will put a zero in the thousands place.

```
      0
25) 6,585
```

Now we move to the hundreds place. How many times will 25 go into 65? Twice. We would say twice because $2 \cdot 25 = 50$ and $3 \cdot 25 = 75$; 75 is greater than 65, so we will choose $25 \cdot 2$.

```
      0 2
25) 6,585
```

Now we multiply $25 \cdot 2$, place this under 65, subtract, and bring down the next digit.

```
      0 2
25) 6,585
      5 0
      1 58
```

Now we ask, "how many times will 25 go into 158?" 6, because $6 \cdot 5 = 150$.

So, we place a 6 in the tens place, multiply, subtract, and bring down the last digit.

```
      0 26
25) 6,585
      5 0
      1 58
      1 50
         85
```

Now, we follow the same process. How many times does 25 go into 85? 3 times. Place a 3 in the ones place, multiply, and subtract.

```
      0 263
25) 6,585
      5 0
       158
       150
         85
         75
          10 ←remainder
```

There is nothing else to bring down, but we have 10 left over. This is our remainder, so we can say that $6{,}585 \div 25 = 263$ with a remainder of 10, or $263\frac{10}{25}$.

The fraction $\frac{10}{25}$ can be simplified, so in simplest terms, this is $263\frac{2}{5}$.

Using Expanded Form

We can also complete division problems using expanded form. In the problem 6,585 divided by 25, we can set up our problem by dividing each place value by 25 and adding them together.

$$(6{,}000 \div 25) + (500 \div 25) + (80 \div 25) + (5 \div 25)$$

$$240 + 20 + \frac{80}{25} + \frac{5}{25}$$

$$260 + \frac{85}{25}$$

$$260 + 3\frac{10}{25}$$

$$263\frac{10}{25}$$

$$263\frac{2}{5}$$

Dividing Decimals

Dividing decimal numbers involves the same process as dividing by whole numbers. The most common, and most efficient, way to solve these problems is to use long division. When using long division to solve decimal problems, you will set up your division problem and multiply the dividend and divisor by base 10 values until you get a value without decimals. The concept is that $2 \div 10$ is equivalent to $20 \div 100$ which is also equivalent to $2{,}000 \div 10{,}000$. If you multiply both values by the same number, you will get the same quotient.

Let's look at the problem 725.6 divided by 0.125. We would need to multiply each number by 1,000 to remove the decimal places.

$$0.125 \times 1{,}000 = 125$$
$$725.6 \times 1{,}000 = 725{,}600$$

Now, we can set this problem up using long division and divide using the long division process. Divide, multiply, subtract, and bring down.

```
      0 05,8 04
125) 7 25,6 00
     6 25
     1,00 6
     1,00 0
          6 0
            0
          6 00
          5 00
          1 00
```

When we are dividing by decimals, we want our answer in decimal form. You may be asked to round your answer to the nearest tenths, hundredths, or thousandths. Typically, you will not have more than 3 decimal places.

So, we can keep dividing by adding a decimal and a zero to the dividend. This is because 725,600 is equivalent to 725,600.0.

```
     005804.8
125) 725600.0
     625
     1006
     1000
        60
         0
       600
       500
       1000
       1000
          0
```

$725.6 \div 0.125 = 5{,}804.8$

Review Video: Dividing Decimals
Visit mometrix.com/academy and enter code: 560690

Dividing Fractions

We use the inverse property to help us solve fraction division problems. The inverse property tells us that dividing by a number is the same as multiplying by its reciprocal. The reciprocal of a number is its "flipped" version, where the numerator is flipped with the denominator. We can multiply the reciprocal of a fraction to get the same value as dividing by the original fraction. To multiply fractions, make sure each term is in fraction form and multiply the numerators and multiply the denominators.

Let's look at the problem $4 \div \frac{1}{2}$.

When we divide by a fraction, we get the same value by multiplying by its reciprocal.

This means that $4 \div \frac{1}{2}$ is equivalent to $4 \times \frac{2}{1}$. Write 4 as a fraction and multiply to find $\frac{4}{1} \times \frac{2}{1} = 8$.

Example

Solve $\frac{3}{4} \div \frac{1}{6}$.

When you see a problem like this, rewrite the problem by inverting the second fraction, then multiply the fractions instead of dividing. We are dividing $\frac{3}{4}$ by $\frac{1}{6}$, so we can also say we are multiplying $\frac{3}{4}$ by $\frac{6}{1}$.

$$\frac{3}{4} \div \frac{1}{6} = \frac{3}{4} \times \frac{6}{1}$$

Now multiply the numerators and denominators.

$$\frac{3}{4} \times \frac{6}{1} = \frac{3 \times 6}{4 \times 1} = \frac{18}{4}$$

The last step is to simplify.

$$\frac{18}{4} = \frac{9}{2}$$

So,

$$\frac{3}{4} \div \frac{1}{6} = \frac{9}{2}$$

Representing Integer Operations on a Number Line

Integer operations include adding, subtracting, multiplying, and dividing using positive numbers, negative numbers, and zero. These operations can be represented on a number line.

We can represent operations of integers on a number line. Think about the problem $4 + (-7)$. This can be represented on a number line by starting at 4 and counting to the left 7 times because we are adding a -1 to 4 each time we move to the left. You can tell we are moving to the left because of the arrows in the figure.

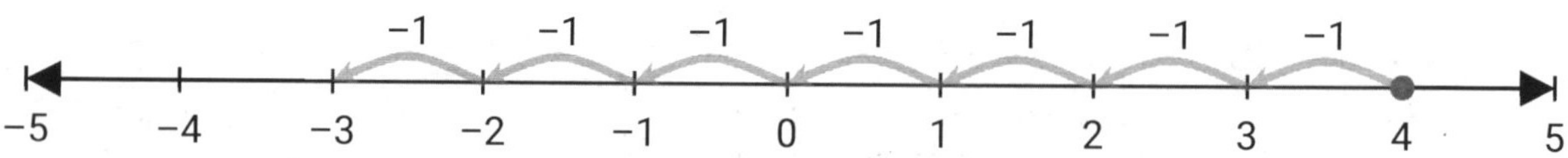

This number line also represents the problem $4 - 7$. We could also say that the number line shows $4 + (7 \times (-1))$ because we started at 4 and moved 7 "jumps" of -1.

Consider this number line that does not have any arrows. What expressions can you generate from this number line?

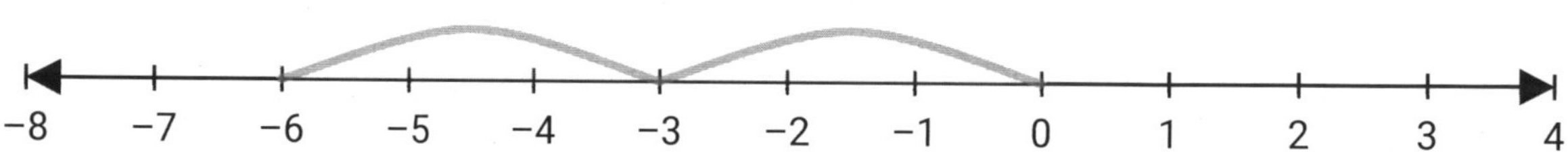

Since there are no arrows, it is open to interpretation. Let's look at our options.

An addition expression can be found. We could say $-6 + 3 + 3$ because it could be viewed that we started at -6 and added 3 twice.

A subtraction expression can be found in this number line. We could say $0 - 3 - 3$ because it could be viewed that we started at 0 and subtracted 3, twice.

A multiplication expression can also be found. We could say that we started at 0 and added -3 times 2. We could say this because there are two "jumps" of -3.

There are other possibilities that can be generated through equivalent expressions. When looking at a number line to find the expression, it is important to break each part down by considering the following questions. Where does the expression start? Which direction are the arrows moving?

How many jumps are there and what is the value of each jump? All these will help you determine the correct expression.

Review Video: Negative and Positive Number Line
Visit mometrix.com/academy and enter code: 816439

Proportionality

Additive Relationships

An **additive relationship** is a pattern where a value is added to x. For example, the two points (4,6) and (6,8) can be used to represent an additive relationship, since both points have a y-value that comes from 2 being added to the x-value. This pattern can also be described as $x + 2$, where x is the previous number and 2 is added to it. Patterns may be expressed with a series of numbers separated by commas, or in a data table or graph.

x	y
2	4
4	6
6	8
8	10

This data table shows an additive relationship, $x + 2$. When describing an additive relationship, we commonly use the equation $y = x + a$. This additive relationship can be written using the formula $y = x + a$ or $x + a = y$. In this example, x is the starting value, adding 2 is what happens to x, and y is the ending value. When we use values from the table to replace x and y in our equation, the sentence is true.

Multiplicative Relationships

A **multiplicative relationship** describes a pattern between x and y where x is multiplied by a number to get to y. Looking at the points (3,9) and (9,27), we can see that each x-value is multiplied by 3 to get the y-value. This is also called the **scale factor**.

x	y
3	9
9	27
27	81
81	243

This data table shows the same relationship in table form. This is a multiplicative relationship because the x-value is being multiplied by a number to get a y-value. We describe this multiplicative relationship using the formula $y = ax$, or $ax = y$, where x is the starting value, a is the scale factor, and y is the ending value. In this example, 3 is being multiplied by x to get to y, or y is 3 times as much as x, or x increases by a factor of 3. The equation to describe this relationship is $y = 3x$ or $3x = y$.

Representing Additive and Multiplicative Relationships

Patterns and relationships can be expressed using tables, equations, and graphs. These representations can be used interchangeably. They are different ways to illustrate the same information. In an additive relationship, a number is being added to x to get y. This is expressed using the equation $y = x + a$. This relationship can also be expressed using a table and a graph. Let's look at the equation $y = x + 3$. In this relationship, 3 is added to all x-values, or all y-values are 3 more than x. We can express this using a table.

x	y
1	4
2	5
3	6
4	7

This information can also be described using a graph by using the x- and y-values as coordinate pairs. We can plot each point on a graph to see the pattern graphically.

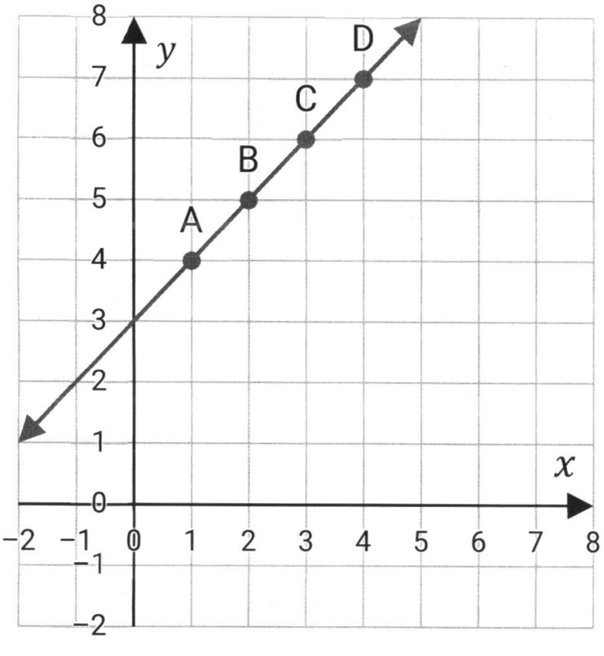

This graph uses the x and y-values from the table to create points. This line illustrates the information in the data table and describes the equation $y = x + 3$.

The equation, table, and graph all describe the same relationship, that y is 3 more than x.

Comparing Relationships and Patterns

We can use tables, graphs, and equations to compare relationships between x and y in additive and multiplicative relationships. To do this, we need to identify a pattern and use that information to compare. You may be given two sets of equations in the form $y = ax$ or $y = x + a$, two data sets, or two graphs, and asked to compare the relationships of x and y. Let's look at two equations and compare.

Equation #1	Equation #2
$y = 5x$	$y = x + 5$

Here we have two equations. You should ask yourself a few questions:

- What is the same in these relationships and how are they different?
- What is happening to x to get y?
- Are these additive or multiplicative relationships?

In this example, both equations have 5 as the a-value. Equation 1 shows a multiplicative relationship where y is 5 times as great as x and equation 2 shows an additive relationship where y is 5 more than x.

Ratios

A **ratio** expresses the relationship between two values. For example, comparisons of the amount of green paint to the amount of white paint, the number of dogs to number of cats, or the volume of flour to volume of sugar could be described using ratios. These items can all be expressed using a value, and the relationship between these values is called a ratio. Ratios are expressed in a few ways: using the ratio symbol, using words, using division, and using equivalent ratios. Let's say a veterinarian sees 35 dogs and 25 cats per week. What is the relationship between the number of animals of each type that are seen? You could use words to explain the ratio of dogs to cats as 35 to 25, or there are 35 dogs seen for every 25 cats seen. You could use the ratio symbol to show the ratio of dogs to cats is $35 : 25$. You can show the ratio of dogs to cats as a fraction, $\frac{35}{25}$. You can simplify a ratio by finding the greatest common factor and dividing each term. In this example the greatest common factor of 35 and 25 is 5. We use the same process used to simplify fractions. So, the ratio of dogs to cats is $7 : 5$, or there are 7 dogs seen for every 5 cats, or the ratio is 7 to 5. We can also express the ratio of cats to dogs. When expressing the ratio of cats to dogs, the same values apply, only reversed. The ratio of cats to dogs is 25 to 35, 5 to 7, $25 : 35$, $5 : 7$, $\frac{25}{35}$, $\frac{5}{7}$, or there are 5 cats seen for every 7 dogs. Ratios can be expressed in a variety of ways, but each way expresses the same relationship between two values.

Review Video: Ratios
Visit mometrix.com/academy and enter code: 996914

Rates

A **rate** is a comparison of two values with different units. A **constant rate** means that the relationship between units remains the same. Some common examples are the comparison of dollars to hour, miles to hours, and beats to seconds. Rates can be expressed in a variety of ways, including using language, as quotients, using equivalent rates, algebraically, using tables, or graphically.

Rates can be expressed through language. Let's say you get your first job working at a store making \$12 for every hour of work. This is a rate, a comparison between two unlike units, dollars and hours. This rate can be expressed through words. We use the word *per* when expressing rates. You could say that you make 12 dollars per hour.

Rates can be expressed as a fraction, or division. If you make 12 dollars per hour, you could express that as $12/hour, or $\frac{12 \text{ dollars}}{1 \text{ hour}}$. You could even say that the rate of dollars per hour is $\frac{12}{1}$.

Rates can be expressed using equivalent rates. $12/hour can be expressed as $24/2 hours. Or, if you work 20 hours per week, you could say you make $240/week. Regardless of the number of hours worked, the number of dollars made per hour remains constant, or the same.

Review Video: Rates and Unit Rates
Visit mometrix.com/academy and enter code: 185363

Solving Problems with Ratios and Rates

To solve problems using ratios and rates, you will use logic and reasoning to make reasonable predictions. The best way to approach ratio and rate problems is to use tables, models, or equivalence to help you solve the problem. Let's say the ratio of dogs to cats at an animal shelter is 5 to 2. This means that for every 5 dogs there are 2 cats, or for every 2 cats there are 5 dogs. We can use this ratio to solve some problems about the number of dogs and cats at this shelter. Let's say there are 25 dogs at this shelter, and the ratio of dogs to cats is still 5 : 2. We can use the ratio of 5 : 2 to help us find how many cats there are.

Use a model. If the ratio of dogs to cats is 5 to 2, our model may look like this.

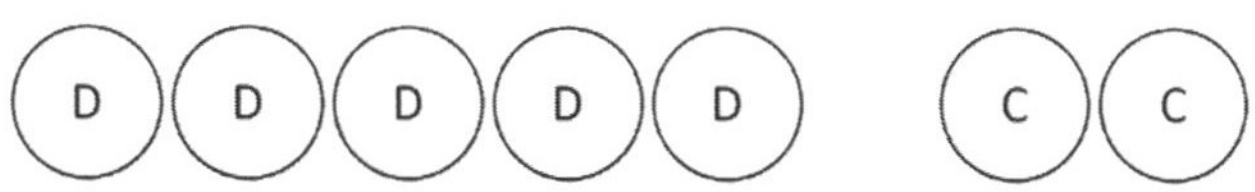

Now, if there are 25 dogs, the ratio needs to stay the same, so we can duplicate our model until we have 25 dogs.

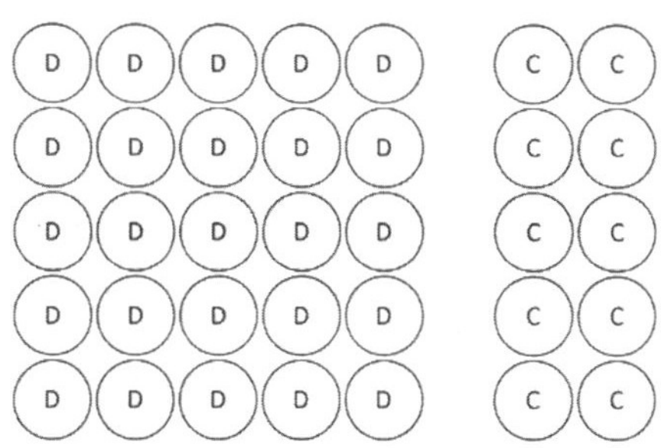

Now, if there are 25 dogs, we can see that there are 10 cats.

We can also use a table to solve this problem. By using a table, we can compare the numbers of dogs and cats. If there are 5 dogs to 2 cats, and there are 25 dogs, our table will look like this.

Dogs	Cats
5	2
25	

Now, we need to find the pattern. It looks like to get from 5 to 25, we multiply by 5. So, if we multiply the value of cats by 5, we will know the number of cats.

Dogs	Cats
5	2
25	10

We can see there are 10 cats.

We can also use equivalent ratios to solve this. We can write the ratio of dogs to cats as a fraction and find an equivalent fraction to solve our problem. In this example we can write the fraction of dogs to cats and in one fraction, the value for cats is missing.

$$\frac{\text{dogs}}{\text{cats}} = \frac{5}{2} = \frac{25}{?}$$

We can find an equivalent fraction my multiplying the numerator and denominator by 5 to find the number of cats.

$$\frac{5}{2} \times \frac{5}{5} = \frac{25}{10} = \frac{\text{dogs}}{\text{cats}}$$

Using each of these methods, the ratio stays the same, 5 : 2, and using any of these strategies, we find that if there are 25 dogs, there are 10 cats.

EXAMPLE

You are making posters for a school election. You make 3 posters in 1 hour. At this rate, how many posters will you make in 4.5 hours?

In this problem, we are given a rate. You are making posters at a rate of 3 posters per hour. And we need to figure out how many posters you can make in 4.5 hours.

To solve this problem, we can use any of the following strategies: draw a model, draw a table, or use equivalence. Models can take a long time, but if you are feeling stuck, sometimes a picture is the best way to make sense of the information. Tables can also take a little while but can help illustrate patterns. Finding equivalent rates and ratios is likely to be the more efficient way to solve these problems. Let's use equivalence to solve this problem.

So, if you are making 3 posters in 1 hour, the rate you are making posters is 3 posters per hour. This can be written in fraction form:

$$\frac{3\text{ posters}}{1\text{ hour}} = \frac{3}{1}$$

Now that we have a rate, we can find an equivalent rate. We do not know how many posters you will be making, but we know that it will take 4.5 hours.

We can write the new fraction using this information, remembering to keep posters and hours in the same part of the fraction by placing both in the numerator or both in the denominator.

$$\frac{3\text{ posters}}{1\text{ hour}} = \frac{?\text{ posters}}{4.5\text{ hours}}$$

Now that we have our two fractions, we can solve for the missing value. We can see that 1 times 4.5 is 4.5, so if you multiply each value by the same number, we will get an equivalent fraction and that will give us an equivalent rate.

$$\frac{3}{1} \times \frac{4.5}{4.5} = \frac{13.5}{4.5}$$

So, if we make posters at a rate of 3 posters per hour and we work for 4.5 hours, we will make 13.5 posters.

Rates, Ratios, and Proportions

We can represent ratios and rates using proportions and scale factors. A **proportion** is an equation with two equivalent ratios. We use proportions to compare ratios and to solve ratio and rate problems. Suppose a recipe requires 2 cups of sugar and 3 cups of flour. This can be described by the ratio $2 : 3$, or $\frac{2}{3}$. Now, that means that for every 4 cups of sugar, we need 6 cups of flour because these ratios are equivalent. This can be expressed by the following proportion.

$$\frac{2}{3} = \frac{4}{6}$$

Now, what if we were making a recipe with 8 cups of sugar? We can use proportions to help us solve this problem where x is the number of cups of flour needed.

$$\frac{2}{3} = \frac{8}{x}$$

Proportions are written in the form:

$$\frac{a}{b} = \frac{c}{d}$$

They can also be written in the form $ad = cb$ when the equation is rearranged.

$$d \times \frac{a}{b} = \frac{c}{d} \times d$$
$$b\left(d \times \frac{a}{b}\right) = c \times b$$
$$d \times a = c \times b$$
$$ad = cb$$

This is also known as **cross multiplying**. When we have a proportion, we can cross multiply to solve.

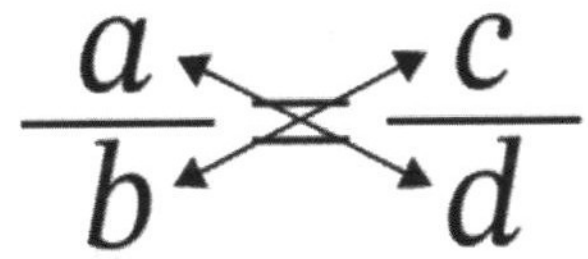

$$ad = cb$$

Now, solve the proportion for the number of cups of flour needed for 8 cups of sugar.

$$\frac{2}{3} = \frac{8}{x}$$
$$2 \times x = 8 \times 3$$
$$\frac{2x}{2} = \frac{24}{2}$$
$$x = 12$$

So, if we are using 8 cups of sugar, we need 12 cups of flour.

$$\frac{2}{3} = \frac{8}{12}$$

These are equivalent ratios.

Review Video: Proportions
Visit mometrix.com/academy and enter code: 505355

Review Video: Cross Multiplying Fractions
Visit mometrix.com/academy and enter code: 893904

Modeling Ratios

Ratios can be expressed through models. You will often encounter ratio models as strip diagrams and picture models. Suppose we are tiling a bathroom floor with a cool design and for every 4 hexagon tiles, there are 6 square tiles. We can express this ratio using a picture model or a strip diagram.

Model 1

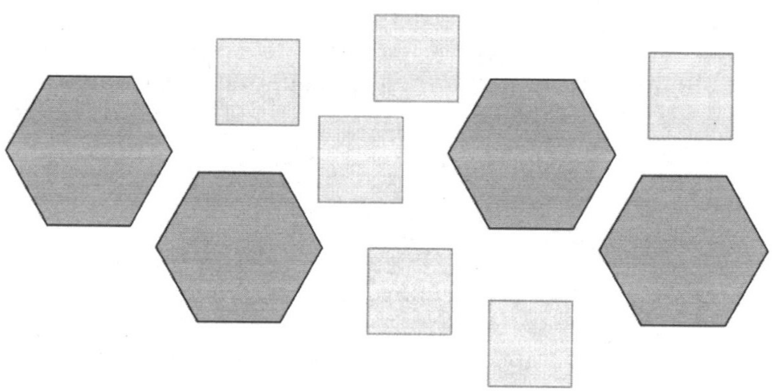

Model 2

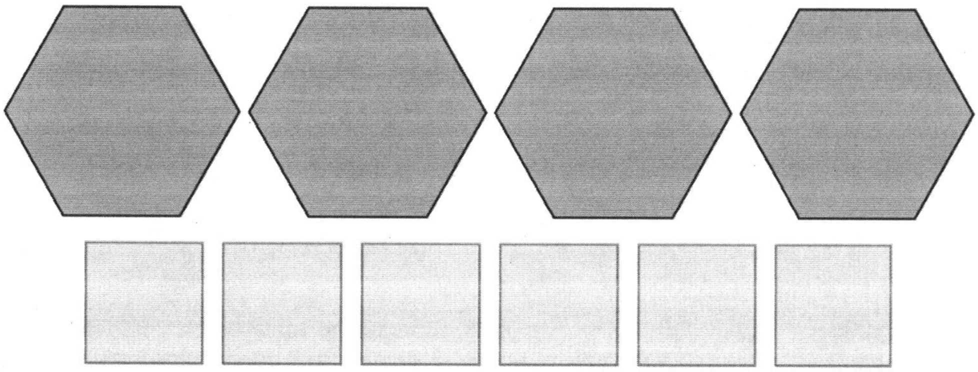

Model 3

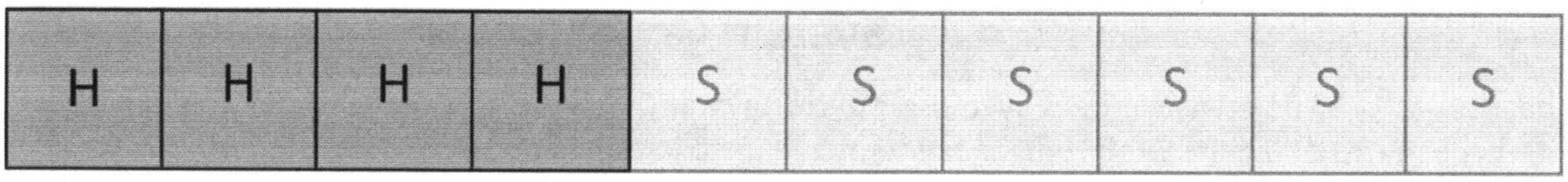

Model 4

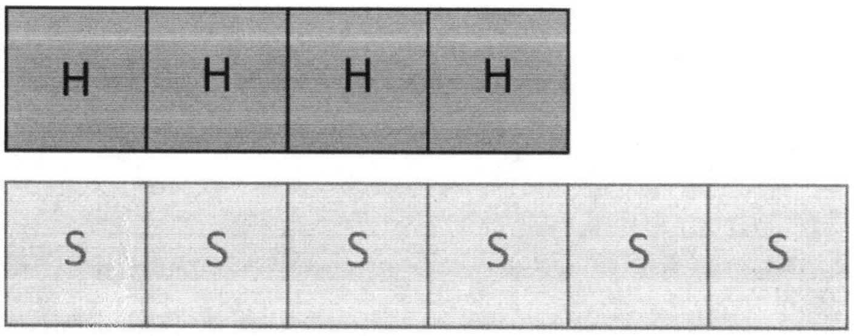

Strip diagrams and picture models can also help you simplify a ratio. You may group like terms to identify a simplified ratio.

Model 5

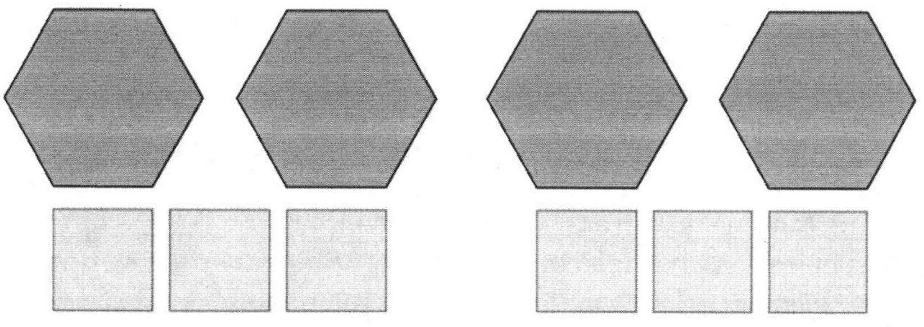

MODEL 6

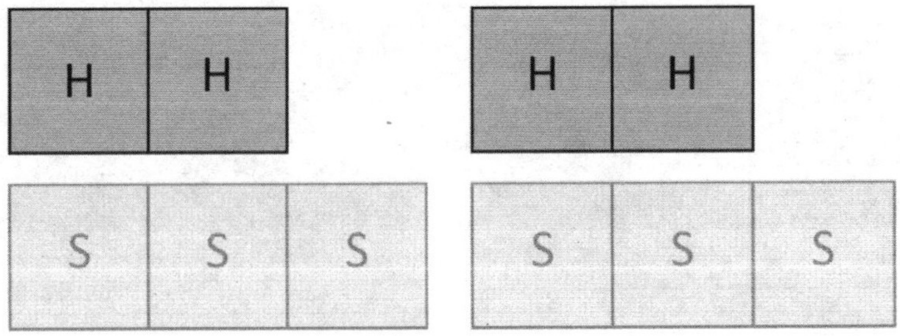

So, from these models, we can conclude that the ratio of hexagon tiles to square tiles is 4 : 6, and we can also express it as 2 : 3 because we can divide our diagrams into two equal groups and in each group, there are 2 hexagons and 3 squares.

Customary System Conversions

There are two basic measurement systems, **customary** and **metric**. Within each unit system, there are three main categories of unit measurements: length, volume, and mass. The customary system uses miles, yards, feet, and inches to measure length. You can convert measurements between these units of measurement. The customary system uses gallons, quarts, pints, ounces, and cups to measure volume or capacity. You can convert units within this volume category. The customary system uses tons, pounds, and ounces to measure weight. We also measure time in seconds, minutes, hours, days, weeks, months, and years. You can covert units within each category.

Common Customary Measurements

Length	Weight	Time	Volume
1 foot = 12 inches 1 yard = 36 inches 1 yard = 3 feet 1 mile = 5,280 feet 1 mile = 1,760 yards	1 pound = 16 ounces 1 ton = 2,000 pounds	1 minute = 60 seconds 1 hour = 60 minutes 1 day = 24 hours 1 week = 7 days 1 year = 12 months 1 year = 365 days	1 cup = 8 fluid ounces 1 pint = 2 cups 1 quart = 2 pints 1 quart = 4 cups 1 gallon = 4 quarts 1 gallon = 16 cups

Converting measurements means using different units to describe the same value. For example, if we are measuring the length of a room, we can measure the room in inches, feet, or yards. The room will be the same length, but the measurement will have a different value for different units. Suppose we measure the room in feet, but we need to know what the length is in yards. We can convert our measurement to yards using a proportion that describes the relationship between feet and yards.

If 1 yard contains 3 feet, then the ratio between yards and feet is 1 : 3. That means that no matter how you describe yards to feet, the ratio will be the same, and the value will be proportional.

$$\frac{1\text{ yd}}{3\text{ ft}} = \frac{x\text{ yd}}{12\text{ ft}}$$

We can write an equivalent expression and see that this proportion can also look like:

$$12 \text{ ft} \times \frac{1 \text{ yd}}{3 \text{ ft}} = \frac{x \text{ yd}}{12 \text{ ft}} \times 12 \text{ ft}$$
$$12 \text{ ft} \times \frac{1 \text{ yd}}{3\text{ft}} = x \text{ yd}$$

When you convert measurements to smaller units, you are typically going to be multiplying. If you are converting to larger units, you will be dividing.

For example, if you are converting feet to inches, you will multiply the number of feet by 12. If you are converting inches to feet, you will divide the number of inches by 12.

$$\frac{12 \text{ in}}{1 \text{ ft}} = \frac{x \text{ in}}{5 \text{ ft}} \qquad 5 \text{ ft} \times \frac{12 \text{ in}}{1 \text{ ft}} = 5 \times 12 = 60 \text{ in}$$

$$\frac{12 \text{ in}}{1 \text{ ft}} = \frac{60 \text{ in}}{x \text{ ft}} \qquad 60 \text{ in} \div \frac{12 \text{ in}}{1 \text{ ft}} = 60 \div 12 = 5 \text{ ft}$$

Review Video: Measurement Conversion
Visit mometrix.com/academy and enter code: 316703

Example

A friend's house is 3 miles from your house. How far away is your friend's house from your house in yards?

In this problem, we are converting measurements of length. There are 1,760 yards in a mile, so we can use this proportion to help us determine how many yards there are in 3 miles.

$$\frac{1{,}760 \text{ yd}}{1 \text{ mi}} = \frac{x \text{ yd}}{3 \text{ mi}}$$

To solve, multiply by 3 miles on each side of the equation.

$$3 \times \frac{1{,}760}{1} = \frac{x}{3} \times 3$$
$$3 \times \frac{1{,}760}{1} = x$$
$$3 \times 1{,}760 = x$$
$$5{,}280 = x$$

We can also use cross multiplication using a proportion.

$$\frac{1{,}760 \text{ yd}}{1 \text{ mi}} = \frac{x \text{ yd}}{3 \text{ mi}}$$
$$1{,}760 \times 3 = 1x$$
$$5{,}280 = x$$

So, 3 miles is equivalent to 5,280 yards. That means that the friend's house is 5,280 yards away.

EXAMPLE

You are baking a cake. The recipe calls for 24 fluid ounces of water. How many cups of water do you need?

In this problem, we are converting fluid ounces to cups.

We first need to identify the relationship between cups and fluid ounces. There are 8 fluid ounces in 1 cup. This can be described using the following proportion.

$$\frac{8 \text{ oz}}{1 \text{ c}}$$

Now, we are converting 24 fluid ounces to cups. So, that can be described using the proportion below.

$$\frac{8 \text{ oz}}{1 \text{ c}} = \frac{24 \text{ oz}}{x}$$

When we are converting from a smaller unit to a larger unit, we use division.

$$24 \text{ oz} \div \frac{8 \text{ oz}}{1 \text{ c}} = 24 \div 8 = 3 \text{ cups}$$

The recipe calls for 24 fluid ounces of water, which is equivalent to 3 cups.

Metric System Conversions

Metric units have a base 10 system where each measurement unit, is a multiple or factor of 10. Each category uses prefixes to describe the value of the unit. Meters are used to describe length. Within the length category, the most common metric measurements we use are kilometers, meters, centimeters, and millimeters. Kilo- means 1,000, so a kilometer is 1,000 meters in length. Centi- means 100, so 100 centimeters are in a meter. Milli- means 1000, so 1000 millimeters are in a meter. Liters are used to measure volume. The most common metric units for volume are kiloliters, liters, and millimeters. As you can see, we see the same prefixes; kilo- and milli-. A kiloliter is 1,000 liters and there are 1,000 millimeters in a liter. Grams are used to measure mass. The most common metric units for mass are kilograms, grams, and milligrams.

Common Metric Measurements		
Length	**Mass**	**Volume**
1,000 m = 1 km	1,000 g = 1 kg	1,000 L = 1 kL
1,000 mm = 1 m	1,000 mg = 1 g	1,000 mL = 1 L
100 cm = 1 m	100 cg = 1 g	100 cL = 1 L
10 mm = 1 cm	10 mg = 1 cg	10 mL = 1 cL

Review Video: Metric System Conversions
Visit mometrix.com/academy and enter code: 163709

EXAMPLE

An apple has a mass of 76 grams. What is the mass of the apple in kilograms?

In this problem, we need to convert 76 grams to kilograms.

There are 1,000 grams in a kilogram.

$$\frac{1{,}000 \text{ g}}{1 \text{ kg}}$$

We want to know how many kilograms is equivalent to 76 grams.

$$\begin{aligned} \frac{1 \text{ kg}}{1{,}000 \text{ g}} &= \frac{x \text{ kg}}{76 \text{ g}} \\ \frac{1}{1{,}000} &= \frac{x}{76} \\ 76 \times \frac{1}{1{,}000} &= \frac{x}{76} \times 76 \\ \frac{76}{1{,}000} &= x \\ 76 \div 1000 &= x \\ 0.076 \text{ kg} &= x \end{aligned}$$

Alternatively, we can use cross multiplication to solve the proportion.

$$\begin{aligned} \frac{1{,}000 \text{ g}}{1 \text{ kg}} &= \frac{76 \text{ g}}{x \text{ kg}} \\ 1{,}000x &= 76 \times 1 \\ 1{,}000x &= 76 \\ \frac{1{,}000x}{1{,}000} &= \frac{76}{1{,}000} \\ x &= 0.076 \end{aligned}$$

The apple weighs 0.076 kilograms.

Modeling Fractions, Decimals, and Percentages

There are a group of fractions, decimals, and percentages that are commonly expressed in the real world and that are very important to understand as reference points when working with other values. One category of common part-whole representations is **base 10 values**. These are $\frac{1}{10}, \frac{2}{10}, \frac{3}{10} \ldots \frac{10}{10}, \frac{11}{10}$ and so on. As decimals they appear as 0.1, 0.2, 0.3...1.0, 1.1 and so on. And as percentages, 10%, 20%, 30%... 100%, 110% and so on.

Another common category is **quarter values**. As fractions they look like $\frac{1}{4}, \frac{1}{2}, \frac{3}{4}, 1, 1\frac{1}{4}$, and so on. As decimals, they look like 0.25, 0.5, 0.75, 1, 1.25, and so on. As percentages, they look like 25%, 50%, 75%, 100%, 125%, and so on.

The last category is **thirds**. As fractions these look like $\frac{1}{3}, \frac{2}{3}, 1, 1\frac{1}{3}$ and so on. As decimals these look like $0.3\overline{3}$, $0.6\overline{6}$, 1, $1.3\overline{3}$, and so on. And as percentages, 33%, 66%, 100%, 133%, and so on.

Benchmark Values

These **benchmark values**, or common values, can be represented through 10 × 10 grids, strip diagrams, and number lines. It is important to be able to identify common fractions, decimals, and percentages using these visual representations.

$$\frac{10}{100} = \frac{1}{10} = 0.1$$

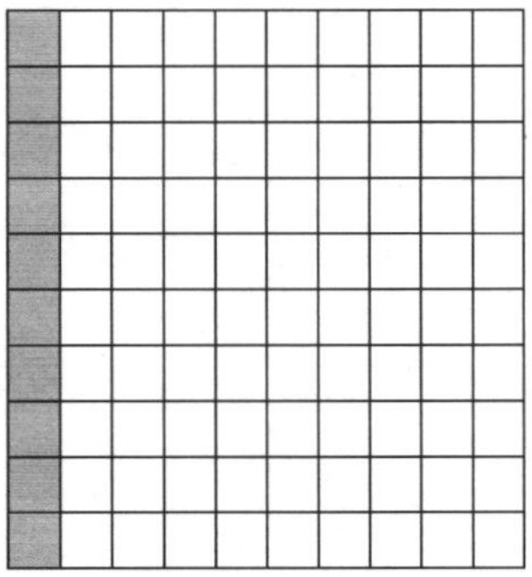

10%

$$\frac{20}{100} = \frac{2}{10} = 0.2$$

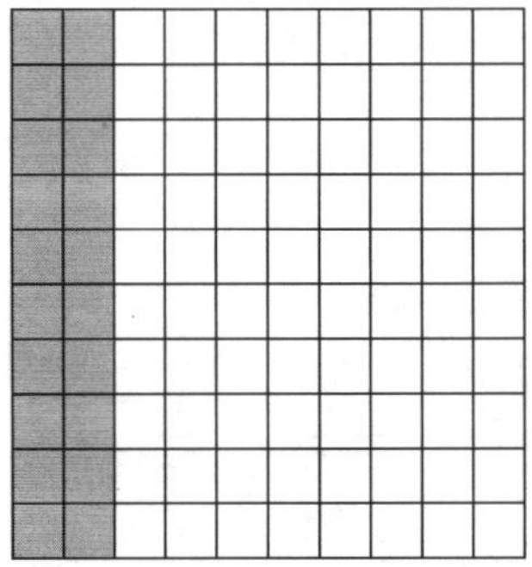

20%

$$\frac{25}{100} = \frac{2.5}{10} = 0.25$$

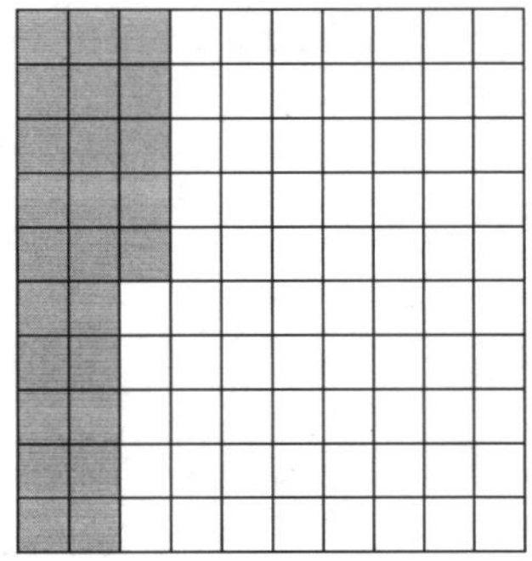

25%

$$\frac{30}{100} = \frac{3}{10} = 0.3$$

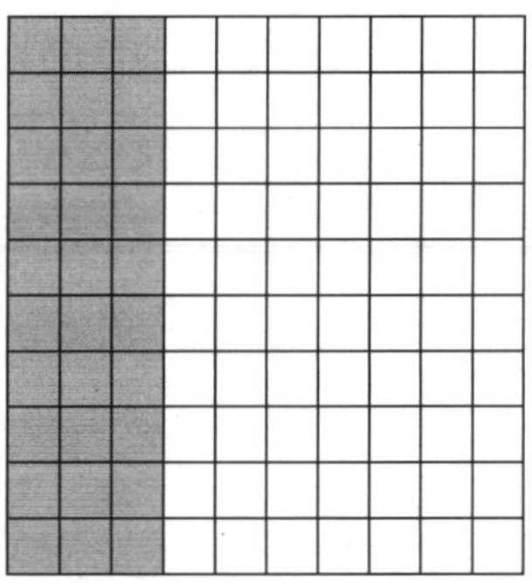

30%

$$\frac{50}{100} = \frac{5}{10} = 0.5$$

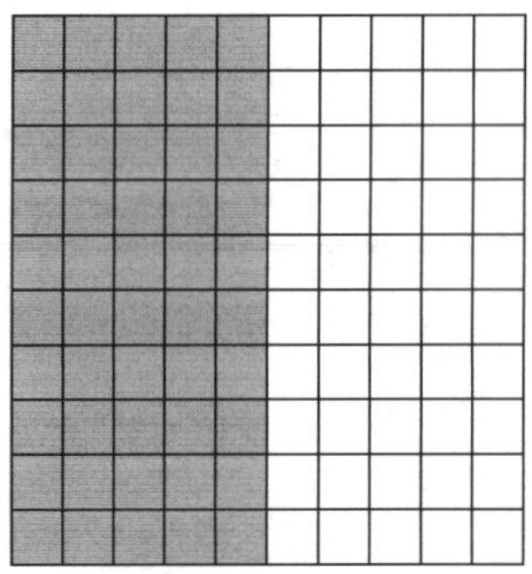

50%

$$\frac{75}{100} = \frac{7.5}{10} = 0.75$$

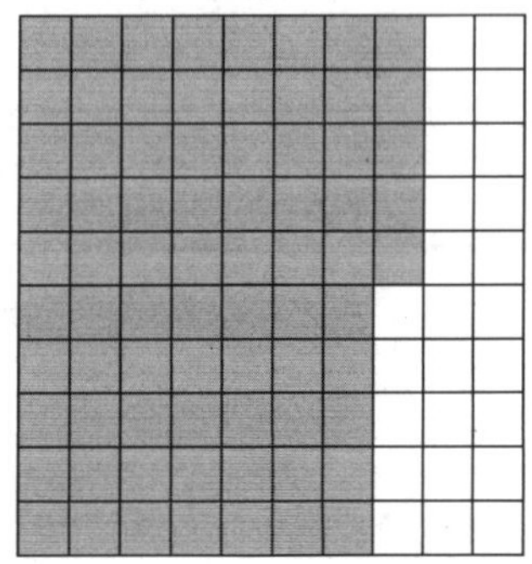

75%

$$\frac{100}{100} = \frac{10}{10} = 1.0$$

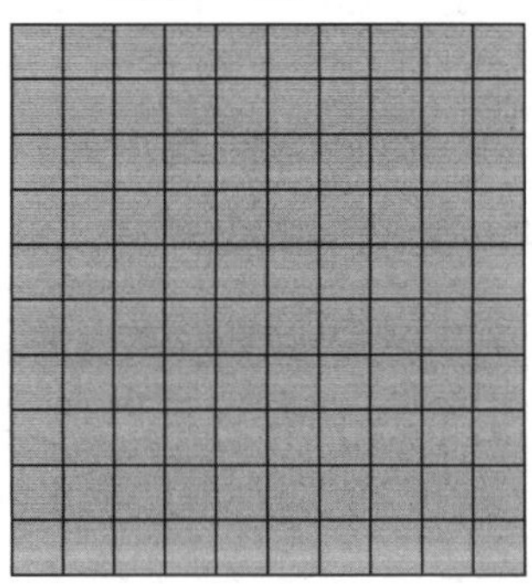

100%

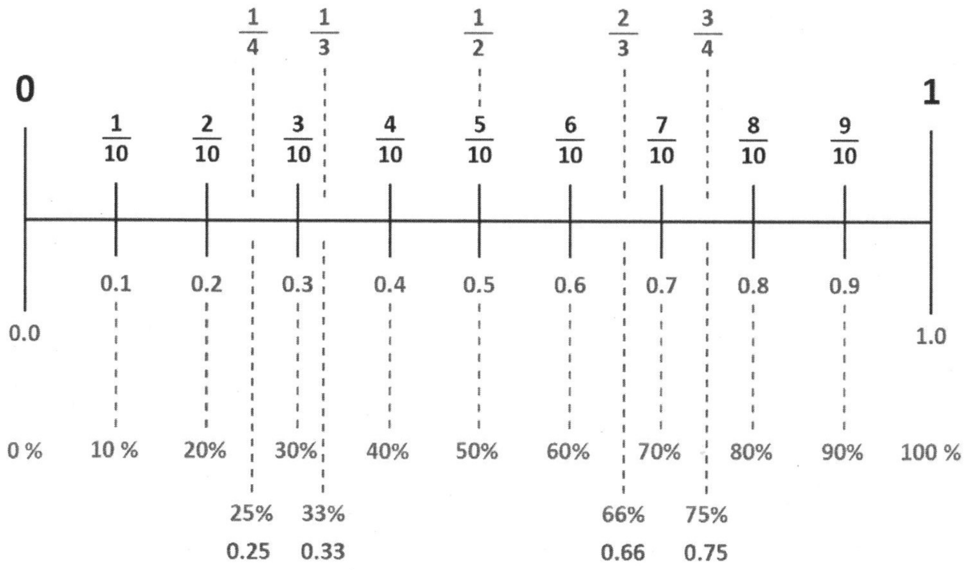

Converting Fractions, Decimals, and Percentages

Fractions, decimals, and percentages compare parts to a whole and are another way to represent division. Sometimes you are required to find equivalent values for given fractions, decimals, and percentages. You can generate equivalent values through models like strip diagrams and number lines, but you can also calculate conversions using multiplication or division.

Converting Fractions to Decimals

To convert a fraction to a decimal, you will divide the numerator by the denominator. For example, $\frac{2}{5}$ can be converted to a decimal by performing the division problem 2 divided by 5 to get the value 0.4, so 0.4 is equivalent to $\frac{2}{5}$.

$$\begin{array}{r} 0.4 \\ 5\overline{)\,2.0} \\ \underline{2\,0} \\ 0 \end{array}$$

$$\frac{2}{5} = 0.4$$

Example

Convert $\frac{7}{20}$ to a decimal.

In this problem, we need to convert a fraction to a decimal. First, rewrite the fraction as a division problem.

$$\frac{7}{20} = 7 \div 20$$

Now, we can solve the new division problem by extending the decimal and using long division.

$$\begin{array}{r} 0.35 \\ 20\overline{)7.00} \\ \underline{6\,0} \\ 1\,00 \\ \underline{1\,00} \\ 0 \end{array}$$

Once we have completed the long division, we can express the conversion as an equation.

$$\frac{7}{20} = 0.35$$

Converting Decimals to Percentages

To convert a decimal to a percent, multiply the decimal by 100 and rewrite using the percent sign. For example, 0.4 can be converted to a percent by performing the calculation 0.4 times 100 to give the value 40, or 40%.

$$0.4 \times 100 = 40$$
$$0.4 = 40\%$$

Example

Convert 0.735 to a percent.

In this problem, we need to convert a decimal to a percentage. Multiply the decimal by 100.

$$0.735 \times 100 = 73.5$$

Now, we can express the conversion as an equation using the percentage sign.

$$0.735 = 73.5\%$$

Example

Convert $\frac{3}{5}$ to a percent.

In this problem we need to convert a fraction to a percentage. First, convert the fraction to a decimal, and then convert the decimal to a percentage.

Rewrite the fraction as a division problem.

$$\frac{3}{5} = 5\overline{)3}$$

Next, we will solve the new division problem by extending the decimal and using long division.

$$\begin{array}{r} 0.6 \\ 5\overline{)3.0} \\ \underline{3\,0} \\ 0 \end{array}$$

Now that we have a decimal form, we can multiply the decimal quotient by 100.

$$0.6 \times 100 = 60$$

Last, we can express the conversion as an equation using the percent sign.

$$\frac{3}{5} = 60\%$$

Another way to approach this problem is to convert the fraction to a value out of 100, and then convert the fraction out of 100 to a percentage.

First, we will use equivalent fractions to convert $\frac{3}{5}$ to a fraction out of 100. We know that $5 \times 20 = 100$, so we can multiply $\frac{3}{5}$ by $\frac{20}{20}$ to get a fraction out of 100.

$$\frac{3}{5} \times \frac{20}{20} = \frac{60}{100}$$

Now, a percentage is a value out of 100, so we can rewrite this value as a percentage with the percentage sign.

$$\frac{60}{100} = 60\%$$

Last, we can rewrite the conversion as an equation.

$$\frac{3}{5} = 60\%$$

Converting Decimals to Fractions

To convert decimals to fractions, keep in mind place value and how a decimal is read. If you can remember the proper way to *read* a decimal, this will really help in generating a fraction that can then be simplified. If reading the decimal is difficult for you, you will need to identify each place value. For example, when you see a decimal like 0.20, you know that you can read this number as 20 hundredths, but also you can see that the smallest value is the zero in the hundredths place, so the fraction will be a part of 100. This can be represented as the fraction $\frac{20}{100}$, also read as 20 hundredths. Since 0.20 is equivalent to 0.2, you may also see this this decimal as 2 tenths and represent the fraction $\frac{2}{10}$, also read as 2 tenths. Once you have this value, you can simplify by finding a common factor between the numerator and denominator to find $\frac{1}{5}$, so $0.20 = \frac{1}{5}$.

$$0.20 = \frac{20}{100} = \frac{2}{10} = \frac{1}{5}$$

Example

Convert 1.225 to a fraction.

In this problem, we need to convert a decimal to a fraction. To approach this problem, we need to identify the place values in this decimal. Notice that there is a 1 in the ones place, a 2 in the tenths place, a 2 in the hundredths place, and a 5 in the thousandths place. We can also read this fraction as one and two hundred twenty-five thousandths.

Next, we will rewrite the decimal as a part compared to the smallest place value. The smallest place value, or the value farthest to the right, is the thousandths place. Because of this, our fraction will be part of 1,000.

$$\frac{1{,}225}{1{,}000}$$

Notice that we are writing this as an improper fraction. As we simplify, we can convert to a mixed number if that is needed. Sometimes improper fractions are easier to work with. It depends on the situation.

Next, we will reduce the fraction to simplest terms. Find the greatest common factor to reduce it in one step or find a common factor and reduce it in multiple steps. Both terms are divisible by 5, so we can start there. We will divide both the numerator and denominator by 5.

$$1{,}225 \div 5 = 245$$
$$1{,}000 \div 5 = 200$$

These terms can be reduced further. The new numerator and denominator are both divisible by 5, so we will divide both values by 5, again.

$$245 \div 5 = 49$$
$$200 \div 5 = 40$$

These terms cannot be simplified further.

The last step is to rewrite the conversion as an equation.

$$1.225 = \frac{49}{40}$$

Converting Percentages to Fractions

To convert percentages to fractions, keep in mind that a percentage is a rate per 100. Any percent can be written as a part of 100. For example, 54% can be converted to a fraction by writing it as $\frac{54}{100}$. Now, this fraction can be simplified using common factors to find that $54\% = \frac{27}{50}$.

Example

Convert 63% to a fraction.

In this problem, we need to convert a percentage to a fraction. We know that a percent is a rate per 100 or a part per 100. This means we can rewrite 60% as a fraction out of 100.

$$60\% = \frac{60}{100}$$

Now that we have written the percentage as a fraction out of 100, we can reduce the fraction to simplest terms. 60 and 100 are divisible by 20, so we will divide both the numerator and denominator by 20.

$$60 \div 20 = 3$$
$$100 \div 20 = 5$$

These terms cannot be simplified further, so the last step is to rewrite the conversion as an equation.

$$60\% = \frac{3}{5}$$

Review Video: Converting Fractions to Percentages and Decimals
Visit mometrix.com/academy and enter code: 306233

Review Video: Converting Decimals to Fractions and Percentages
Visit mometrix.com/academy and enter code: 986765

SOLVE PROBLEMS INVOLVING DECIMAL, PERCENTAGE, AND FRACTION CONVERSIONS

You Bought a Milkshake with $4 out of the $20 in Your Wallet. What Percentage Represents the Amount of Your Money That Was Spent?

a. 2%
b. 20%
c. 16%
d. 5%

In this problem, you are given a story. You used $4 out of the $20 in your wallet and need to find what percent represents the amount you spent.

To approach this problem, we need to understand what information is given, and what you need to find. If you spent $4 out of $20, that means that you spent 4 out of 20, which can be written as the fraction $\frac{4}{20}$.

We want to find what percentage this represents. We can use conversions to find the equivalent percentage to $\frac{4}{20}$.

To convert a fraction to a percentage, we can use equivalent fractions, or we can use division.

Let's start with division. Remember, fractions are another way to write a division problem, so $\frac{4}{20}$ is the same thing as 4 divided by 20. We can set this up using long division.

$$\begin{array}{r} 0.2 \\ 20\overline{)\,4.0} \\ \underline{0} \\ 4\,0 \end{array}$$

So, if you spent $4 out of a total of $20, you spent 0.2 of your money. We want this as a percent, so we can multiply this decimal number by 100, to find the percent.

$$0.2 \times 100 = 20$$

So, you spent 20% of your money.

We can also find this value using equivalent fractions. To use equivalent fractions to find a percentage, we want to find an equivalent fraction where the denominator is 100. We can see that

20 times 5 is 100, so if we multiply the numerator and denominator by 5, we will get an equivalent fraction out of 100.

$$\frac{4}{20} \times \frac{5}{5} = \frac{20}{100} = 20\%$$

$\frac{20}{100}$ is equivalent to 20%, so this also shows that we spent 20% of our money.

The correct answer is B.

Showing Equal Parts

Fractions, decimals, and percentages share a common function: they each compare a part to a whole. One example of this is a quarter. A quarter is 25 cents, or $0.25. We can express the relationship between quarters and dollars multiple ways. We could express this as a fraction. A quarter is $\frac{25}{100}$ of a dollar because it is 25 cents out of 100 cents. This could be simplified to $\frac{1}{4}$ of a dollar. We could express this as a decimal. A quarter is 0.25 of a dollar. And we could express this as a percent. A quarter is 25% of a dollar. Each of these representations show the same *value* of part compared to the whole. You may use strip diagrams or similar models to show equivalent values with fractions, decimals, and percentages.

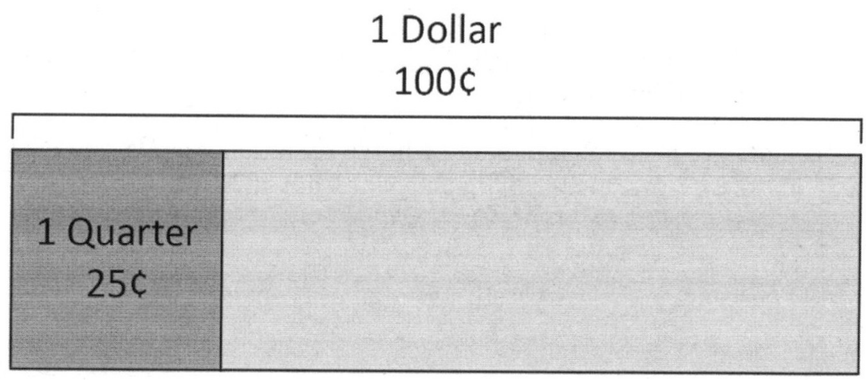

Percentage Problems

Percentage problems come in three possible categories: missing part, missing whole, and missing percent. Within every percentage problem, there is a whole value, a percent of the whole, and a value of the part. First, let's dissect the relationship between whole, percent, and part. Consider a value of 20, which will represent our whole value.

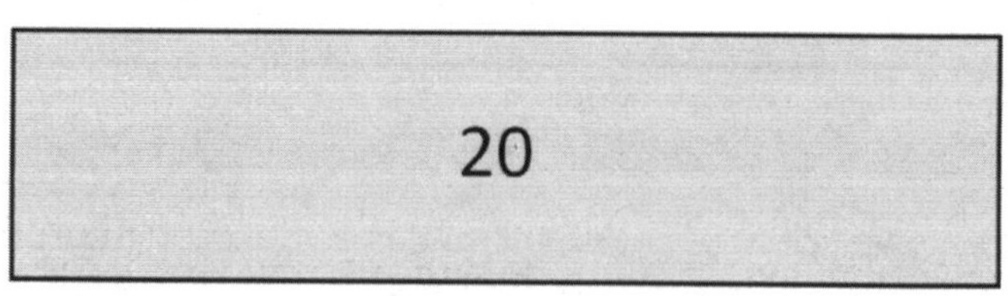

Now, any percent is going to be part of this whole value of 20.

50% would be half of the value of 20, which is 10.

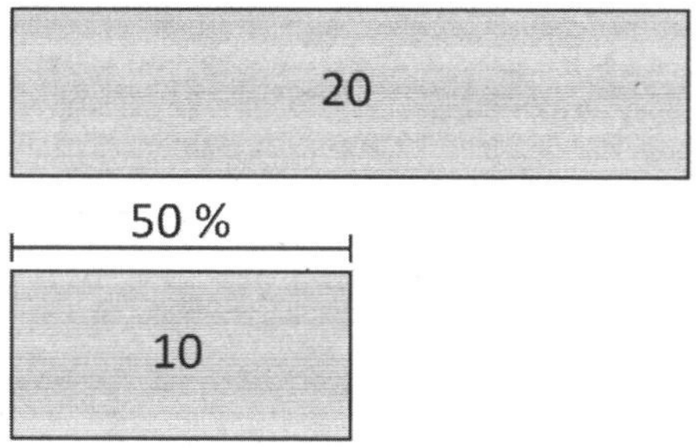

What is the relationship between these parts? How do we use equations to solve this?

Missing Part

Let's start with a missing part problem. This would look like, "What is 50% of 20?"

In this problem, we need to find 50% of a whole value 20. We know that 50% of 20 is 10, but let's figure out how we can solve this mathematically, so we have a strategy to solve more difficult problems.

To find the value of the missing part, we multiply the whole by the percent in decimal form. The decimal form of 50% is 0.5, so we multiply 20 by 0.5 to find the value of the part.

$$20 \times 0.5 = 10$$

So, in a missing part problem, our equation is:

$$\text{whole} \times \text{percent as a decimal} = \text{part}$$

Missing Whole

Now, let's look at missing whole problems. This will look like, "10 is 50% of what value?"

In this type of problem, we know the part, we know the percentage, but we need to find the value of the whole.

To find the value of the whole, we need to divide the value of the part by the decimal form of the percent. In this example, we need to divide 10 by the decimal form of 50%, which is 0.5.

$$10 \div 0.5 = 20$$

So, in a missing whole problem, our equation is:

$$\text{part} \div \text{percent as a decimal} = \text{whole}$$

Missing Percent

Lastly, we will look at a missing percent problem. A missing percent problem will look like, "10 is what percentage of 20?"

In this problem, we have a whole value and a part value, but we need to find the percent.

To find the percent, we need to divide the part by the whole. Our answer will be in decimal form, so we will need to convert it to percent form by multiplying by 100%. In this example, we need to take

10 (the part) and divide it by 20 (the whole) and multiply the answer by 100% to get the percent value.

$$10 \div 20 = 0.5 \times 100\% = 50\%$$

So, in a missing percent problem, our equation is:

$$\text{part} \div \text{whole} = \text{decimal} \times 100 = \text{percent}$$

Expressions, Equations, and Relationships

Independent and Dependent Quantities

When there is a relationship between two quantities, there is an independent quantity and a dependent quantity in the relationship. An **independent quantity** is the quantity that stands alone. This is the value that starts the relationship. A **dependent quantity** is reliant on the other quantity; it is dependent on the independent value. In a mathematical relationship, there is a value, something is done to that value, and then you have an ending value. An additive relationship is an example of a relationship with an independent and a dependent quantity. In an additive relationship, there is a value, something is added to the value, and then you have an ending value. This can be described by the equation $y = x + a$. In this equation, x is the independent quantity. It stands alone; it is the quantity that is being changed. The ending value, the value that is dependent on x, is y; this is the dependent value. The value of y is dependent on the value of x. When looking at independent and dependent quantities in tables, the x-value and the y-value can also be understood as the **input** and the **output**.

Let's look at an algebraic relationship:

You get hired for your first job and make $10 an hour. In this scenario, the relationship is between dollars and hours worked. Which quantity is dependent on the other? The number of dollars you make is dependent on how many hours you work. So, we can say that dollars is the dependent value, the y-value, and hours is the independent value, the x-value.

Review Video: Identifying Independent and Dependent Variables
Visit mometrix.com/academy and enter code: 627181

Representing Algebraic Relationships

We can describe algebraic relationships using tables and equations. When you are given a table, there is an independent quantity and a dependent quantity. There is a starting value, the value that an operation is done to, and there is an end value, the value that occurs after the operation. We often see algebraic relationships in the form $y = x + b$ or $y = kx$. When subtraction and division are involved, we can see these equations in the form of $y = x + (-b)$, or $y = x - b$, and $y = \frac{x}{k}$. We can use any variable to describe these relationships, but there will be an independent value, the value that the operation is happening to, and a dependent value, the outcome of the operation. We see these relationships often shown in tables; they are sometimes called "in and out tables", where an independent value goes "in", and a dependent value comes "out". When we have a table that shows a relationship, we can write an equation to describe the relationship. In the table, we will have an independent quantity, an operation, and a dependent quantity. Once we can identify those parts, we can write an equation to describe the relationship.

Representing Real-World Algebraic Relationships

Algebraic relationships can be described using tables, graphs, and equations. Algebraic relationships are relationships between independent and dependent variables and appear in real-world situations. It is important to be able to identify equations, tables, and graphs that illustrate real-world algebraic relationships. You may see a scenario that describes a relationship and need to choose the correct graph or table that describes the relationship. You may see an equation that illustrates an algebraic relationship and need to identify a story that the equation best describes. In either type of question, it is important to start by identifying the independent and dependent variables and then identify the pattern. In other words, identify the x-values, the y-values, and the operation. Once you have identified these three main parts of an algebraic relationship, you can convert that meaning to an equation, a table, a graph, or a story.

EXAMPLE

Elyse bought x stickers from a local artist for \$3.25 per sticker. She spent y dollars on stickers. Which equation matches Elyse's situation?

a. $3.25x = y$
b. $y = x + 3.25$
c. $3.25 = x + y$
d. $y = x - 3.25$

In this problem, we are given a situation and a list of equations. We need to choose the equation that matches the situation.

To approach this problem, we need to review the situation and write an equation to match Elyse's situation.

If Elyse bought x stickers for \$3.25, the total number of dollars spent is $\$3.25x$. If she bought 5 stickers, we would multiply \$3.25 by 5 to get the total, or if she bought 10, we would multiply 10 by \$3.25 to get the total.

One side of our equation will be $\$3.25x$.

We also know that the total number of dollars spent is y. That means that y is going to be on the other side of our equation.

The equation that matches this story is $y = 3.25x$.

The equation $y = 3.25x$ is equivalent to $3.25x = y$, and this matches one of our choices.

The correct answer is A.

EXAMPLE

The graph shows the average number of sandwiches, y, a restaurant sells per day, x.

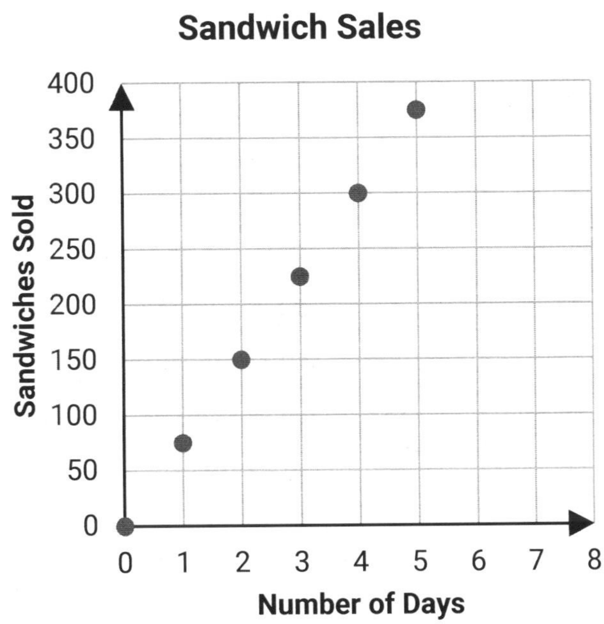

Which equation best represents the relationship between x and y represented by the graph?

a. $y = 75x$
b. $y = 75 + x$
c. $y = 150 + x$
d. $y = 150x$

In this problem, we are given a graph and four equation choices. Examine the graph and select the equation that best represents the relationship between x and y on the graph.

Identify the relationship between x and y on the graph. To do this, we need to first recognize the x- and y-axis and the values of the coordinates.

When we look at this graph, we can see that the number of days is represented along the bottom, the x-axis, and the number of sandwiches is represented along the left side, the y-axis. So, sandwiches are the y-values, and days are the x-values.

Now, we need to list the values that we see on the graph.

We can see that our first point is at (0,0). This means that after zero days, the restaurant sells zero sandwiches.

The next point is at (1,75). This means that after 1 day, the restaurant sells 75 sandwiches.

The next point is at (2,150), followed by (3,225), (4,300), and (5,375).

The best way to examine these values is to make an x and y table and observe the pattern.

x	y
0	0
1	75
2	150
3	225
4	300
5	375

Now that we can observe the values, we can see that the restaurant sells about 75 sandwiches per day because on day 1, they sell 75, and the y-value increases by 75 each day, so the pattern is times 75.

This means that the relationship between the x- and y-values can be represented by the equation $y = 75x$ because the total number of sandwiches, y, can be found by multiplying 75 by the number of days, x.

Our equation, $y = 75x$, matches answer choice A.

The correct answer is A.

EXAMPLE

Tamila is playing a ball game with her brother where they get 3 points for each trick shot they make. Which graph best shows the relationship between the number of trick shots made and the number of points?

a.

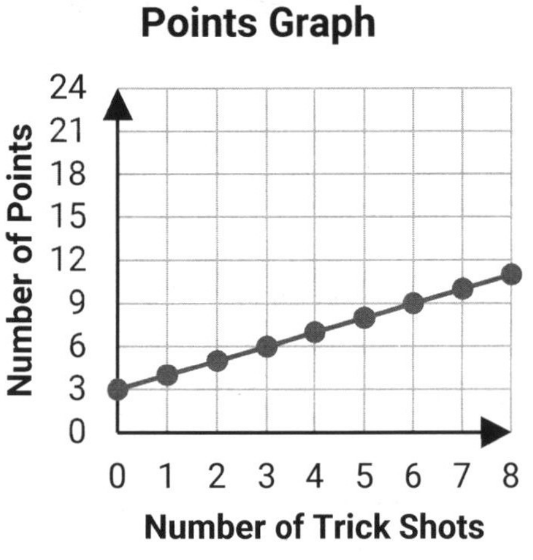

c.

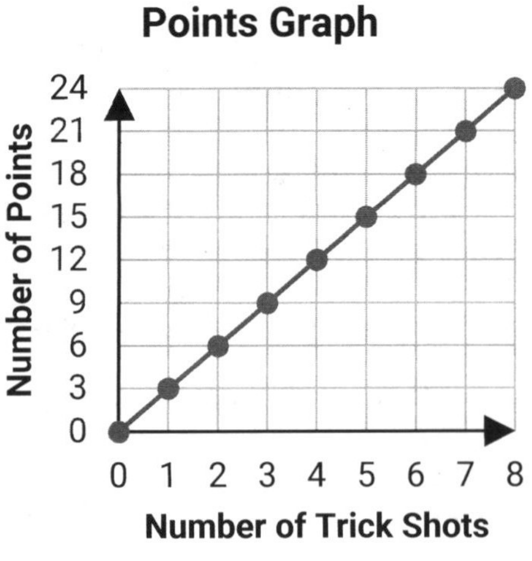

b.

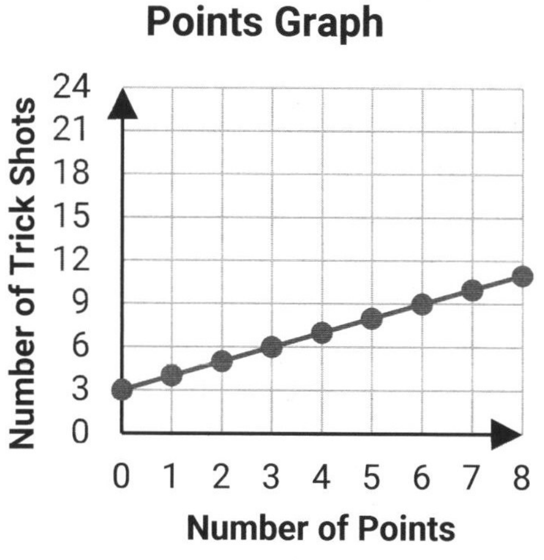

d.

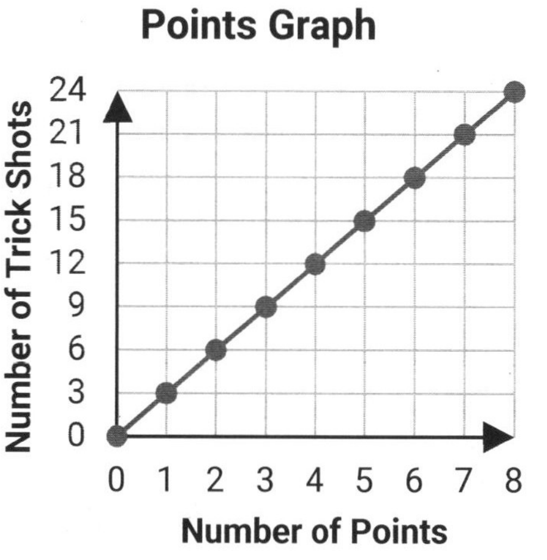

In this problem, we are given a story and four graphs. We need to examine the relationship between trick shots and points and select the graph that best represents the relationship.

In the story, we know that Tamila and her brother are playing a game where they try to make trick shots and they get 3 points for each trick shot made. We should ask ourselves, what is the pattern in this story? There are a few ways to approach this.

One way to approach this is to complete a table. If Tamila makes 0 trick shots, she will have 0 points. If she makes 1 trick shot, she will have 3 points. If she makes 2 trick shots, she will have 6 points. If she makes 3 trick shots, she will have 9 points, and so on. We can include this data in a data table.

x	0	1	2	3	4	5	6	7	8
y	0	3	6	9	12	15	18	21	24

We can also think about the pattern. If Tamila is getting 3 points for each trick shot, we know that this is a multiplication pattern.

Based on the pattern from the story and the table, the equation for this story is $y = 3x$, where y is the total number of points and x is the total number of trick shots made.

Now, we need to examine the graphs and select the graph that best represents this equation and pattern.

If we look at our graph choices, we can see a few main differences.

Choices A and C show the number of trick shots along the x-axis and number of points along the y-axis.

Choices B and D show the number of points along the x-axis and the number of trick shots along the y-axis.

The first difference is in the placement of the x- and y-values.

We can also see a difference in the lines on the graphs. The lines shown in options C and D are steeper than the lines shown in options A and B.

Let's examine these graphs a little more closely.

Choices A and B show a graph that is less steep than choices C and D.

If we observe the data points on graphs A and B, we will see that the data points are (0,3), (1,4), (2,5), (3,6), (4,7), (5,8), (6,9), (7,10), (8,11).

By looking at these data points, we can see that the pattern is adding 3. This would mean that choices A and B represent the pattern $y = x + 3$. This does not match the story.

If we observe the data points on graphs C and D, we will see that the data points are (0,0), (1,3), (2,6), (3,9), (4,12), (5,15), (6,18), (7,21), and (8,24).

By looking at these data points, we can see that the pattern is multiplying by 3 because if you multiply each x-value by 3, you will get the y-value. This would mean that options C and D represent the pattern $y = 3x$. This matches our story.

This means that the correct answer is either C or D. What is the difference between these two graphs? The difference is the x- and y-axis.

In graph C, we can see that the x-axis represents the number of trick shots, and the y-axis represents the number of points.

In graph D, we can see that the x-axis represents the number of points, and the y-axis represents the number of trick shots.

We have already identified the pattern is $y = 3x$ because the total number of points is the number of trick shots made times the number of points for each trick shot, 3. This means that the number of points is represented by the y-values and the y-axis, and the number of trick shots is represented by the x-values and the x-axis.

Graph C correctly represents this information.

The correct answer is C.

Order of Operations

The **order of operations** is a mathematical term to describe the correct sequence of steps to simplify an expression or solve an equation. The order of operations is very specific and important to remember. The acronym **PEMDAS** is used to help remember the order of operations.

The first two operations are **parentheses** and **exponents**. This is the PE in PEMDAS. When given an expression or equation that includes parentheses or exponents, these items should be dealt with first. If you have an expression or equation with both items, or more than one, you will first simplify or solve the items in parentheses, then the items with exponents.

If there are parentheses or exponents within other parentheses or exponents, you should simplify from the inside out. For instance, given the expression $3 \times (5 - 2)^2$, you first solve the part inside the parentheses, $5 - 2$, and then solve the exponent, 3^2. But given the expression $3 \times (5 - 2^2)$, you first solve the exponent, 2^2, and then the parentheses, $5 - 4$.

The next group is **multiplication** and **division**. This is the M and D in PEMDAS. When given an expression or equation that includes multiplication or division, these operations are dealt with *after* parentheses and exponents if they are present. If multiplication and division are present, simplify from left to right. For example, given the expression $24 \div 4 + 3 \times 5$, we would simplify the expression $24 \div 4$ and then the expression 3×5.

The last category is **addition** and **subtraction**, the A and S in PEMDAS. This is the last category that is dealt with when simplifying an expression. Addition and subtraction are dealt with after parentheses, exponents, multiplication, and division, and when there is more than one addition or subtraction operation, they are solved or simplified from left to right. For example, given the expression $2 + 4 - 3 + 7$, we would simplify from left to right. First, $2 + 4$, then $6 - 3$ (note that we are using the result of the previous expression because it is simplified first), and last, $3 + 7$.

Review Video: Order of Operations
Visit mometrix.com/academy and enter code: 259675

Prime Factorization

A **factor** is a number that can be multiplied to get a given number. It is part of a multiplication or division relationship. Factors can be multiplied together to get a given number, and a number can be divided by a factor to get another factor. For example, you can find the factors of 24. Let's start by thinking about what groups of numbers can be multiplied to get 24. 24×1, 12×2, 3×8, and 4×6 can all be multiplied to get 24. So, the factors of 24 are 24, 12, 8, 6, 4, 3, 2, and 1. Numbers with more than two factors are called **composite numbers**. 24 is a composite number.

Some numbers are **prime numbers**. A prime number's only factors are itself and 1. 3 is a prime number because the only whole numbers that can be multiplied together to get 1 are 3 and 1, as in 3×1 or 1×3.

1 and 0 are neither prime nor composite numbers.

The **prime factorization** of a number is a process to find the prime factors of a given number. To find the prime factors of a given number, we often use what is called a **factor tree**. This is a visual process to find the prime factorization of a given number.

Review Video: Prime Factorization
Visit mometrix.com/academy and enter code: 760669

Example

Find the prime factorization of 24.

In this example, we will divide factors down to the groups of prime numbers.

24

To find the prime factorization of 24 we will start with a factor of 24. There are a lot of factors to choose from. When finding prime factors, you can begin with any set of factors, except 1 and the given number. In this example, let's start with the smallest prime number factor, which is 2. $12 \times 2 = 24$, so, 12 and 2 are factors. We can notate this on our factor tree.

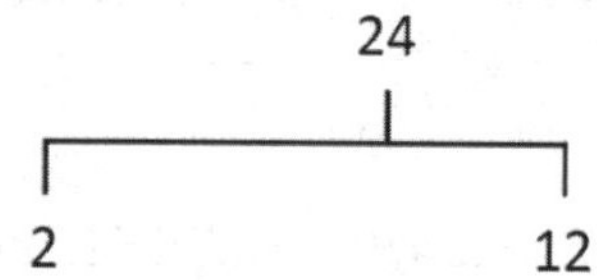

2 is a prime number so it is one of the prime factors. We can circle this on our factor tree to show that this is a prime factor. 12 is not a prime number and can be divided further.

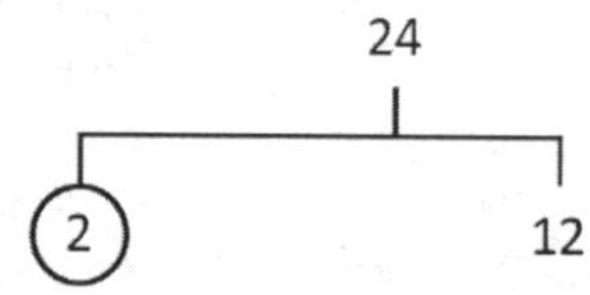

We will now find factors of 12. We know that we can get 12 by multiplying 2×6 and 3×4. It does not matter which factor groups we start with, so in this example, let's use 3 and 4. We can notate these on our factor tree.

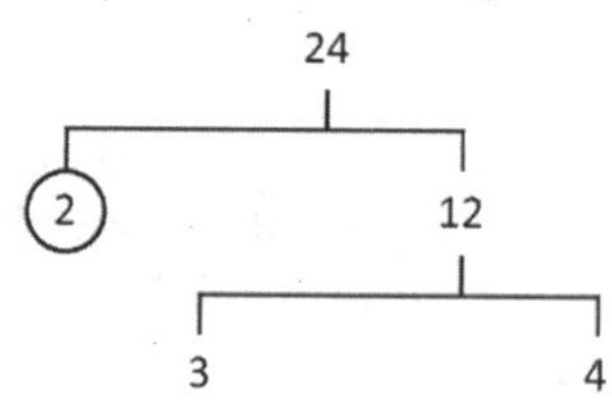

3 is a prime number, 4 is not a prime number. We can show that 3 is a prime number using a circle.

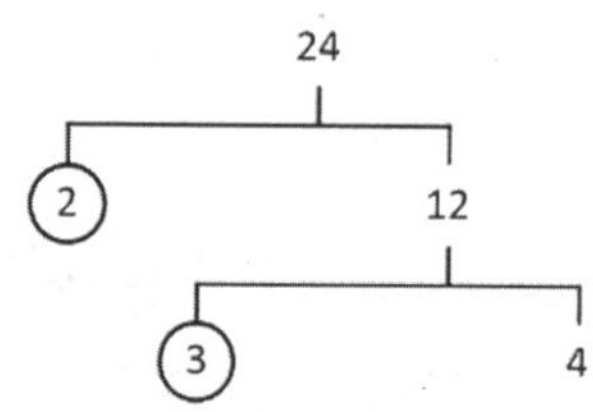

Now, we need to find the factors of 4. 4×1 and 2×2 are the only factors of 4. Since 1 is not a prime number, so we should use 2 and 2. We will notate this on the factor tree.

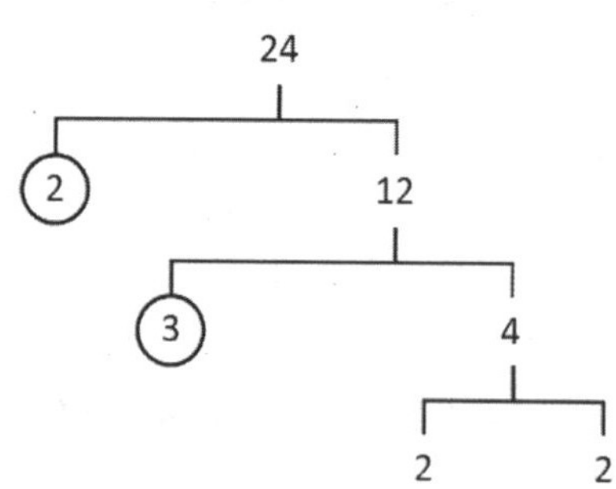

2 is a prime number, so the terms cannot be simplified any further. We can circle both terms in our factor tree.

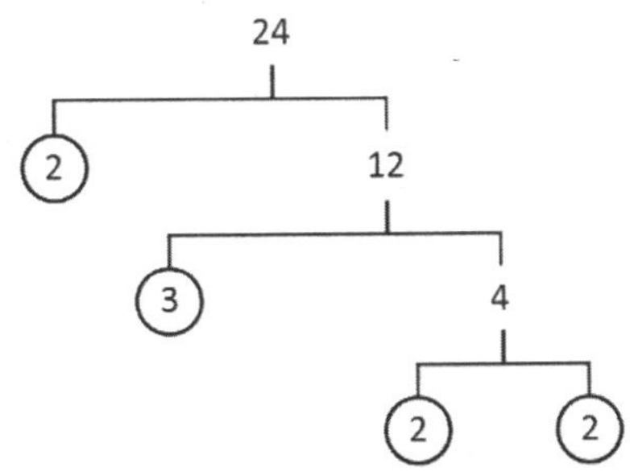

Now we have a list of prime factors: 2, 3, 2, and 2. These are the prime factors of 24. This means that if we multiply all these terms together, we will get 24, or that $2 \times 3 \times 2 \times 2 = 24$.

The last step in finding the prime factorization is to simplify our expression. Our current expression for the prime factorization is $2 \times 3 \times 2 \times 2$. Simplify by grouping like terms.

$2 \times 2 \times 2$ can be rewritten using an exponent. This is equivalent to 2^3. The 3 in our expression is already simplified.

$$2 \times 3 \times 2 \times 2$$
$$2^3 \times 3$$

So, the prime factorization of 24 is $2^3 \times 3$.

Example

Below is the incomplete prime factorization of 252. Find the missing prime factors.

$$3^2 \times 7 \times \_\_$$

In this problem, we are required to find the missing prime factors of 252. To begin this problem, we will first need to find an equivalent expression and solve for the missing value.

We can simplify the expression by first finding the value of the exponent. 3^2 is equivalent to 9. We can notate this in our simplification.

$$9 \times 7 \times \_\_$$

Next, we can simplify 9×7 to 63.

$$63 \times \_\_$$

We are finding the prime factorization of 252, so we can ask ourselves what number multiplied by 63 will give us 252, or what is 252 divided by 63. We can do a quick calculation to find that $252 \div 63 = 4$.

So, $3^2 \times 7 \times 4 = 252$.

Remember, we are finding missing prime factors, but 4 is not prime. So, we must take it a step further and find the prime factors of 4.

The factors of 4 are 2 and 2, and 2 is a prime number. We also know that $2^2 = 4$.

Now we know our missing values.

The prime factorization of 252 is $3^2 \times 7 \times 2^2$ and the missing value is 2^2.

We can check our work by simplifying the expression.

$$3^2 \times 7 \times 2^2$$
$$9 \times 7 \times 4$$
$$63 \times 4$$
$$252$$

Identifying Equivalent Expressions

Expressions Versus Equations

An **expression** includes numbers, variables, or numbers and variables separated with operation signs. Anything that stands alone or could belong on one side of an equal sign, is an expression. $3x + 4$ is an example of an expression. It contains numbers, a variable, and an operation. A single number is also considered an expression. Often, expressions are simplified. $2x + 4x - 1x$ is an example of an expression because there is no equal sign. It cannot be solved; you cannot solve for x in an expression, but it can be simplified. The expression below is simplified.

$$2x + 4x - 1x$$
$$6x - 1x$$
$$5x$$

Each step gives a more simplified version of the same expression. Each step in the simplification gives an equivalent expression.

Identify Equivalent Expressions with Variables

A **variable** is any unknown value represented by a letter or symbol, most commonly x. A **term** is a number or a number multiplied by a variable, like 3, or $3x$. Numerical expressions will include variable terms, and you may be required to identify or generate equivalent expressions that include these variable terms. When you encounter variables, it is important to remember that with each variable, any repetition of that variable is a **like term**. For example, x and y are not like terms because they are different unknown values. Also, x and 4 are not like terms because 4 is a whole number and x is an unknown term. However, x and $3x$ are like terms because they share the same variable. When encountering an expression with like terms, you may be required to simplify or expand the expression to find equivalent expressions.

Simplify the expression $4x + 2x + 7$.

Given the expression $4x + 2x + 7$, you have two like terms. We simplify these terms to find an equivalent expression. We can combine $4x + 2x$ to $6x$ because they are like terms.

So, $4x + 2x + 7$ is equivalent to $6x + 7$.

Expand the expression $4x + 2x + 7$.

Given the same expression $4x + 2x + 7$, we can expand the variable terms to find an equivalent expression. For example, $4x$ can be expanded to $(x + x + x + x)$, and $2x$ can be expanded to $(x + x)$.

So, $4x + 2x + 7$ is equivalent to $(x + x + x + x) + (x + x) + 7$.

When identifying equivalent expressions with variables, like terms can be combined, simplified, or expanded to generate an equivalent expression.

Using the Order of Operations

An **equivalent expression** is part of a set of expressions that have an equivalent value. The order of operations is essential to finding and identifying equivalent expressions. Finding equivalent expressions may require you to simplify or expand an expression. You may simplify the whole expression, or just part of the expression. For example, you may be required to simplify or identify an equivalent expression like $3(2 + 4) - 5$. There are many equivalent expressions that can be generated by this example. These are just a few possibilities.

Simplification

$3(6) - 5$ is an equivalent expression. The part of the expression in parentheses was simplified.

$18 - 5$ is an equivalent expression. The parentheses and multiplication parts of the expression were simplified.

13 is an equivalent expression. All components of the expression have been simplified.

Expansion

$3(2 + 2^2) - 5$ is an equivalent expression. The term 4 has been expanded to include an exponent.

$3(2 + 4) - (5 \times 1)$ is an equivalent expression. The term 5 has been expanded as 5×1.

There are many variations of the same expression. You may be required to simplify or expand an expression to identify equivalence.

Using Exponents

An **exponent** is used to identify a multiple of the same factor. The symbol for an exponent is a small number to the top right of a whole number. The small number shows how many times the whole number should be multiplied by itself. For example, 2^3 is equivalent to $2 \times 2 \times 2$, or 8. When identifying equivalent expressions using exponents, you may be required to simplify exponents, expand exponents, or generate exponents.

Simplification

Given the expression $4^2 + 2 - 3$, you may find an equivalent expression by simplifying the exponent. In this case, the exponential expression is 4^2. This can be simplified by finding the value of 4^2, which is 16. So, an equivalent expression to $4^2 + 2 - 3$ is $16 + 2 - 3$.

Expansion

You may be required to expand an expression including an exponent. Given the expression 4×2^3, you may expand this exponent. In this case, the exponential expression is 2^3. This can be expanded to $2 \times 2 \times 2$. So, an equivalent expression to 4×2^3 is $4 \times (2 \times 2 \times 2)$.

Generate Exponents

You may be required to generate an exponent to identify an equivalent expression. Given the expression $8 + 4 + 36$, you may convert each of these values to an exponential expression. 8 can be rewritten as 2^3, 4 can be rewritten as 2^2, and 36 can be rewritten as 6^2. So, an equivalent expression to $8 + 4 + 36$ is $2^3 + 2^2 + 6^2$.

When identifying equivalent expressions with exponents, these values can be simplified, expanded, or generated to identify equivalent expressions.

Review Video: Exponents
Visit mometrix.com/academy and enter code: 600998

USING MODELS

We can use models to illustrate and compare expressions to tell if they are **equivalent**. This can be a helpful strategy when starting out comparing expressions. Models are another way to write an expression in expanded form. We can compare expressions using common models, like strip diagrams, hanging models, and tiles. Using models is not the most efficient way to compare expressions and is not recommended to use during testing because it is time consuming. However, models can be helpful when you run out of strategies, or you are just starting out comparing expressions.

HANGING MODELS

Compare expressions with hanging models.

Hanging models are used to illustrate if two expressions are equivalent. One expression is illustrated on each side of the model to compare. Consider the expressions $3x + 2x$ and $7x - 2x$. These expressions can be compared using a hanging model.

We will start by illustrating one expression on each side of the model.

We can illustrate $3x + 2x$ as:

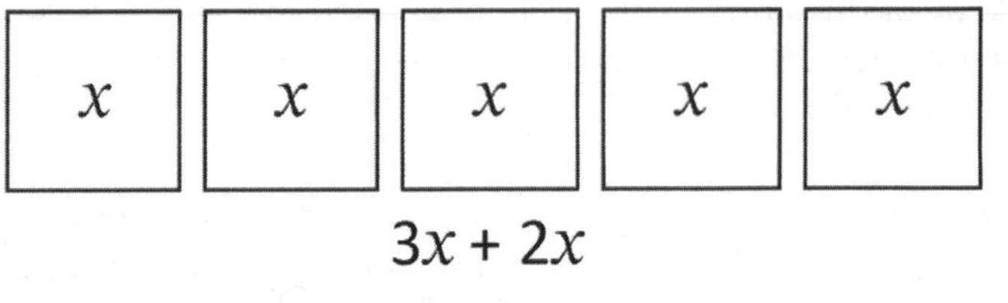

because $3x + 2x$ can be expanded to $(x + x + x) + (x + x)$.

Now, we can model the second expression. We can illustrate $7x - 2x$ as:

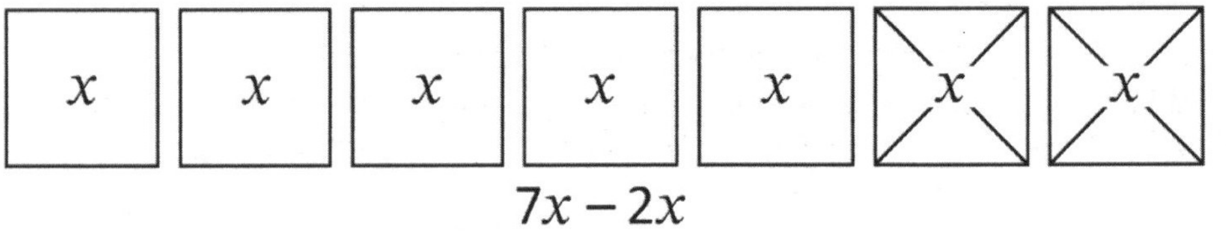

because it can be expanded to $(x + x + x + x + x + x + x) - (x + x)$.

A completed hanging model would look like this.

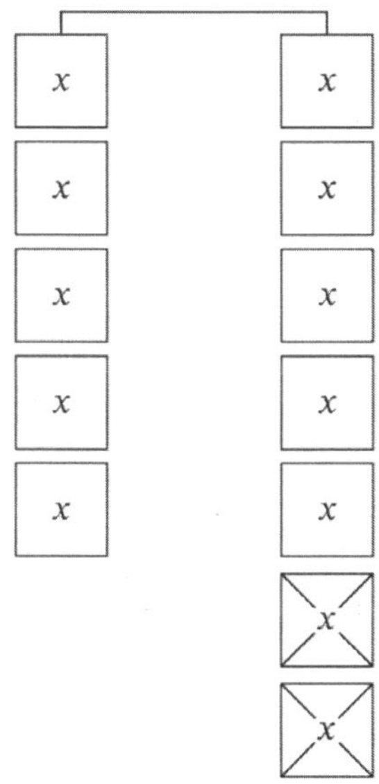

Now that we have a complete hanging model, we can see that each expression is equivalent. Both sides are balanced, since the number of x's on the left side and the number of x's on the right side are equal.

Strip Diagrams

Compare expressions with strip diagrams.

Strip diagrams can be used to illustrate expressions and make it easy to determine if they are equivalent. Let's use a strip diagram to see if $3x + 5$ and $2x + 7$ are equivalent.

First, we need to illustrate each expression in a strip diagram.

$3x + 5$ can be illustrated as:

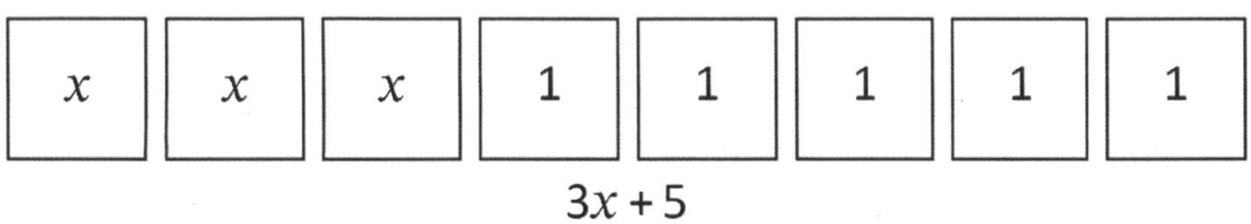

The expression $3x + 5$ can be expanded to $x + x + x + 1 + 1 + 1 + 1 + 1$.

$2x + 7$ can be illustrated as:

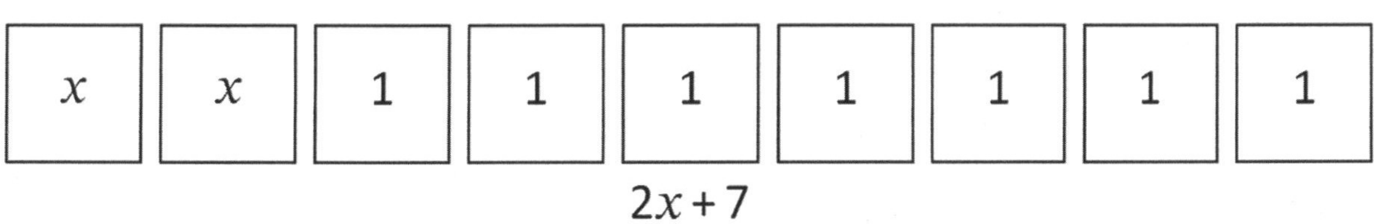

The expression $2x + 7$ can be expanded to $x + x + 1 + 1 + 1 + 1 + 1 + 1 + 1$.

Now that each expression is illustrated by a strip diagram, we can compare. Are these expressions equivalent?

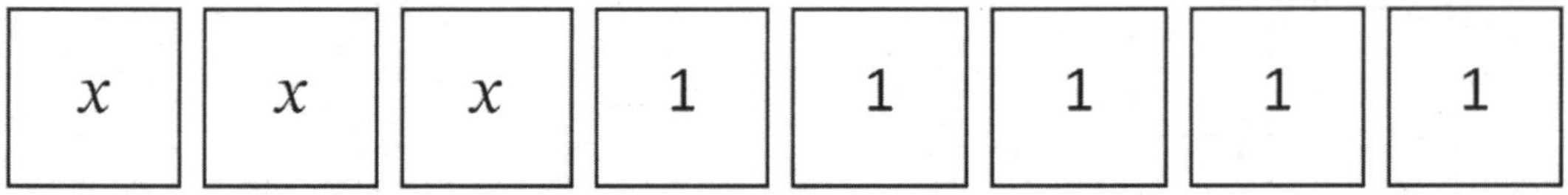

$3x + 5$

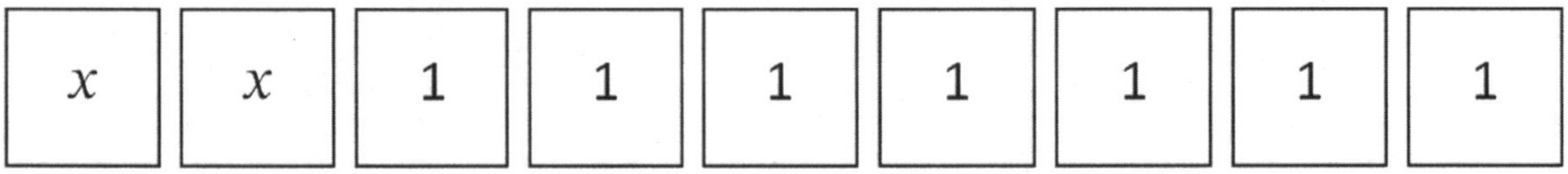

$2x + 7$

No. They each have a different number of x's and a different number of 1's. These expressions are not equivalent.

TILES

Compare expressions using tiles.

Tiles are used to illustrate expressions. In class, you may experience using virtual or physical tiles. They can also be drawn to help compare expressions. Let's use tiles to see if $2(3 + x)$ and $6 + 2x$ are equivalent.

We can start by building an illustration for $2(3 + x)$.

First, we will illustrate the expression $3 + x$.

This can be illustrated with tiles as:

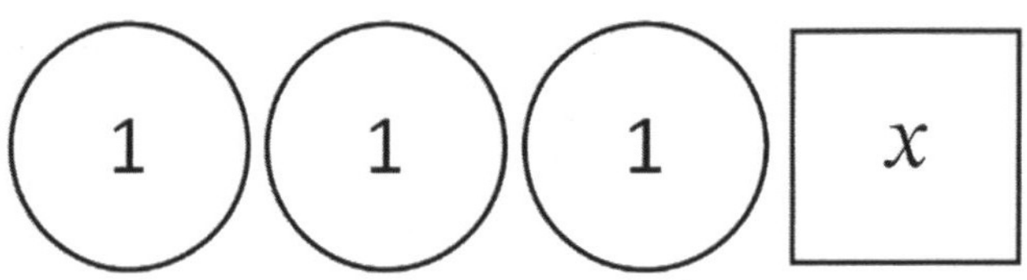

In this expression, $3 + x$ is being multiplied by 2, so let's double that expression.

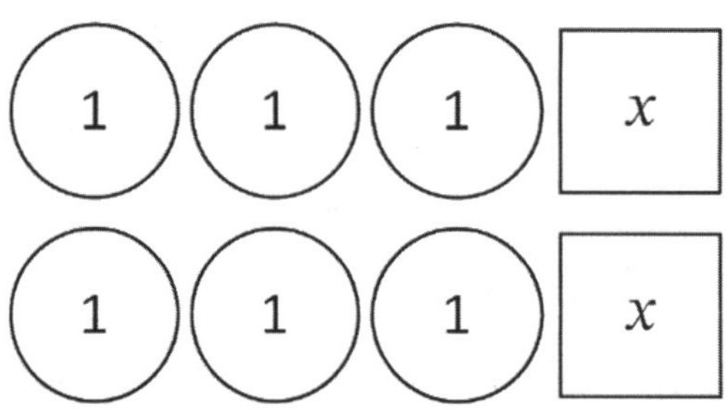

Now that we have one expression illustrated, we can illustrate $6 + 2x$. This can be illustrated with tiles as:

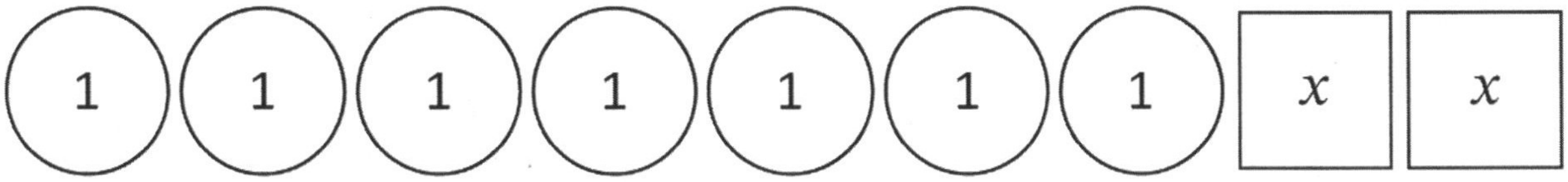

Now we can compare these values. Are these expressions equivalent? Each expression has the same number of x tiles and the same number of 1 tiles. So, they are equivalent.

Generating Equivalent Expressions

Using the Inverse Property

The **inverse property of addition** states that the sum of a number and its opposite is always equal to 0. Remember, the opposite of a number is a number that is opposite on the number line from zero, or the same number with the opposite sign. For example, −4 is opposite to 4, and 1,726.9 is opposite to −1,726.9. So, the inverse property of addition states that if you add opposite numbers, their sum is zero. For example, $5 + (-5) = 0$ and $-5 + 5 = 0$.

The **inverse property of multiplication** states that a number multiplied by its reciprocal is always equal to 1. The **reciprocal** of a number is its "flipped" fraction. For example, the reciprocal of 5 is $\frac{1}{5}$, or the reciprocal of $\frac{2}{3}$ is $\frac{3}{2}$. The inverse property of multiplication can be applied for these values, $5 \times \frac{1}{5} = 1$ and $\frac{2}{3} \times \frac{3}{2} = 1$. This is because when you multiply across, you get a fraction that is equal to 1.

$$\frac{2}{3} \times \frac{3}{2} = \frac{6}{6} = 1$$

Examples

Equivalent expressions can be generated using these inverse properties. There is an endless number of possibilities. Let's look at a few examples.

Given the expression $12 \times 0 + (4 - 6)$, we can use the inverse property of addition to generate equivalent expressions.

Using the inverse property of addition, we can say that $12 \times 0 + (4 - 6)$ is equivalent to $12(3 + -3) + (4 - 6)$. Alternatively, the expression $12 \times 0 + (4 - 6)$ is also equivalent to $12(-36 + 36) + (4 - 6)$.

We can do this because the sum of opposite numbers is equal to 0. In this example, we used $(3 + -3)$ and $(36 + -36)$ as equivalent expressions to 0. We could replace the 0 in the original expression with any expression that is equivalent to 0.

Given the expression $1 + (4 - 6)$, we can use the inverse property of multiplication to generate equivalent expressions. Using the inverse property of multiplication, we can say that $1 + (4 - 6)$ is equivalent to $\left(2 \times \frac{1}{2}\right) + (4 - 6)$, or $\left(\frac{5}{4} \times \frac{4}{5}\right) + (4 - 6)$. We can do this because when we multiply a number and its reciprocal, we get 1.

Using the Identity Property

The **identity property of multiplication** states that when a number is multiplied by 1, you get the same number. That is, anything multiplied by 1 is itself. For example, $2 \times 1 = 2$, or $1 \times -36 = -36$. Using the identity property of multiplication, we can identify and generate equivalent expressions. Let's say that we are given the expression $15 - (3 \times 4)$. We can generate equivalent expressions using the identity property. One equivalent expression example would be $(15 \times 1) - (3 \times 4)$. Another example would be $15 - (1 \times 3 \times 4)$. We can say these expressions are equivalent because the identity property of multiplication states that we can multiply any portion of an expression by 1 to get the same value.

The **identity property of addition** states that when 0 is added to a number, you get the same number. For example, $2 + 0 = 2$, or $0 + -3 = -3$. We can also use this property to identify and generate equivalent expressions. For example, if we are given the expression $2 \times (1 + 2)$, we could write the equivalent expressions $2 \times (0 + 1 + 2)$ or $(2 + 0) \times (1 + 2)$.

Using the Commutative Property

The commutative property applies to addition and multiplication and states that these operations can be completed in any order. The **commutative property of addition** states that numbers and terms can be added together in any order to still get the same value. For example, $3 + 4 = 7$ and $4 + 3 = 7$. Also, we can use the commutative property of addition to show that $3x + 4 + 2^2$ is equivalent to $4 + 3x + 2^2$ and $2^2 + 4 + 3x$. When adding terms, you can add in any order and get the same value.

The **commutative property of multiplication** states that numbers and terms can be multiplied in any order to get the same value. For example, 12×3 is equivalent to 3×12. Additionally, we can use the commutative property of multiplication to assume that $(5 + 3) \times (36 - 6)$ is equivalent to $(36 - 6) \times (5 + 3)$. You can multiply terms in any order and still get the same value.

Using the Associative Property

The **associative property of addition** states that if three or more terms are being added together, the value is the same regardless of the groupings.

For example, given the expression $3 + 4 + 6$, these terms can be grouped and added in any form. $3 + 4 + 6$ is equivalent to $(3 + 4) + 6$ and is also equivalent to $3 + (4 + 6)$. This can be applied to write equivalent expressions in a variety of ways.

For example, suppose we are given the expression $5 + (y + 2) + 4$. We can generate equivalent expressions knowing the associative property. Knowing that when three or more terms are added, the grouping is irrelevant, we can say that this expression is equivalent to $5 + y + (2 + 4)$, and it is equivalent to $(5 + y) + (2 + 4)$. It is even equivalent to $5 + y + 2 + 4$.

The **associative property of multiplication** states that if three or more terms are being multiplied together, the value is the same regardless of the grouping. We can use this property to identify and generate equivalent expressions.

For example, given the expression $2 \times 7 \times 3$, these terms can be grouped in any way and still get the same value. $2 \times 7 \times 3$ is equivalent to $(2 \times 7) \times 3$ or $2 \times (7 \times 3)$.

We can use this information to generate and identify equivalent expressions. Knowing that terms can be grouped in any way when dealing with multiplication, we can find equivalent expressions by regrouping terms.

An example would be given the expression $5 \times (2 \times y) \times 4$. Using the associative property of multiplication, we know that when three or more terms are multiplied, we can group them in any way, so $5 \times (2 \times y) \times 4$ is equivalent to $(5 \times 2) \times (y \times 4)$. It is also equivalent to $(5 \times 2) \times y \times 4$ and $5 \times 2 \times (y \times 4)$. It is even equivalent to $(5 \times 2 \times y) \times 4$ and $5 \times (2 \times y \times 4)$.

Using the Distributive Property

The distributive property is one of the most used properties when generating equivalent expressions. This concept is tested very often, so it is important to be able to use this property effectively. The **distributive property** states that when the sum of two or more terms is multiplied by a number, it is the same as adding the product of each term multiplied by that number. Let's look at the expression $4(3 + 2)$. With the distributive property, we can say that this expression is equivalent to $(4 \times 3) + (4 \times 2)$. This also applies to more simplified multiplication problems. For example, 6×87 can be expressed as $6(80 + 7)$ which is equivalent to $(6 \times 80) + (6 \times 7)$. This is very useful when simplifying expressions, especially when generating or identifying equivalent expressions.

Review Video: Commutative, Associative, and Distributive Properties
Visit mometrix.com/academy and enter code: 483176

Example

Use the **distributive property** to identify an equivalent expression.

Which of the following is equivalent to the expression $2(y + 5) - 3$?

a. $2 + y + 2 + 5 - 3$
b. $2 \times y \times 2 \times 5 - 3$
c. $2 \times y + 2 \times 5 - 3$
d. $2 \times y \times 2 + 5 - 3$

We can approach this problem in a few ways. For this example, let's expand the given expression using the distributive property to identify an equivalent expression from the choices.

In the expression $2(y + 5) - 3$, we have the term $y + 5$ being multiplied by 2. This means that each term can be multiplied by 2 to give the same value.

So, $2(y + 5)$ is equivalent to $(2 \times y) + (2 \times 5)$.

Now, we have one operation left in our expression, –3. In this expression, $2(y + 5) - 3$, the entire expression $2(y + 5)$ has 3 subtracted by it. This comes at the end of the simplification, so we can place this at the end of our expression.

So, we can say that $2(y + 5) - 3$ is equivalent to $(2 \times y) + (2 \times 5) - 3$.

Review the answer choices. It looks like our options do not have parenthesis. Let's look at what we have so far: $(2 \times y) + (2 \times 5) - 3$.

Knowing order of operations and the fact that the multiplication operation is done before the addition and subtraction operation, we can rewrite this expression without parentheses.

This means $(2 \times y) + (2 \times 5) - 3$ is equivalent to $2 \times y + 2 \times 5 - 3$.

Review our choices. Choice C is the expression that is equivalent to the given expression.

Equations

WRITING EQUATIONS TO REPRESENT PROBLEMS

We can use **equations** to represent real-world math problems. When we write equations from problems, we need to understand what information we are provided, and what value is missing. If we can see what we know, and identify what we need to find, we can use numbers and symbols to illustrate any problem. When writing equations, we use variables to stand for the unknown values.

Let's say you are given this story: You get paid $250 every month from your new job. You have been working there for 2 months and have $820 in your account. How much money was in your account when you started the job?

In this problem, we know how much money you get per month, we know how many months you have been working, and we know how much money you have now.

What do we not know? We do not know how much money you started with. We are trying to find how much money you had in your account before the 2 months.

We can use d for the number of dollars in your account before you started working.

If we know a total, we can usually assume this can go on one side of our equal sign because we are doing some math and then we end up with $820.

$$\$820 =$$

Now we have 1 side of our equation. How will we get to $820? We will start with something and then add 2 months of pay. So, we know we will start with a number and then add to it. We can add this to the other side of the equation.

$$\$820 = d +$$

Now, we started with d and then added 2 payments of $250. So, we added 2 payments of $250 to d. We have two options here to show this. We could say that we added $500 to d.

$$\$820 = d + \$500$$

We can also say that we added $2 \times \$250$ to d.

$$820 = d + 2(250)$$

Because of the associative property, this equation can be written in multiple ways.

$$820 = d + 2(250)$$
$$d + 2(250) = 820$$
$$820 = 2(250) + d$$
$$2(250) + d = 820$$

When writing an equation, it is important to identify what you know and what you do not know. You will use a variable for the unknown value. Then you can start understanding what the problem is saying. Every problem has a starting point, something that happens, and an ending point. When you can identify these things, you can build an equation.

REPRESENTING EQUATIONS ON A NUMBER LINE

One-step equations can be represented on a number line. You may be asked to identify a number line that represents an addition, subtraction, multiplication, or division equation. These equations may include a variable. When representing equations on a number line, it is important to identify the starting point, the end point, and what happens in the middle.

In an addition equation, you will have a starting point, add a value, and have an ending point.

$2 + 3 = 5$ can be represented on a number line:

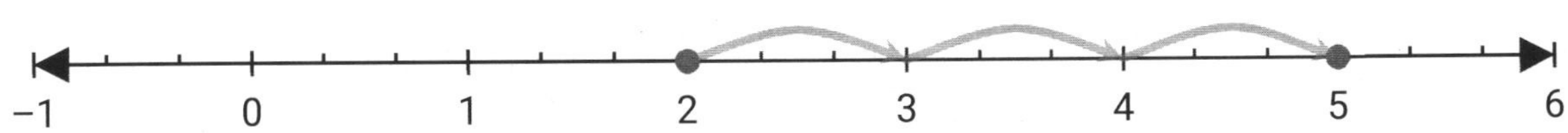

In a subtraction equation, you will have a starting value, a value decreased, and an ending value.

$5 - 2 = 3$ can be represented on a number line:

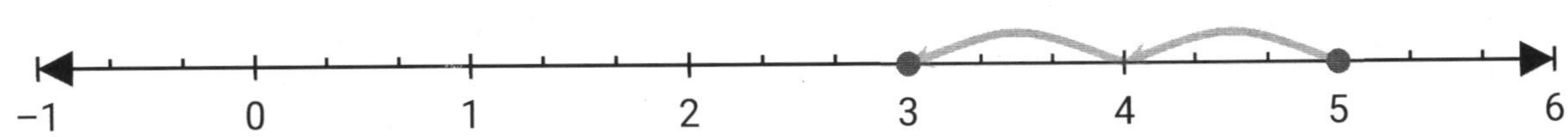

In a multiplication equation, you will start with zero, have a series of equal increases, and have an ending value.

$2 \times 3 = 6$ can be represented on a number line:

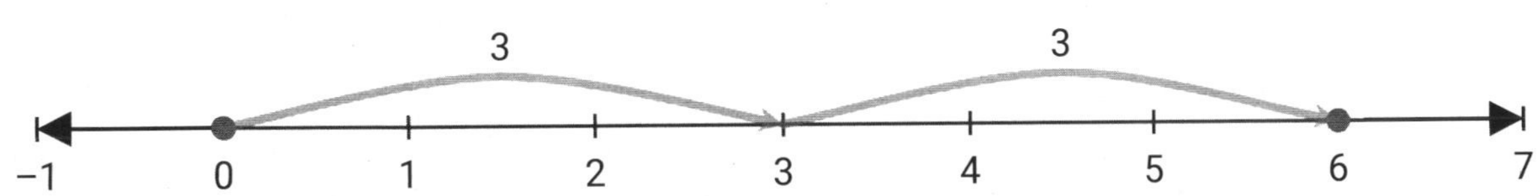

In a division equation, you will have a starting point, a series of regular partitions, an ending point at zero, and a value per partition.

$\frac{6}{2} = 3$ can be represented on a number line:

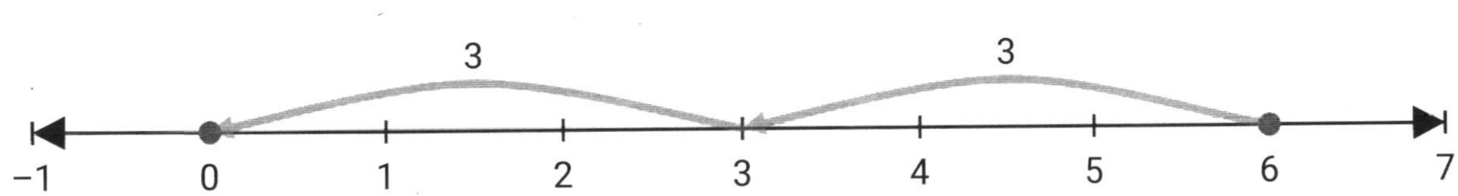

Using Equations to Express Scenarios

Stories and scenarios can be expressed through equations. You can write an equation to match a story or write a story to match an equation. It is important to understand what is going on in an equation, so you can choose a story that makes sense. An addition equation will include adding a value to an existing value and ending with a total. A subtraction equation will include a starting value, an ending value, and a value being taken away. A multiplication equation will usually have a certain number of groups of a value, or a value being replicated a certain number of times, with an ending value. And a division equation will usually have a starting value and that value being broken into segments or groups a certain number of times. Once you identify what is happening in an equation, you can match a story to the problem.

Solve Equations with a Variable

Equations with **variables** include an **unknown value**. When you are solving an equation with a variable, you are finding the value of that unknown quantity. You are finding the value of the variable. Sometimes logic is enough to solve these problems, sometimes you need to complete a series of steps, and sometimes you may need to try different values to check yourself.

Say you are given the equation $-6 + x = 10$, and you are asked what value of x will make this sentence true. There are a few ways to solve this.

The first step to solve this problem is using logic. Do you know this using mental math? Can you solve this problem just by looking at it? Perhaps. If you can use mental math, that is a great place to start. If you use mental math on a test, it is always a good idea to check your answer on paper just to be sure.

The next step to solve an equation is to solve for the variable. Given the equation $-6 + x = 10$, we can solve for x by performing operations to isolate x and get our variable on one side of the equation by itself.

In this example, we want to get x by itself on one side of the equation. We can do this by adding 6 to both sides of our equation.

$$\begin{aligned} -6 + x &= 10 \\ +6 &= +6 \\ x &= 16 \end{aligned}$$

We can do this because if we add, subtract, multiply, or divide the same value on both sides of the equation, the sentence will still be true. For instance, if $2 = 2$, then $2 + 3 = 2 + 3$.

$$\begin{gathered} 2 = 2 \\ 2 + 3 = 2 + 3 \end{gathered}$$

Now we know that the solution for $-6 + x = 10$ is $x = 16$. This means that if x equals 16, the sentence will be true.

The last strategy would be to use the values of x to test the solution. In this example, we have 16 as a possible solution, so we can use 16 in place of x to see if the equation is true.

$$\begin{aligned} -6 + x &= 10 \\ -6 + (16) &= 10 \\ 10 &= 10 \end{aligned}$$

When we simplify with 16 as the x-value, we get 10 on both sides of our equal sign, so our sentence is true and 16 is the solution.

EXAMPLE

What is the solution to the equation $-4x = 16$?

a. −4
b. 4
c. 12
d. −12

In this problem, we are given an equation and some possible solutions. We have two strategies to solve this problem. We can solve the equation, or we can use the given values to check to see if the sentence is true.

Let's solving the equation.

The goal of this is to get x by itself on one side of the equation. Right now, x is being multiplied by −4, so we need to do the opposite operation of multiplication, which is division. Divide each side of the equation by −4.

$$\frac{-4x}{-4} = \frac{16}{-4}$$

$\frac{-4}{-4} = 1$, so x is by itself.

$\frac{16}{-4} = -4$ because dividing a positive number by a negative number gives a negative number.

$x = -4$, so choice A is correct.

EXAMPLE

The area of a rectangle is 735 square feet. The base of the rectangle is 49 feet. What is *h*, the height of the rectangle?

In this problem, we are given some measurements of a rectangle and are tasked to find the other measurement. This can be written as an equation with a variable.

In this example, we know the area and we know the base of the rectangle and we need to find the height.

To find the area of a rectangle, multiply the base and the height.

Let's use this information to write an equation we can solve.

$$A = b \times h$$
$$735 = 49 \times h$$

Now, solve for h. We can see that h is being multiplied by 49, so we need to perform the inverse operation on both sides of the equal sign.

$$\frac{735}{49} = \frac{49h}{49}$$
$$735 \div 49 = h$$

You may need to do some long division to find the value of h. The division problem will show that $735 \div 49 = 15$.

So, now we know that $h = 15$.

We can check our answer by using 15 for the value of h.

$$735 = 49h$$
$$735 = 49(15)$$
$$735 = 735$$

This value makes the sentence true, so the height of the rectangle is 15 feet.

Determining if a Value Makes an Equation True

To determine if a value makes an equation true, we need to use that value in an equation with a variable. You may be given a value for a variable and asked to choose an equation that makes the sentence true. If both sides of an equal sign are the same value, then you can determine that the sentence is true. Let's say you are given the value $x = 3$. What are some possible equations that $x = 3$ would be a solution to? There are an infinite number of possibilities, but some examples would be $2 + x = 5$, $4 - x = 1$, $10x = 30$, and $\frac{12}{x} = 4$. In all these examples, 3 is the solution.

$$2 + x = 5$$
$$2 + 3 = 5$$

$$4 - x = 1$$
$$4 - 3 = 1$$

$$10x = 30$$
$$10(3) = 30$$

$$\frac{12}{x} = 4$$
$$\frac{12}{3} = 4$$

We have to test the value of x in each option to see if the sentence is true and the equation is balanced.

Inequalities

Writing Inequalities to Represent Problems

An **inequality** is a math sentence that connects two expressions with a comparison. These expressions are compared using a greater than, $>$, less than, $<$, greater than or equal to, $\geq$, or less than or equal to, $\leq$, sign. These signs are used in inequalities.

There are some stories that can be illustrated by inequalities. In these scenarios, we need to identify what we know, what we do not know, and the comparison. For example, suppose you need to go to the grocery store to buy avocados that are $0.75 each. You only brought 5 dollars. How many avocados can you buy? This is an example of an inequality because you have a maximum or minimum to meet. You need to get avocados, but you cannot go over the 5-dollar maximum. You can set up an inequality to illustrate this.

We know that avocados are \$0.75 each. We know that you cannot spend more than \$5. You do not know how many avocados you can buy, so this is the unknown.

We can write an inequality using a for avocados.

We cannot go over \$5, so the \$5 must be greater than or equal to the total price of the avocados at a rate of \$0.75 per avocado.

$$5 \geq$$

Now, we want avocados and each one is \$0.75, so the other side of our inequality is \$0.75 times the number of avocados.

$$5 \geq 0.75a$$

This could also be written as

$$0.75a \leq 5$$

Solving Inequalities on a Number Line

Inequalities can be represented on a number line. Inequalities are written using two expressions connected by a greater than, less than, greater than or equal to, or less than or equal to sign. We express solutions to these sentences using number lines and series of arrows, open circles, and closed circles. Inequalities show that a number or term is greater than, less than, greater than or equal to, or less than or equal to another term. You may be asked to draw or identify the number line that represents an inequality, including inequalities with variables.

When representing solutions to an inequality on a number line, we are identifying the number or group of numbers that makes the sentence true.

We can represent the inequality $2 + x > 10$.

In this inequality, x is a number that, when added to 2, is greater than 10. What are the possibilities? x has to be at least 8, because any number less than 8, added to 2, is not greater than 10.

The number must be greater than 8, but not exactly 8, so we will identify 8 on our number line with an open circle.

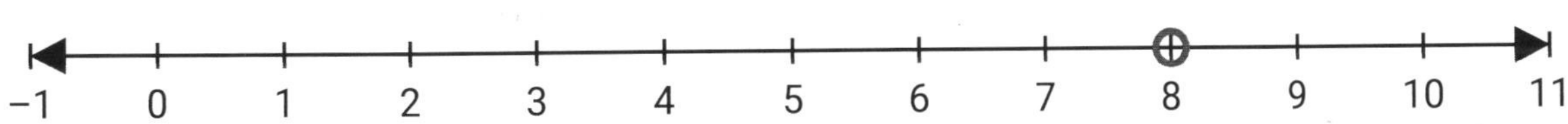

All numbers greater than 8 can be a solution, so we will place an arrow to the right to identify all numbers greater than 8.

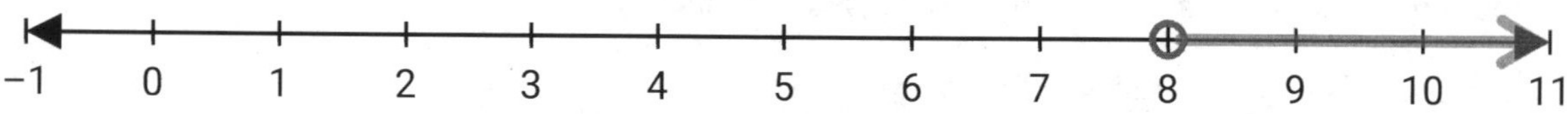

We can represent $2 + x \leq 10$ on a number line.

In this inequality, x is a number that when added to 2 is less than or equal to 10. What are the possibilities? x can be less than 8, and can be exactly 8. 8 would make both sides equal, and that is one option. Because x can be equal to 8, we will represent 8 on the number line with a closed circle.

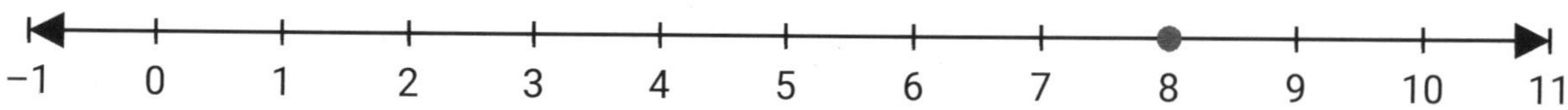

Now, we need to find the other solutions to make the sentence true. What can be added to 2 and be less than 10? Anything less than 8 will make this sentence true. So, we can identify these values by placing an arrow to the left of 8 to identify all values less than 8.

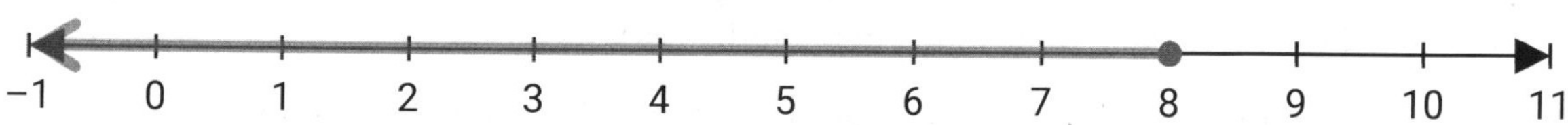

Review Video: Graphing Solutions to Inequalities
Visit mometrix.com/academy and enter code: 391281

Using Inequalities to Express Scenarios

Real-world scenarios can be expressed through inequalities, and we can also write situations based on an inequality. Inequalities usually use the language, "fewer than," "more than," "no more than," "no less than," "a maximum of," "a minimum of," etc. This language gives us clues that we are dealing with values that are greater than, less than, greater than or equal to, or less than or equal to a quantity.

If it is said a value is no more than 5, that means the value is less than or equal to 5. If there is a value that is more than 10, that means the value is greater than 10. If there is a value that is at least 25, that means the value is greater than or equal to 25. If the value is less or more, you will use greater than or less than. If the value is less or more, but can also be that number, you will use less than or equal to, or greater than or equal to. It takes a little practice and logic to really think about what is happening in the situation.

Solve Inequalities with Variables

Inequalities with a variable include an unknown value and instead of having one single solution, the solution will be a range of values. When we solve inequalities, we use a similar process to solving equations with variables. Sometimes we will be given stories instead of inequalities and will need to write an inequality from a story before solving.

Suppose you are given the inequality $7 + x \geq 4$.

We can solve this using the same strategy we used to solve equations. You want to perform the inverse operation on each side of the inequality so x is by itself.

$$7 + x \geq 4$$
$$7 + x - 7 \geq 4 - 7$$
$$x \geq -3$$

The solution for this inequality is $x \geq -3$. This means that the solutions that make this sentence true are all values that are greater than or equal to −3. Some possible solutions could be −3, −1, 0, 5.5, or 23. Any value that is greater than or equal to −3 is a solution.

Review Video: Solving Inequalities Using All 4 Basic Operations
Visit mometrix.com/academy and enter code: 401111

Example

You have set a personal goal to run more than 10 miles. You run 2.5 miles per day. Which inequality could be used to find the number of days, *d*, you need to run to meet your goal of more than 10 miles?

a. $d < 4$
b. $d > 4$
c. $d > 25$
d. $d < 25$

This problem is asking you to write an inequality that matches the story.

We know that you want to run more than 10 miles, and you run about 2.5 miles per day. You want to know how many days, d, you need to run 2.5 miles to meet your goal of more than 10 miles.

2.5 miles every day for an unknown number of days is a multiplication expression, $2.5d$.

Your goal is to run more than 10 miles, so $2.5d$ must be more than 10.

$$2.5d > 10$$

Now that we have our inequality, we can solve for d, the number of days.

$$\frac{2.5d}{2.5} > \frac{10}{2.5}$$
$$d > 4$$

This matches one of our options, so B is the correct answer.

EXAMPLE

You are building a fence for your dog to run in the backyard. Your dog needs at least 2,100 square feet within the fence. The width of the yard is 17.5 feet. Which inequality shows all the possible lengths, x, that the yard could have to give your dog at least 2,100 square feet?

a. $120 \leq x$
b. $252 \leq x$
c. $252 \geq x$
d. $120 \geq x$

In this example, we are given a story, but no inequality.

The first step in solving this inequality is to write an inequality to match the story.

We are building a rectangular fence with at least 2,100 square feet of space for your dog to run. The units of square feet indicate this is an area problem.

We know that you can find area by multiplying the height and width of the rectangle.

In this example, the width of the rectangle is 17.5 feet and we are trying to find the height, x, and the total area is at least 2,100 square feet. We can start our inequality.

$$17.5x\ [\leq, =, \text{or} \geq]\ 2{,}100$$

The story says that the total area needs to be "at least" 2,100 square feet. This means that the fence could have an area of exactly, or more than 2,100 square feet, but not less. So, if we multiply the height and width of the rectangle fence, it needs to be more than or equal to 2,100 square feet. So, $17.5x$ should be greater than or equal to 2,100.

$$17.5x \geq 2{,}100$$

We can solve for x by performing the inverse operation to get x by itself on one side of the inequality. In this case, we would divide each side by 17.5.

$$\frac{17.5x}{17.5} \geq \frac{2{,}100}{17.5}$$
$$x \geq 120$$

D is the correct answer.

DETERMINING IF A VALUE MAKES AN INEQUALITY TRUE

Inequalities include two expressions separated by a comparison and tell a story about a value that is greater than, less than, greater than or equal to, or less than or equal to another expression. When there is a variable in an inequality, we can test numbers to see if they are possible solutions. If you are given a possible value, you can use this value in place of the variable, simplify, and compare. If the given value makes the sentence true, then that value is a possible solution. If the value does not make the sentence true, it is not a solution.

Let's look at the inequality $3x < 30$.

What are some possible solutions?

One possible solution is $x = 2$. If $x = 2$, then the sentence is true because $3(2) = 6$ and 6 is less than 30.

Another possible solution is $x = -5$. If $x = -5$, the sentence is true because $3(-5) = -15$ and -15 is less than 30.

What about $x = 10$? If $x = 10$, the sentence is not true. 3(10) is equal to 30, so $x = 10$ is not a solution to the inequality.

Triangles

Angles

There are a few rules about triangles that are important to remember that have to do with angles and side lengths. The first rule is that the angles in a triangle add up to **180 degrees**. You can remember this because we know that a square's angles add to 360 degrees because each angle in a square is a right angle, or 90 degrees, and $90° + 90° + 90° + 90° = 360°$. Half of a square is a triangle, so all angles in a triangle add up to half of 360 degrees, which is 180 degrees.

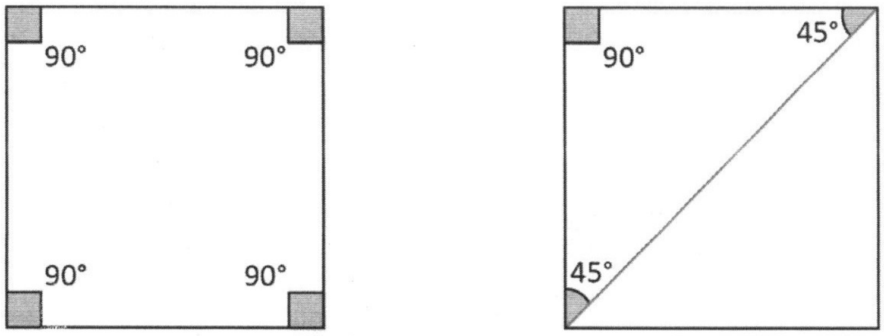

You can use this information to solve problems about angle measures of triangles. If we know two angle measurements, we can calculate the third. If we are given three angle measurements, we can conclude whether they could possibly create a triangle. Suppose a triangle has two angle measures, 90° and 45°, we can find the measure of the third angle. We know that all three angles of a triangle must add up to 180°, so the missing angle must measure 45°.

$$90° + 45° + x = 180°$$
$$x = 45°$$

Side Lengths

The second rule about triangles is about side lengths. For three sides to form a triangle, the sum of two side lengths must be greater than the length of the third side. This goes for any two sides in a triangle. This is true because if two side lengths are smaller than the third side, the triangle would form an open figure. Let's say we have three lengths: length A is 6 inches, length B is 3 inches, and length C is 1 inch. This can never make a triangle. We can see this mathematically. The sum of two side lengths must be greater than the third side length.

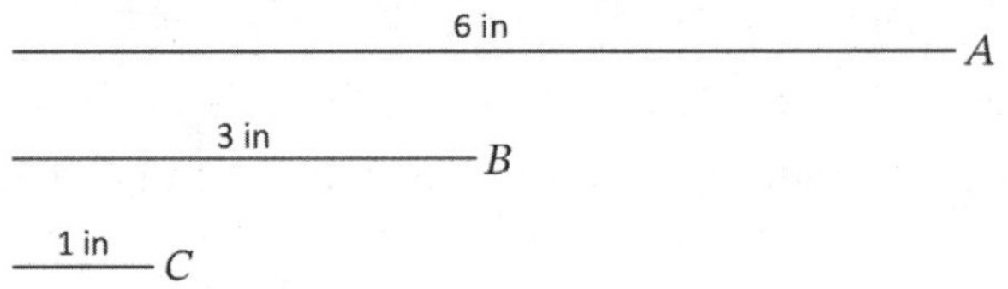

$A + B > C$ $6 + 3 > 1$ $9 > 1$ TRUE	$A + C > B$ $6 + 1 > 3$ $7 > 3$ TRUE	$B + C > A$ $3 + 1 > 6$ $4 > 6$ FALSE

So, because the sum of length B and C is smaller than length A, these lengths can never form a triangle. The figures below show how the three sides cannot connect with the given lengths.

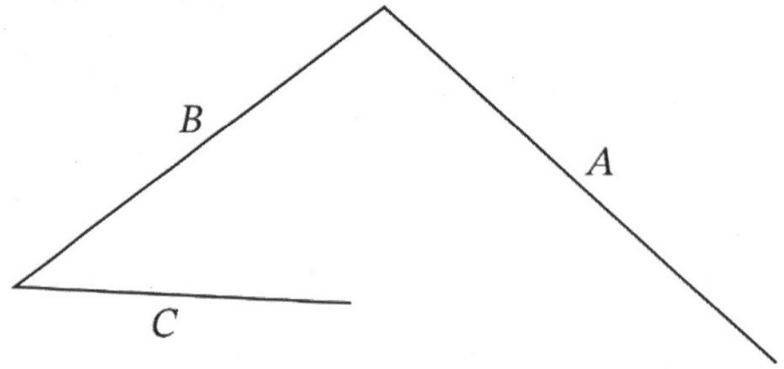

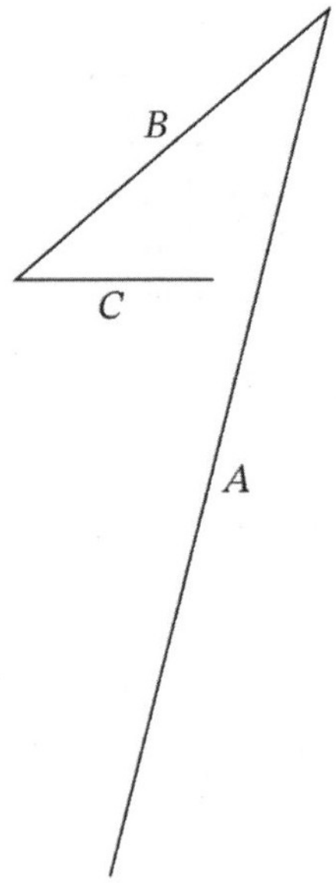

Neither of these are examples of triangles.

Now, if we had the lengths 6 inches, 3 inches, and 5 inches, we could make a triangle.

We can see this mathematically.

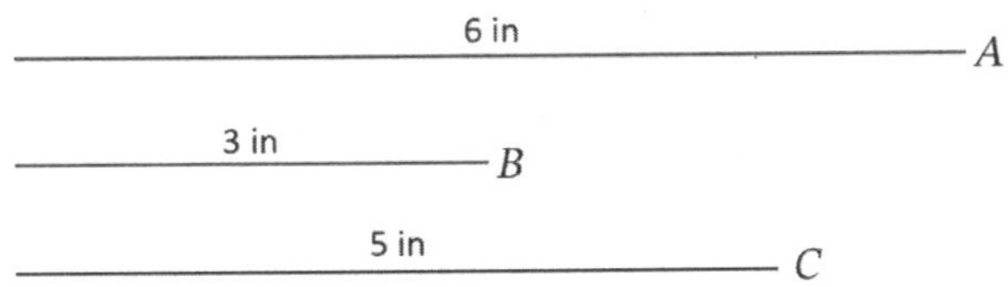

$A + B > C$	$B + C > A$	$A + C > B$
$6 + 3 > 5$	$3 + 5 > 6$	$6 + 5 > 3$
$9 > 5$	$8 > 6$	$11 > 3$
TRUE	TRUE	TRUE

And visually.

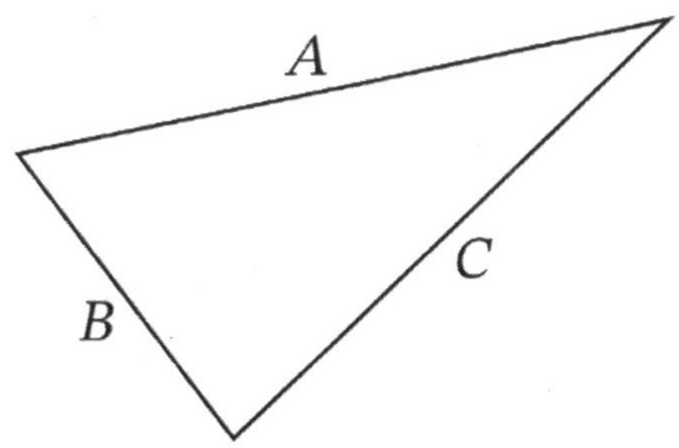

Review Video: General Rules for Triangles
Visit mometrix.com/academy and enter code: 166488

Area of a Rectangle

The **area** of a polygon describes the total measure of the amount of space inside the polygon. We describe area using **square units** because area can be described as the number of squares that cover the inside of a polygon. A rectangle is a polygon with four sides, two sets of parallel sides, and four right angles.

If we have a rectangle that is 5 inches by 3 inches, we can count the number of square inches inside the rectangle to find the area.

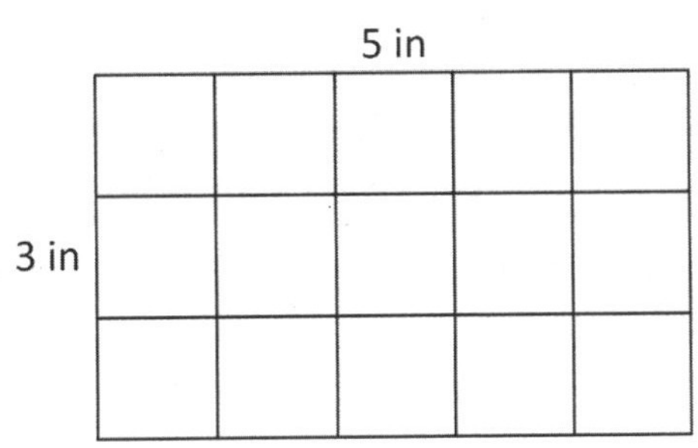

By counting the square inches in this rectangle, we can see that the area is 15 square units.

AREA FORMULA FOR RECTANGLES

We can also use formulas to find the area of a rectangle. Instead of counting the square units, we can find the area of a rectangle by multiplying the base and the height, or multiplying perpendicular sides. **Perpendicular sides** create right angles. Sides can be described as a base and a height, or length and width.

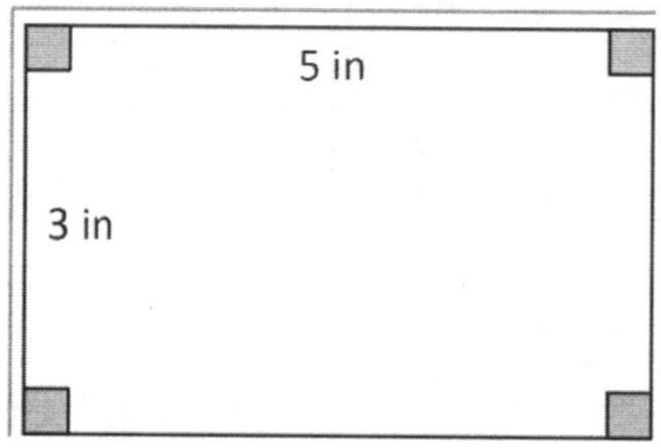

$$5 \text{ in} \times 3 \text{ in} = 15 \text{ sq in}$$

The side length that is 3 inches is perpendicular to the side length that is 5 inches, so the area is 15 square inches.

The area of a shape does not change if it is positioned differently. Consider the rectangle below.

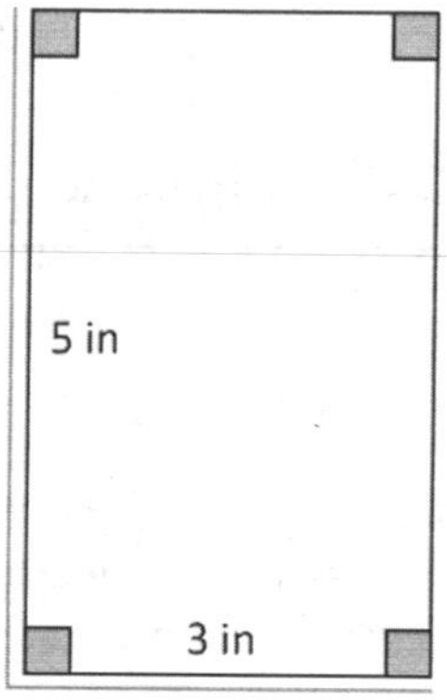

In this example, the base is 3 inches and the height is 5 inches. These sides are still perpendicular to each other, so we can still multiply the base and height to find the area.

$$\text{Area} = \text{base} \times \text{height}$$
$$A = b \times h$$
$$A = 3 \text{ in} \times 5 \text{ in}$$
$$A = 15 \text{ square inches}$$

The formula for finding the area of a rectangle is area equals the base times the height, or $A = b \cdot h$, where the base and height are perpendicular.

EXAMPLE

If we have a rectangle with a given area and a given side length, we can use the area formula to find a missing side length.

A rectangle has an area of 20 square units, and a base of 5 units, we can use the area formula to find the height.

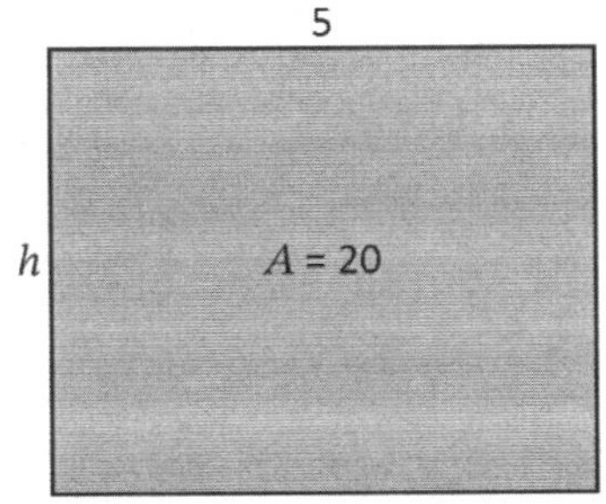

$$A = b \times h$$
$$\frac{20}{5} = \frac{5 \times h}{5}$$
$$\frac{20}{5} = h$$
$$h = 4$$

If we have a rectangle with an area of 20 square units, and a base of 5 units, the height is 4 units because 20 divided by 5 is 4.

We can use equivalent equations to find alternative area formulas. For example, to find a missing height, we can use the equation $h = \frac{A}{b}$, or to find a missing base, we can use the equation $b = \frac{A}{h}$. We can divide the total area by the side length to find the missing perpendicular side length.

$\frac{A}{b} = \frac{b \times h}{b}$ $\frac{A}{b} = h$ $h = \frac{A}{b}$	$\frac{A}{h} = \frac{b \times h}{h}$ $\frac{A}{h} = b$ $b = \frac{A}{h}$

EXAMPLE

A garden has an area of A square feet. The length of the garden is 15 feet and the width of the garden is x feet. Which equation represents the width of the garden?

a. $x = A \times 15$
b. $x = A - (2 \times 15)$
c. $x = \frac{A}{15}$
d. $x = \frac{15}{A}$

In this problem, we are given some elements of a rectangle and need to select the equation that can be used to find a missing side length.

The best way to start a problem like this is to draw a picture. Pictures are useful in geometry because they can help you get an idea of what is really being asked in the question. Draw a rectangle and label the given information.

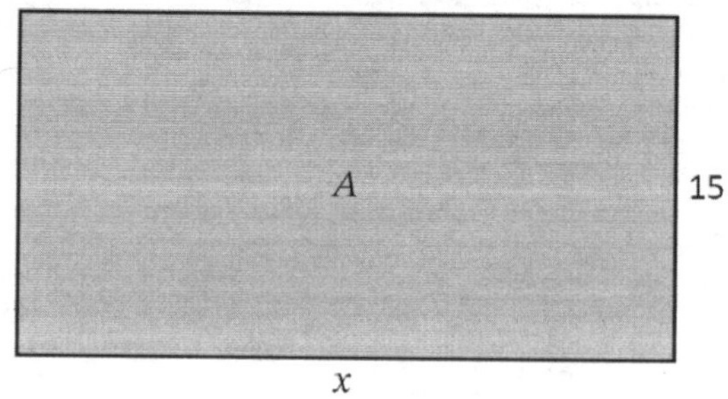

The area formula for a rectangle is $A = b \cdot h$. So, we can use the equation $A = b \cdot h$ and use equivalent equations to describe the width, x.

First, we need to input our given values. The area is A; the length, or height, is 15; and the width, or base, is x.

$$\mathrm{A} = 15 \times x$$

Now, divide both sides by 15.

$$\frac{A}{15} = \frac{15 \times x}{15}$$
$$\frac{A}{15} = x$$

Now, we can reverse the sides so x is on the left side of the equal sign.

$$x = \frac{A}{15}$$

The correct answer is C.

EXAMPLE

Josie is designing a mural. The wall that the mural will be painted on is a rectangle where the height is 8 feet and the width is 11.5 feet. What is the total area of the space in square feet?

In this problem, we are given the perpendicular sides of a rectangle and need to calculate the area. We will use the area formula to help us.

Let's draw a picture and label the given values to help us visualize the problem.

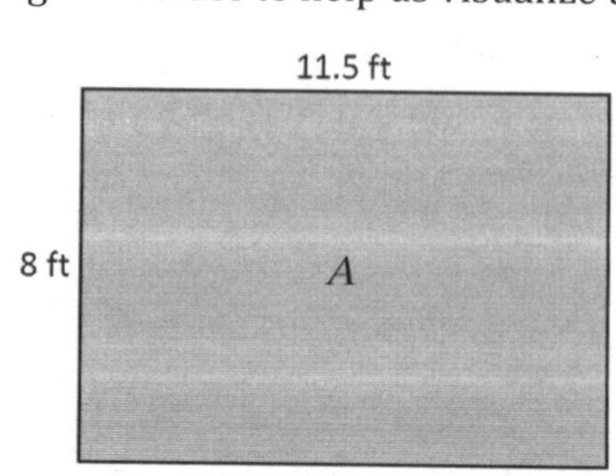

We know that the area of a rectangle is calculated by multiplying the base and the height, or the length and the width. We can use the formula $A = b \cdot h$ and input the given values in the formula.

$$A = b \times h$$
$$A = 11.5 \times 8$$

Multiply to find the area.

$$A = 11.5 \times 8$$
$$A = 92.0$$
$$A = 92 \text{ ft}^2$$

The area of the space is 92 square feet.

EXAMPLE

The area of a rectangle is $4\frac{1}{2}$ square centimeters. The height of the rectangle measures $\frac{1}{2}$ centimeters. What is the base of the rectangle in centimeters?

In this problem, we are given the area and one side length of a rectangle, and we need to find a missing side length.

Let's start by drawing a picture and labeling the given values to visualize the problem.

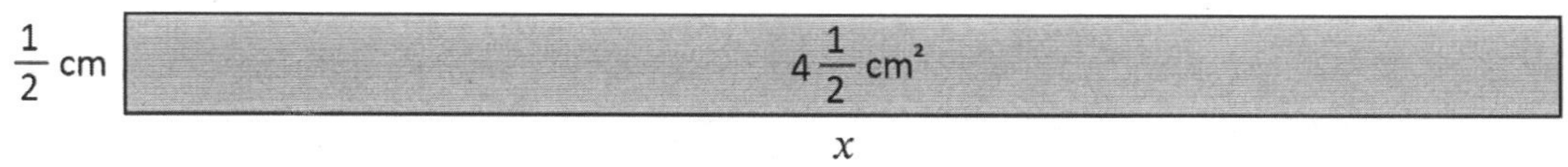

We know that the area of a rectangle is found by multiplying the base times the height, but when we have missing side lengths, we can find a missing side length by dividing the area by the given side length, in this case area divided by the height.

$$A = b \times h$$
$$h = \frac{A}{b}$$

Now, we can input the given values and solve. Remember that dividing by a fraction is equivalent to multiplying by the reciprocal.

$$h = \frac{a}{b}$$
$$h = 4\frac{1}{2} \div \frac{1}{2}$$
$$h = 4\frac{1}{2} \times \frac{2}{1}$$
$$h = 4\frac{1}{2} \times 2$$
$$h = 9$$

The base of the rectangle is 9 centimeters.

Area of a Triangle

We can dissect and rearrange simple shapes to find the areas of difficult shapes. The formula for the area of a rectangle is $A = b \cdot h$, and we can use this formula to help us model the area of a triangle.

A triangle has half of the area of a rectangle with the same base and height measurements as the triangle. We can represent this visually.

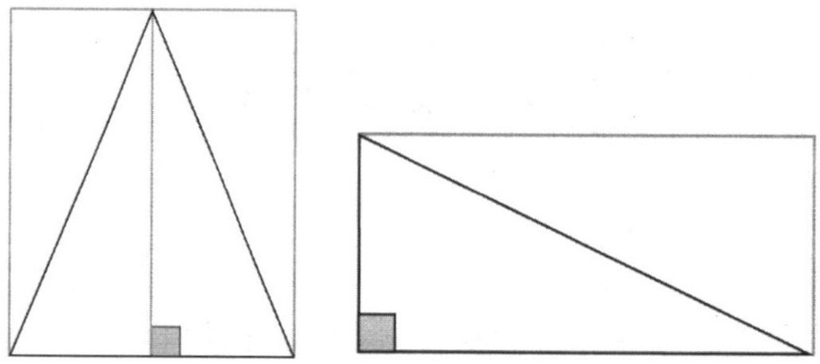

When looking at an obtuse triangle in this way, the triangle will extend outside the rectangle formed by the base and height. But the area of the triangle is still equal to half the area of the rectangle made from the base and height.

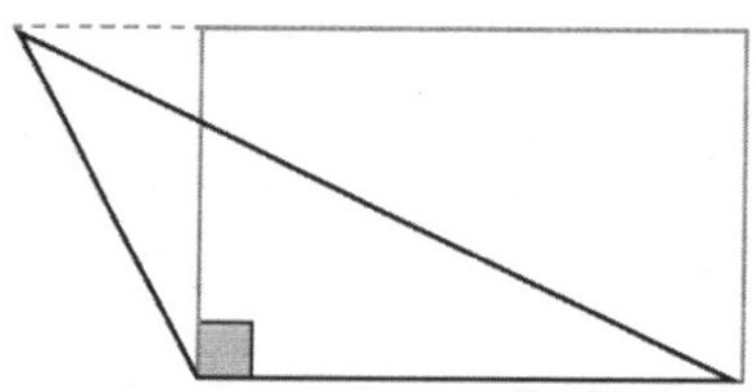

Remember, the base and height of a polygon will always be perpendicular and will create a right angle.

Area Formula for Triangles

Knowing that a triangle is half of a rectangle with the same base and height, we can determine that the area of a triangle can be found by multiplying the base and height of the triangle and dividing this product by 2.

When we multiply the base and height of a triangle, we are finding the area of the surrounding rectangle which is twice the area of the triangle. We need to divide this area by 2 to find the area of the triangle. The formula $A = \frac{1}{2}bh$ is used to find the area of a triangle.

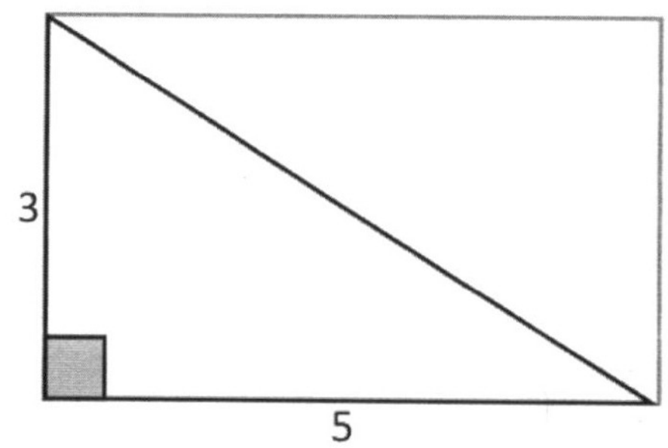

$$A = \frac{1}{2}(3 \times 5)$$

$$A = 7.5$$

The area of a rectangle with a base and height of 5 and 3 is 15 square units. A triangle with the same base and height will be half of that, so 7.5 square units.

Review Video: Area and Perimeter of a Triangle
Visit mometrix.com/academy and enter code: 853779

EXAMPLE

A small triangular tile has a base of $\frac{1}{2}$ inch and a height of $3\frac{1}{2}$ inches. What formula can be used to find the area, *A*, in inches?

a. $A = \frac{1}{2} \times 3\frac{1}{2}$
b. $A = \frac{1}{2}\left(\frac{1}{2} \times 3\frac{1}{2}\right)$
c. $A = 2\left(\frac{1}{2} \times 3\frac{1}{2}\right)$
d. $A = \frac{1}{2} + 3\frac{1}{2}$

In this problem, we are given the height and base measurement of a triangle and need to select the equation that represents the area, A, of the triangle.

Let's start by drawing a picture and labeling the given values to visualize this problem.

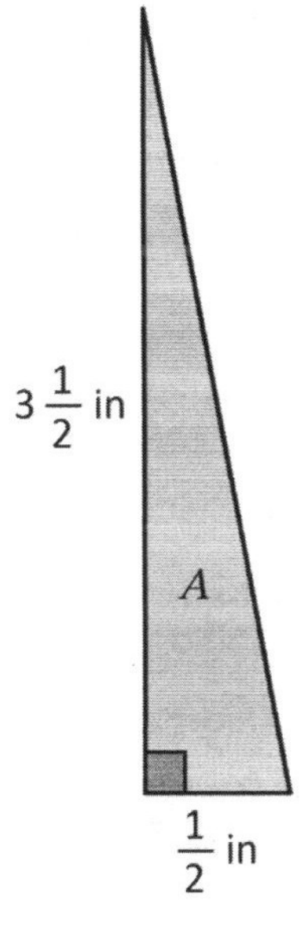

Now that we can see what is being asked, let's think about the area of a triangle. We know that the area of a triangle is half of the area of the surrounding rectangle, and the formula for the area of a triangle is $A = \frac{1}{2}b \times h$. We can use this formula and substitute the given values.

$$A = \frac{1}{2}b \times h$$
$$A = \frac{1}{2}\left(\frac{1}{2} \times 3\frac{1}{2}\right)$$

The correct answer is B.

EXAMPLE

A triangle is pictured below. What is the area of the triangle in square meters?

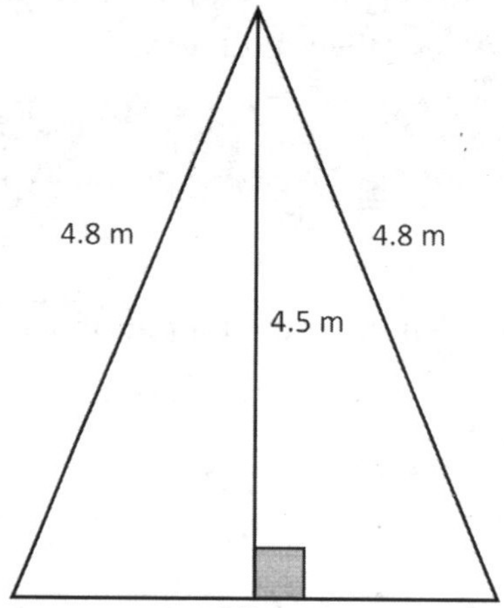

In this problem, we are given a picture of a triangle with the base, height, and all side lengths labeled. We need to first identify the base and the height out of all these measurements.

Remember, the base and height will always be perpendicular and will form a right angle, and only two measurements form a right angle, which is depicted by a square in the corner.

The base of the triangle is 3.2 meters and the height of the triangle is 4.5 meters.

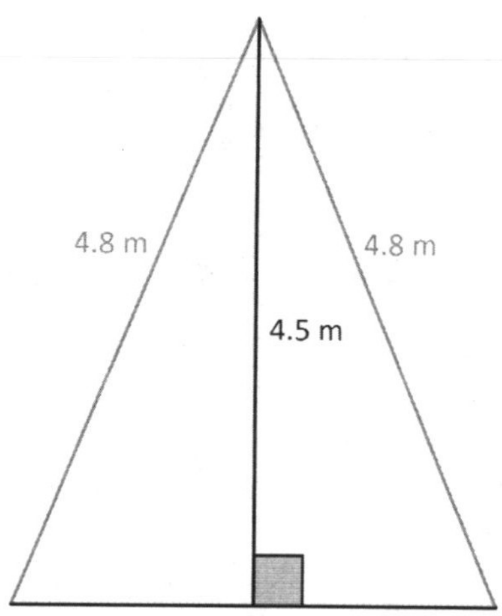

Now that we have identified the base and height of the triangle, we can use the triangle formula to find the area in square meters.

The triangle area formula is half of the base times the height, or half of the area of the surrounding rectangle. We can use the triangle area formula, input the given values, and solve.

$$A = \frac{1}{2}b \times h$$
$$A = \frac{1}{2}(3.2 \times 4.5)$$

$$A = \frac{1}{2}(14.4)$$
$$A = 7.2 \text{ m}^2$$

The area of the triangle is 7.2 square meters.

Area of a Parallelogram

The area of a **parallelogram** can be found by dissecting the shapes within the parallelogram. Within a parallelogram, there are rectangles and triangles. The area of a polygon remains the same whether it is decomposed or rearranged. Consider the following rectangle that is split into two squares.

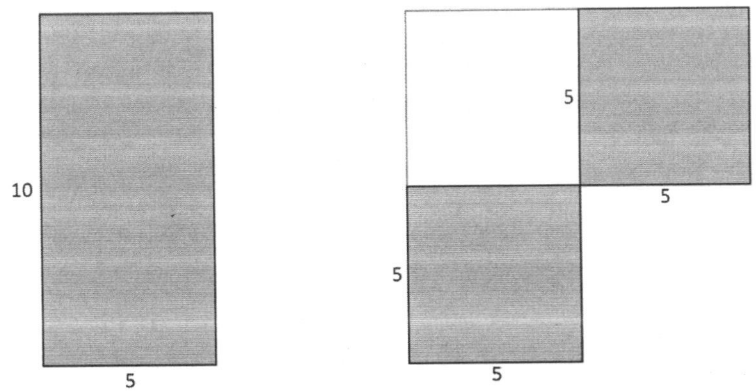

These shapes have the same area even though the area is decomposed, split apart, and rearranged, moved around. The shaded area is still 50 square units regardless of placement.

Area Formula for Parallelograms

When we are dealing with polygons, we can divide the shape into easier-to-calculate shapes and add these smaller areas together. The area of a polygon is the same as the sum of its parts, so we can use what we know about rectangles and triangles to find the area of the parallelogram.

A parallelogram has two sets of parallel sides. As you can see, this means that a parallelogram has two identical triangles on either side.

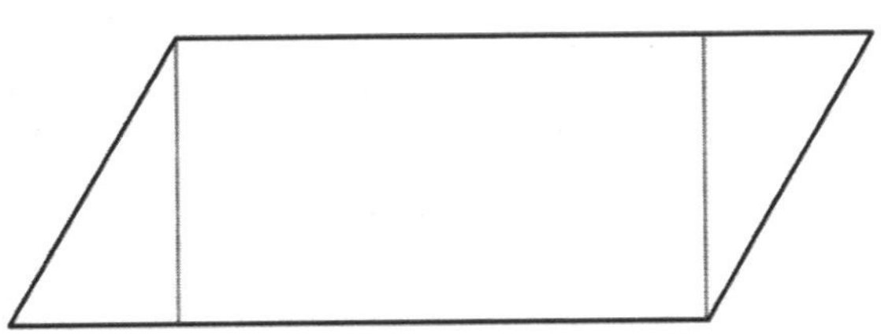

If we rearrange these "triangle ends" we can see that a rectangle with the same measurements is formed. We know that the area of a rectangle can be found using the formula $A = b \cdot h$, which is the same formula as a parallelogram. The area of a parallelogram is equivalent to the area of a rectangle with the same base and height measurements.

$$A = 5 \times 2$$

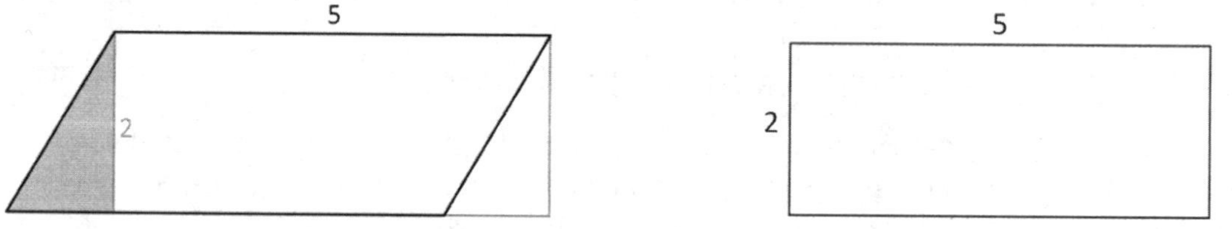

Remember, bases and heights are perpendicular, so the base and height of a parallelogram is the set of perpendicular measurements.

These parallelograms have the same area. The base and height are depicted. As you can see, the base and height can be found by identifying the base and height of the equivalent rectangle. The "slanted" side length is not used to find area.

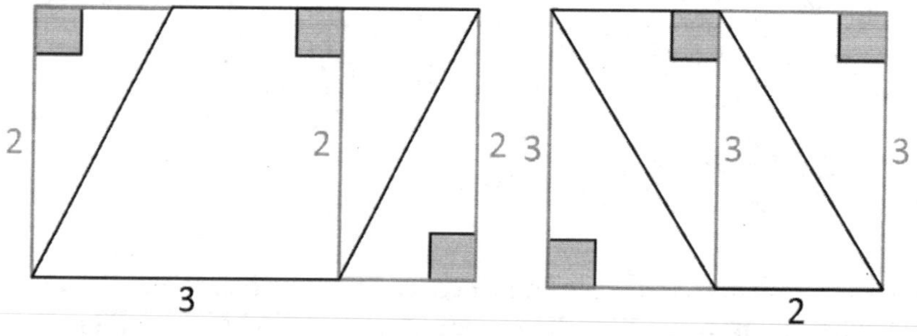

Review Video: Area and Perimeter of a Parallelogram
Visit mometrix.com/academy and enter code: 718313

Example

A parallelogram is shown.

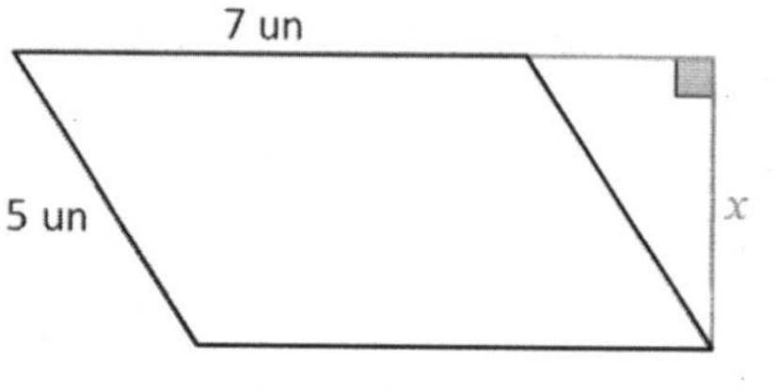

Which equation can be used to find the area, *A*, in square units?

a. $A = 7x$
b. $A = 5x$
c. $A = 7 \cdot 5$
d. $A = 7 \cdot 5 \cdot x$

In this problem, we are given a parallelogram with labeled sides, and we need to select the equation that can be used to find the area, A.

First, we need to remember the area formula for a parallelogram. A parallelogram's area is equal to the area of a rectangle with the same base and height, so the area formula is $A = b \cdot h$.

Now, identify the base and height of the parallelogram. Remember that the base and height of a polygon are always perpendicular. Knowing this, we can see that the perpendicular side lengths of the parallelogram are x and 7.

Now we can input these values in our formula.

$$A = b \times h$$
$$A = 7 \times x$$

$A = 7 \times x$ is equivalent to $A = 7x$, so choice A is the correct answer.

EXAMPLE

A park is shaped like a parallelogram. The dimensions are shown below.

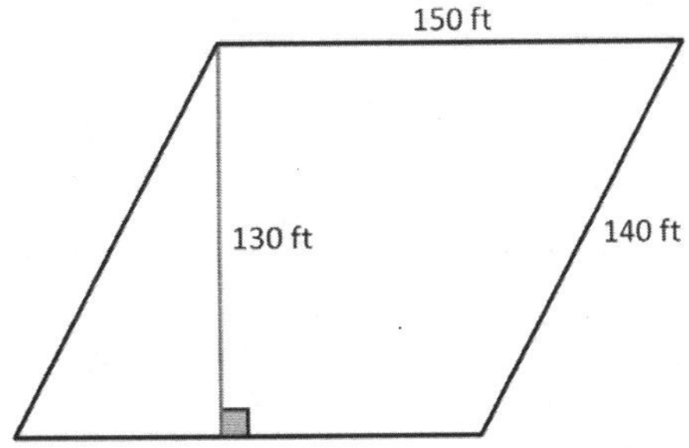

What is the total area of the parallelogram in square feet?

In this problem, we are given the dimensions of a parallelogram and need to calculate the total area in square feet.

The area of a parallelogram can be found using the formula $A = b \cdot h$, where the base and height are perpendicular lines.

In this diagram, the perpendicular pair is 150 feet and 130 feet. We will not use the 140 ft measurement because this side length is not part of a perpendicular pair. We will input these values in our formula and multiply.

$$A = b \times h$$
$$A = 150 \times 130$$
$$A = 19{,}500 \text{ ft}^2$$

The area of the park is 19,500 square feet.

Area of a Trapezoid

A **trapezoid** can be viewed as a collection of rectangles and triangles. A trapezoid has two bases because there are two different sides that are perpendicular to the height.

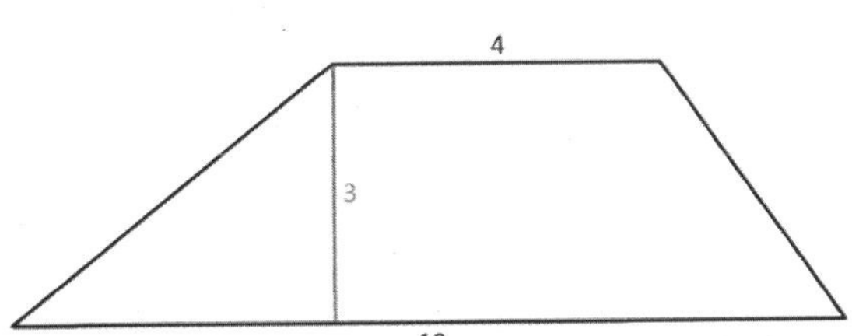

One way to find a formula for the area of a trapezoid is to suppose we have a second copy of the trapezoid. If we rotate one copy 180° and put it next to the original trapezoid, we get a parallelogram:

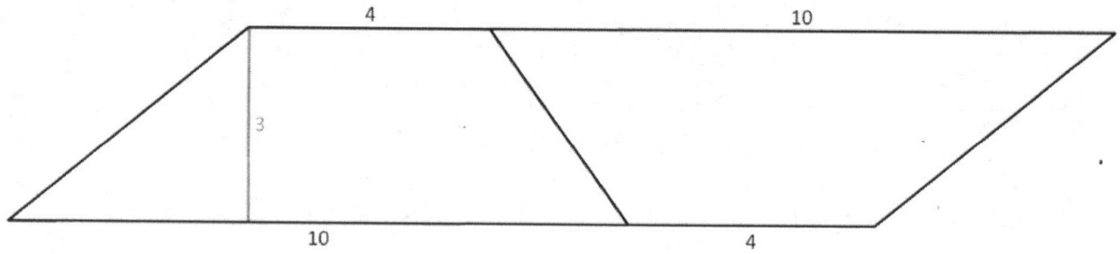

Area Formula for Trapezoids

We have already seen that the area of a parallelogram is equal to its base times height. What are the base and height of the parallelogram made from the two trapezoids? The height is the same as the height of the trapezoid. The base is equal to the sum of the bases of the trapezoids, since the base of the parallelogram is made up of the large base of one trapezoid and the small base of the other.

We can use h to refer to the height of the trapezoid, b_1 to refer to the measurement of one of its bases, and b_2 to refer to the measurement of the other base. The height of the parallelogram is h and the base of the parallelogram is $b_1 + b_2$. The area of the parallelogram is $(b_1 + b_2) \times h$.

But the parallelogram is made up of two copies of the trapezoid. That means the area of the parallelogram is twice the area of the original trapezoid. To find the area of the trapezoid, we need to divide the area of the parallelogram by 2, or multiply it by $\frac{1}{2}$. This gives the formula: $A = \frac{1}{2}(b_1 + b_2) \times h$.

So, to find the area of the trapezoid shown above, we can substitute values into the formula and simplify.

$$A = \frac{1}{2}(b_1 + b_2) \times h$$
$$A = \frac{1}{2}(4 + 10) \times 3$$
$$A = \frac{1}{2}(14 \times 3)$$
$$A = \frac{1}{2}(42)$$
$$A = 21 \text{ units}^2$$

The area of the trapezoid is 21 square units.

Review Video: Area and Perimeter of a Trapezoid
Visit mometrix.com/academy and enter code: 587523

EXAMPLE

The face of a roof is shaped like a trapezoid. The dimensions are shown below.

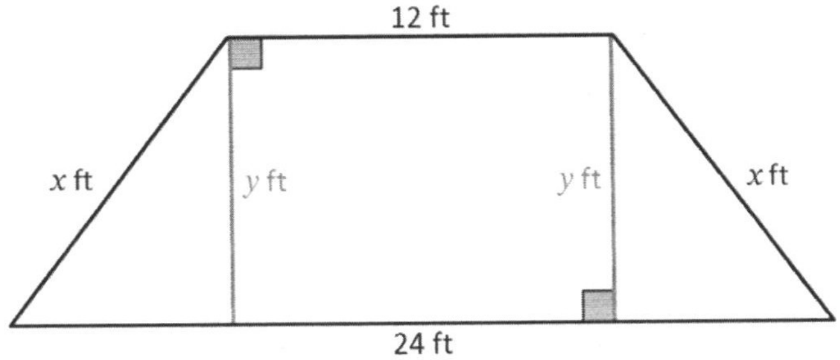

Which equation can be used to find the area, *A*, of the face of the roof in square feet?

a. $A = \frac{1}{2}(12 + 24)x$
b. $A = \frac{1}{2}(12 + 24)y$
c. $A = \frac{1}{2}(24 + y)12$
d. $A = \frac{1}{2}(24 + x)12$

In this problem, we are given a diagram of the face of a roof, and we need to select the equation that can be used to find the area.

The face of the roof is in the shape of a trapezoid, so first, we need to consider the formula for the area of a trapezoid.

The formula for a trapezoid is: $A = \frac{1}{2}(b_1 + b_2) \times h$.

Now that we have the formula, we need to identify the measurements of both bases and the height. The height will be perpendicular to each base and the bases will be parallel.

The parallel pair in the trapezoid is the line measuring 12 feet and the line measuring 24 feet. These are the two bases. It does not matter which base is b_1 and which is b_2.

The measurement that is perpendicular to the bases is the height. In the diagram, this is the line measuring y feet.

The line measuring x feet does not apply to our area formula.

Now we can input the given values into the formula. There are two possible equations we can make, since the bases can be represented in two different orders.

$$A = \frac{1}{2}(b_1 + b_2)h \qquad A = \frac{1}{2}(b_1 + b_2)h$$
$$A = \frac{1}{2}(12 + 24)y \qquad A = \frac{1}{2}(24 + 12)y$$

Let's review our options.

- Choice A gives the area of the trapezoid as half of the sum of the bases multiplied by x. The x value in the diagram is the slanted end of the trapezoid, and this is not used in the area formula. This equation cannot be used to find the area.

- Choice B gives the area of the trapezoid as half of the sum of the bases multiplied by y. The y value in the diagram is the height because it is perpendicular to the bases. This equation can be used to find the area.
- Choice C and D give 24 and x or y as base measurements and 12 as the height measurement. We know that bases are parallel, but these options do not use parallel sides as bases, so neither of these options can be used to find the area.

The correct answer is B.

EXAMPLE

The dimensions of a trapezoid-shaped tabletop are shown below.

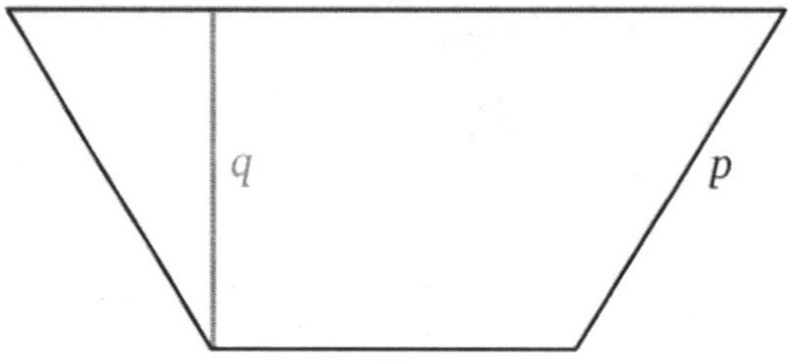

Which equation can be used to find the area, *A*, of the tabletop?

a. $A = \frac{1}{2}(p + q)n$
b. $A = \frac{1}{2}(n + p)q$
c. $A = \frac{1}{2}(m + n)p$
d. $A = \frac{1}{2}(n + m)q$

In this problem, we are given a diagram of a trapezoid and need to select the equation that can be used to find the area, A.

We are not given any number measurements or units, but instead each measurement is represented by a variable.

Let's start with the bases. With a trapezoid, the two bases are parallel sides. In this diagram, line n is parallel to line m, so n and m are the bases.

Now, find the height. The height is always perpendicular to the bases. In this diagram, side q is perpendicular to sides m and n, so q is the height.

We can use the area formula of a trapezoid and input the given values. There are two options because of the placement of the two bases.

$$A = \frac{1}{2}(b_1 + b_2)h$$
$$A = \frac{1}{2}(m + n) \times q$$

$$A = \frac{1}{2}(b_1 + b_2)h$$
$$A = \frac{1}{2}(n + m) \times q$$

These equations match one of our choices. The only choice that gives m and n as the bases and q as the height is choice D. So, the correct answer is D.

EXAMPLE

Calculate the area of the trapezoid.

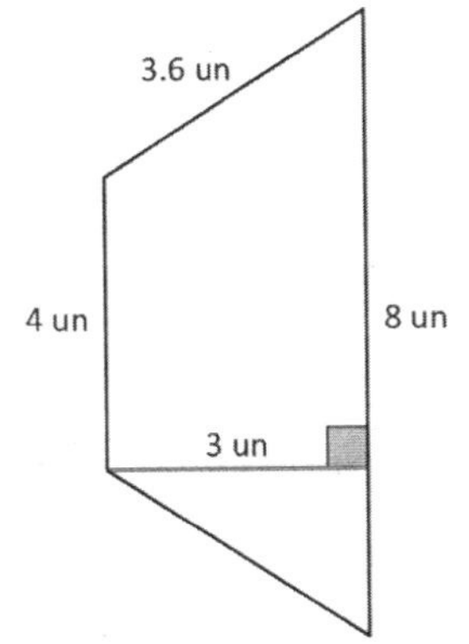

In this problem, we are given a diagram of a trapezoid and need to calculate the area.

First, we need to identify the area formula for a trapezoid. The area formula is $A = \frac{1}{2}(b_1 + b_2)h$.

Now, we need to identify the bases and the height of the trapezoid. The bases are always parallel to each other, and in the diagram, the line measuring 4 units and the line measuring 8 units are parallel. These are the values for our bases.

The height of a trapezoid is always perpendicular to the bases. In the diagram, the line measuring 3 units is perpendicular to the bases. This is the value for the height.

Now, we can substitute the given values and simplify.

$$A = \frac{1}{2}(b_1 + b_2) \times h$$
$$A = \frac{1}{2}(4 + 8) \times 3$$
$$A = \frac{1}{2}(12) \times 3$$
$$A = \frac{1}{2}(36)$$
$$A = 18 \text{ un}^2$$

We have calculated area, so the units are square units. The area of the trapezoid is 18 square units.

Volume of a Rectangular Prism

Volume is the measurement of space inside a three-dimensional shape or object. We use **cubic units**, which can be thought of as cubed units, to describe volume because volume is the number of unit cubes it takes to fill a space. A **rectangular prism** is a three-dimensional shape that has 6 rectangular faces.

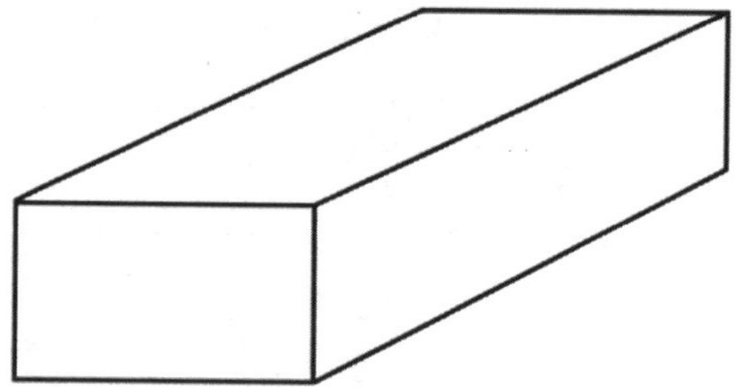

If we have a rectangular prism with side lengths that are measured in centimeters, the volume of the rectangular prism is the total number of cubic centimeters that it would take to fill the inside space.

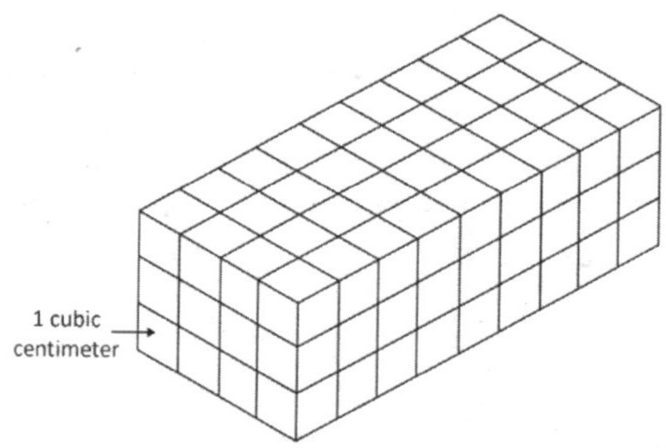

We can fill a physical rectangular prism with smaller unit cubes to find the total volume. We can count the number of cubes in each "layer" and add them up to find the total volume, but the most efficient way to find the volume of a rectangular prism is by using the volume formula.

To find the volume of a rectangular prism, we find the area of a face and multiply that by the height of the prism. In other words, we find the volume of the first layer, and multiply that by how many layers make up the prism.

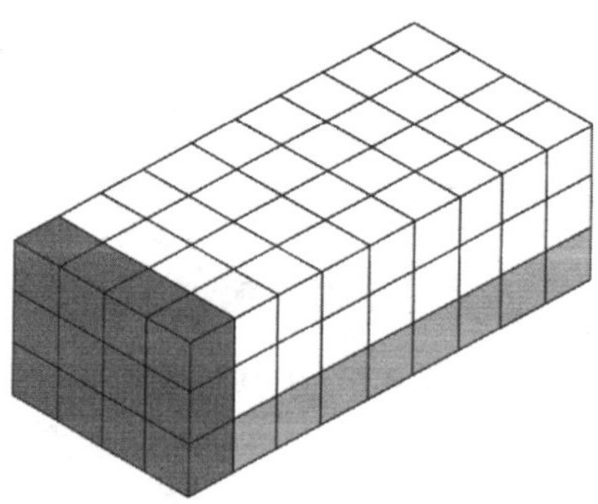

More simply put, the volume of a rectangular prism is the length times the width times the height, or $V = l \cdot w \cdot h$.

If we have a rectangular prism with a length of 9 cm, a width of 4 cm, and a height of 3 cm, we will multiply these values to find the volume in cubic centimeters.

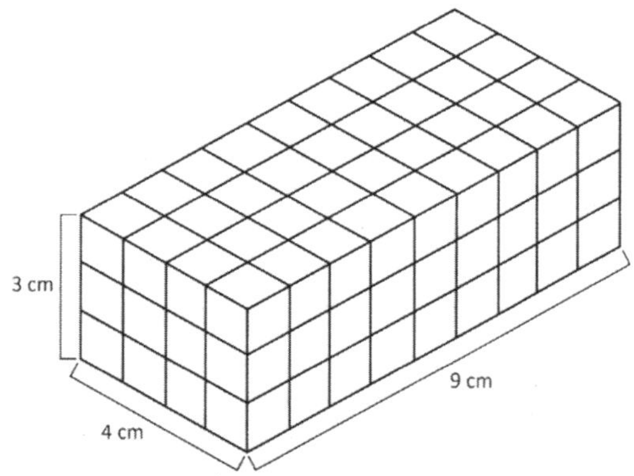

$V = l \times w \times h$
$V = 9 \times 4 \times 3$
$V = 9 \times 12$
$V = 108$ cubic centimeters

Example

A rectangular prism is shown below.

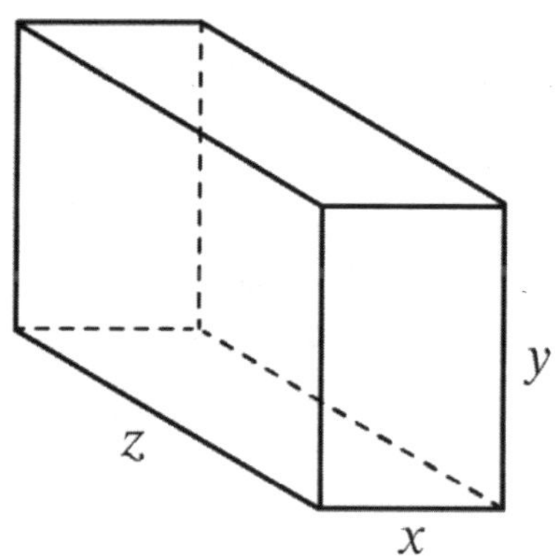

What equation can be used to calculate the volume of the rectangular prism?

a. $V = x + y + z$
b. $V = x \cdot y \cdot z$
c. $V = (x \cdot y) + z$
d. $V = (x + y) \cdot z$

In this problem, we are given a rectangular prism with the dimensions labeled by variables, and we need to determine which equation can be used to calculate the volume of the prism.

The formula for volume of a rectangular prism is $V = l \cdot w \cdot h$.

Because of the associative property, it does not matter the order that we multiply these values, so the actual labels of length, width, and height do not matter and depend on how the prism is placed. Instead, we need to know that we need to multiply all three values.

In the diagram, we see that the length, width, and height of the rectangular prism are labeled using the variables x, y, and z. So, to find the volume of the prism, we need to multiply all side lengths, or multiply x, y, and z.

$$V = x \cdot y \cdot z$$

Because of the associative property and the fact that you can multiply values in any order, there are many equations that can be used to find the volume of this figure, but only one of the answer choices above will work. The correct answer is B.

EXAMPLE

A **cube** has 6 congruent square faces.

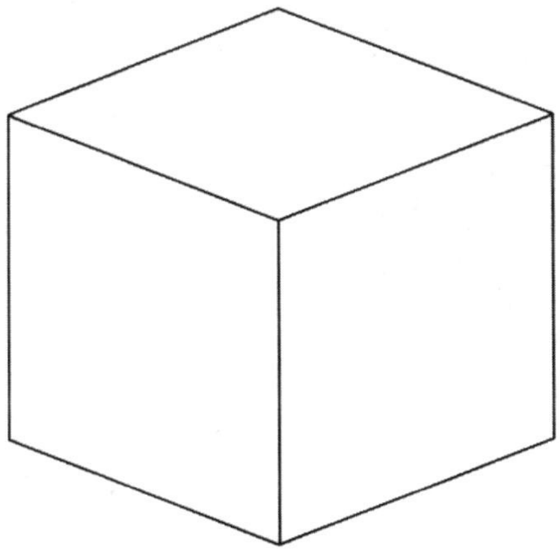

If we have a cube with side measurements of 5 inches, the volume of the cube is the total number of cubic inches that it would take to fill the inside space.

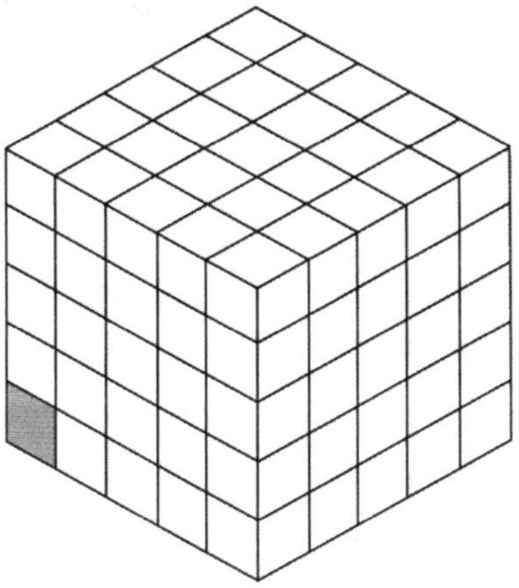

1 cubic inch

We can fill a physical cube with smaller cubes to find the total volume. We can count the number of cubes in each "layer" and add them up to find the total volume, but the most efficient way to find the volume of a cube is by using the volume formula. The volume formula for a cube is the same as for a rectangular prism, just like a square has the same area formula as a rectangle, but it can be written in a different format.

To find the volume of a cube, we find the area of the face and multiply that by the width of the cube, or length times width times height, or $V = l \cdot w \cdot h$.

With a cube, all side lengths are the same because the faces are equivalent squares, so the volume of a cube is side length times side length times side length because the length, width, and height are going to have the same value.

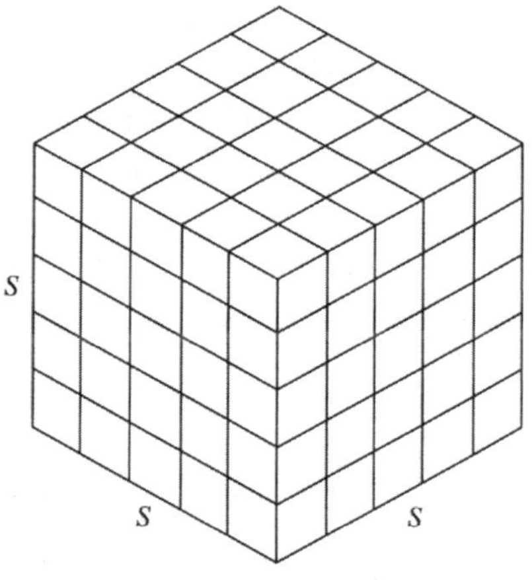

$$V = s \times s \times s$$
$$V = s^3$$

The formula for the volume of a cube is $V = s \cdot s \cdot s$. We know that when we multiply a value by itself it is squared, and when we multiply a value by itself three times, it is cubed. So, we can say the volume of a cube is the side length cubed, or $V = s^3$. We get the term "cubed" from the volume of a cube! This is also why volume is described using cubic units.

So, if we have a cube with the side length measure of 5 inches, the volume will be 5^3.

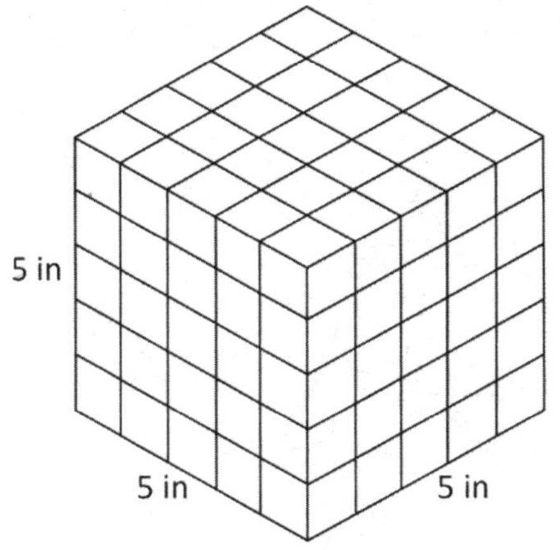

$$V = s^3$$
$$V = 5^3$$
$$V = 5 \times 5 \times 5$$
$$V = 25 \times 5$$
$$V = 125 \text{ in}^3$$

Just like with square units, cubic units can be written a few ways. You can write this as 125 cubic inches, 125 inches cubed, and 125 in^3. We can use in^3 because we are multiplying inches by inches by inches, and we know what when we multiply something by itself 3 times, that value is **cubed**, or raised to the third power.

EXAMPLE

The relationship between side lengths and volumes of cubes is described in the table.

side length (s)	2	3	4	5
volume (V)	8	27	64	125

What equation can be used to describe the relationship between side length and volume?

a. $V = s + s + s$
b. $V = s \cdot s$
c. $V = s + s$
d. $V = s \cdot s \cdot s$

In this problem, we are given a table with the side lengths and volumes of 4 different cubes that share the same relationship. We need to identify the equation that can be used to describe the relationship between side length and volume.

This question is a complicated way to ask which equation can be used to find the volume of a cube.

We know that a cube is a three-dimensional shape, a rectangular prism with 6 equivalent square faces. We also know that the formula for the volume of a rectangular prism is $V = l \cdot w \cdot h$.

This formula is not one of our choices, but we also know that a cube is a special rectangular prism where all side lengths are equivalent, which means we can describe the formula for volume as $V = s^3$, or $V = s \cdot s \cdot s$.

Choice A describes adding all side lengths. This will not give us the volume and does not match the relationship in the table.

Choice B describes multiplying two side lengths. This will give us the area of a face, but not the volume of a prism.

Choice C describes adding two side lengths. Again, this will not give us the volume and does not match the relationship in the table.

Choice D describes multiplying 3 side lengths. This will give us the volume of a cube and describes the relationship in the table. It also matches our volume formula.

We can check our answer by testing our formula with the given values.

For example, the first side length is 2, and the volume is 8. We can input the values in our equation to see if it is true.

$$V = s \cdot s \cdot s$$
$$8 = 2 \cdot 2 \cdot 2$$
$$8 = 4 \cdot 2$$
$$8 = 8$$

This equation is true.

We should test at least two values, so let's test the side length of 3, and the volume of 27.

$$V = s \cdot s \cdot s$$
$$27 = 3 \cdot 3 \cdot 3$$
$$27 = 9 \cdot 3$$
$$27 = 27$$

Both relationships match the formula $V = s \cdot s \cdot s$.

The correct answer is D.

Measurement and Data

Representing Data

Coordinate Planes

A **coordinate plane** is a way to graph data by plotting points on a grid. On a coordinate plane, there is an x-axis and a y-axis. The center point is called the **origin**, and its coordinates are (0,0). The x-axis runs horizontally, and the y-axis runs vertically. We use the x- and y-axis to graph ordered pairs. **Ordered pairs** are sets of values that tell us the coordinates of a point. They are written using parentheses and separated by a comma. (3,2) is an example of an ordered pair. In an ordered pair, the first number is the x-value, and the second number is the y-value. In this example, (3,2), $x = 3$ and $y = 2$. We use these values to plot points on a graph. The point (3,2) lies three units to the right of the origin along the x-axis and two units up along the y-axis. The point also lies at the intersection point of the lines $x = 3$ and $y = 2$. Positive values always run to the right along the x-axis and up along the y-axis. Negative values always run to the left along the x-axis and down along the y-axis.

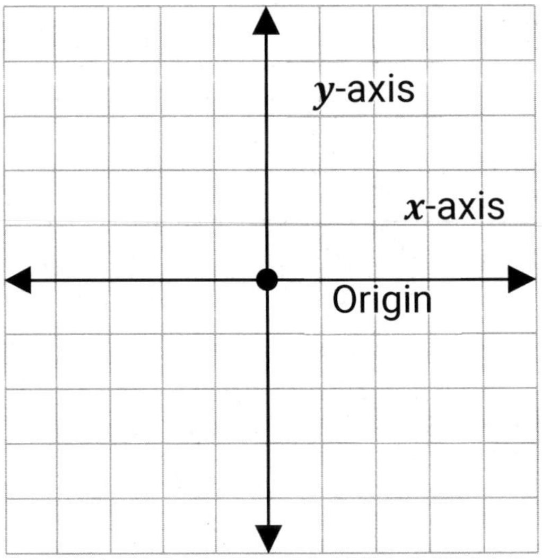

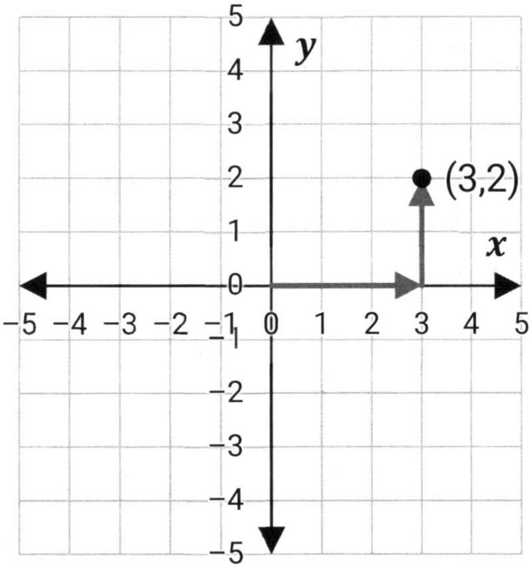

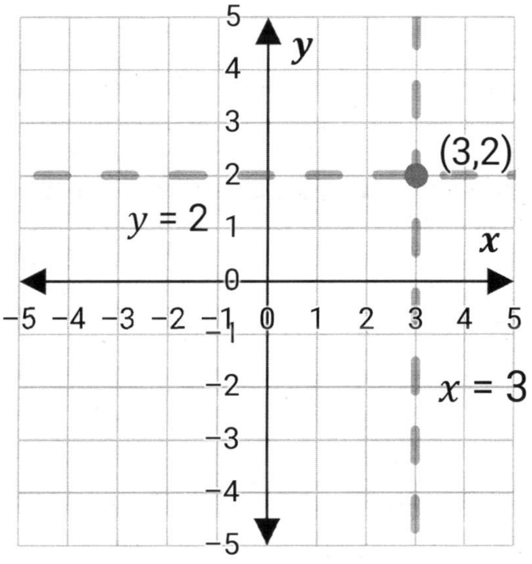

Review Video: Cartesian Coordinate Plane and Graphing
Visit mometrix.com/academy and enter code: 115173

EXAMPLE

Place $(5, -2.5)$ on the coordinate plane.

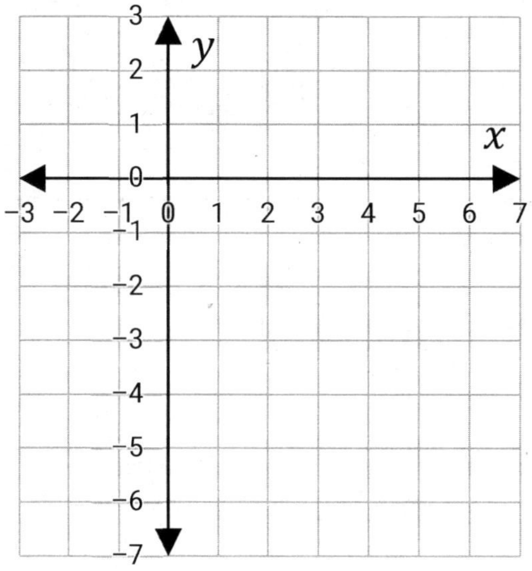

In this problem, we are given the pair $(5, -2.5)$. The x-value in this ordered pair is 5 and the y-value is –2.5.

We will start by finding the x-value, 5, on the coordinate plane. So, we will start at the origin and count 5 units to the right because it is a positive 5.

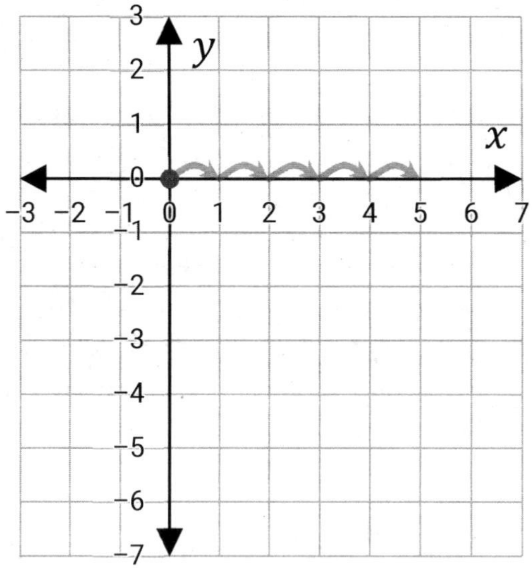

For the ordered pair $(5, -2.5)$, our y-value is –2.5. That means that we will count down 2.5 units. We will count down because it is a negative value.

−2.5 is not labeled on our coordinate plane, but we know that −2.5 is located halfway between −2 and −3. We can also count down 2 units and then a half of a unit. This is where we plot our point.

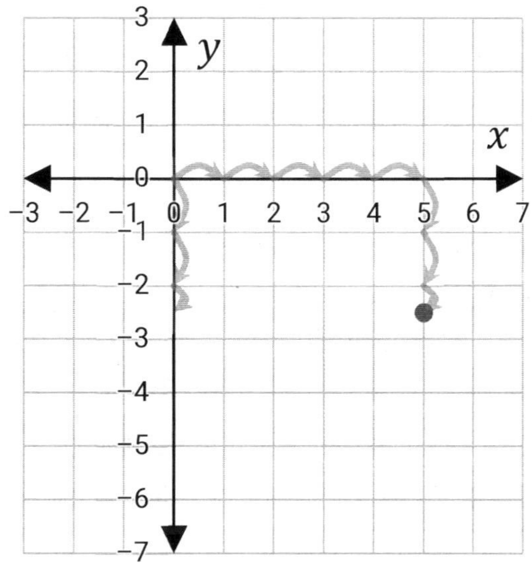

Now, we can double check that our point is placed in the correct location. Let's identify the ordered pair of the plotted point.

First, we will count how many units away from the origin along the x-axis our point is to find the x-value.

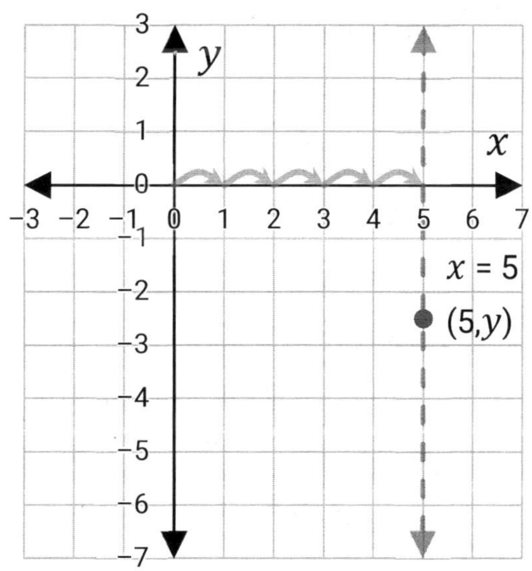

The x-value is 5 units to the right of the origin. Now, we can count how many units away from the origin along the y-axis our point is to find the y-value.

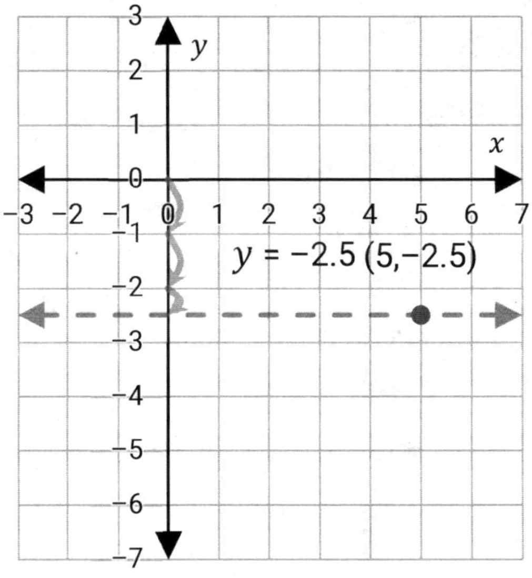

The y-value is 2.5 units below the x-axis, so −2.5 is the y-value. Our point is located at $(5, -2.5)$.

Example

Which point best represents the ordered pair $(-3, 1)$ on the coordinate plane?

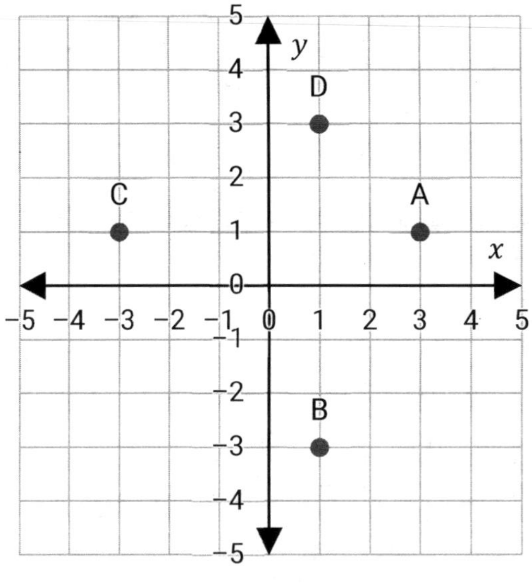

a. Point A
b. Point B
c. Point C
d. Point D

In this problem, we are given four points plotted on a coordinate plane. One of these points represents the ordered pair $(-3,1)$.

The most efficient way to solve this problem is to find the location of $(-3,1)$ and see what point lies in that location.

To find the location of $(-3,1)$, we need to identify which value is the x-value and which is the y-value. In an ordered pair, the first value is the x-value and the second value is the y-value. That means that $x = -3$ and $y = 1$.

So, this location is at the intersection point of $x = -3$ and $y = 1$.

Let's start by finding the location of $x = -3$.

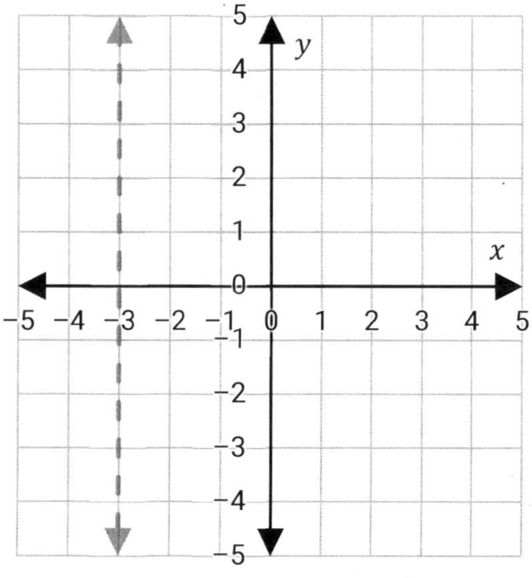

Now, we can find the location of $y = 1$.

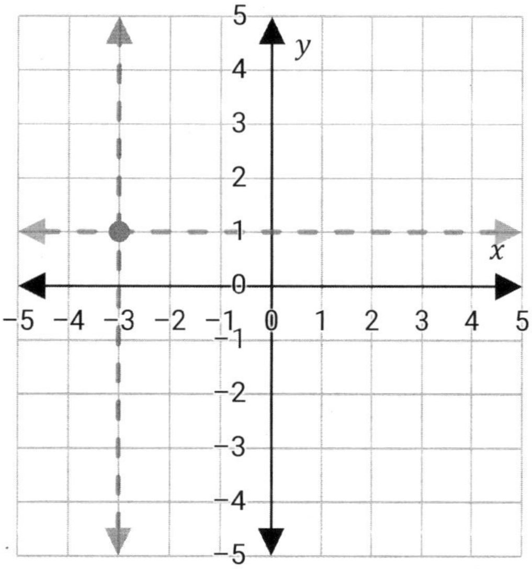

The location of $(-3,1)$ is the point where these two lines cross.

We can also find this point by counting 3 spaces to the left of the origin and up 1 unit from the x-axis.

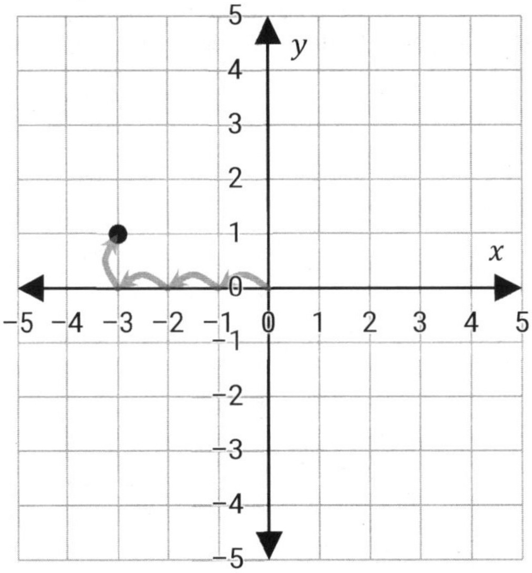

Now that we know the location of $(-3,1)$, we can compare this to our choices. Choice C is the best representation of the ordered pair $(-3,1)$.

The correct answer is C.

EXAMPLE

Which ordered pair describes the point that is located 3 units to the right of the origin and 4 units below the x-axis?

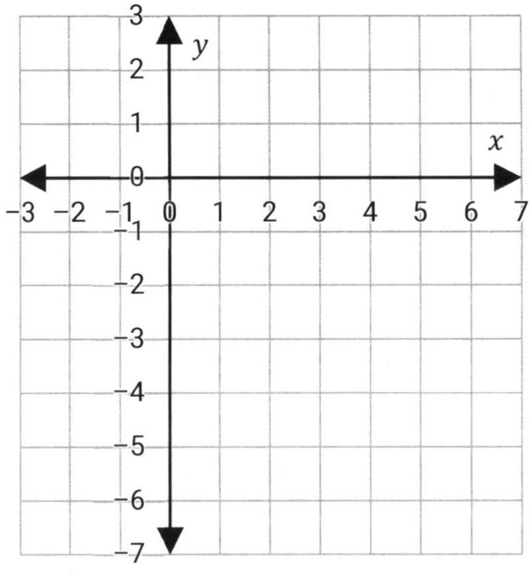

a. $(3,-4)$
b. $(4,3)$
c. $(-3,-4)$
d. $(-3,4)$

In this problem, we are given directions to find a point on a coordinate plane and four options of ordered pairs. To approach this problem, we will follow the directions to locate a point, identify the ordered pair, and match this with the options.

Let's start with following the directions to the location on the coordinate plane.

This point is located 3 units to the right of the origin and 4 units below the x-axis. So, we will start at the origin and count 3 units to the right of the origin.

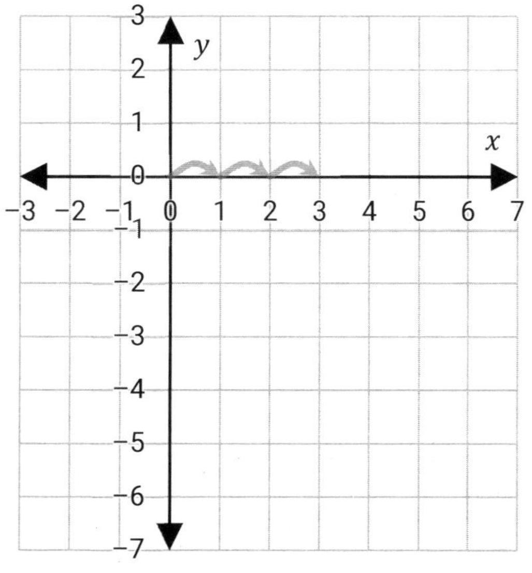

Now, we will count 4 units below the x-axis.

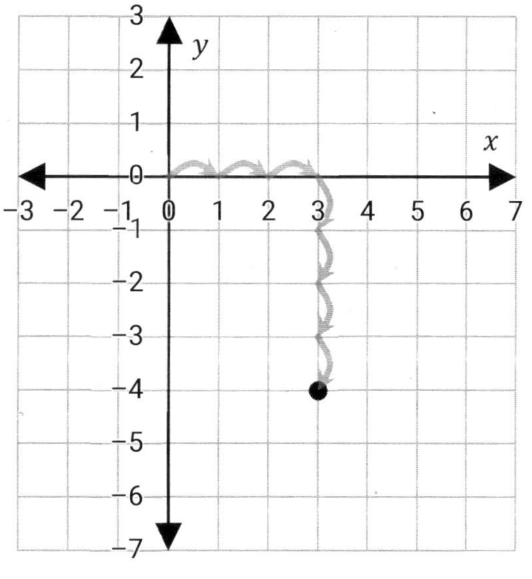

This is our point. Now, what is the ordered pair that best represents this point? Let's find the x- and y-values by identifying the crossing points.

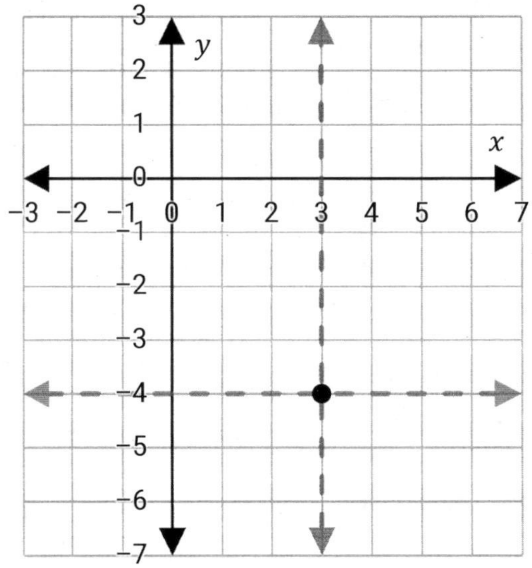

For this point, $x = 3$ and $y = -4$ because the point is 3 units to the right (positive 3) and 4 units down (negative 4). The ordered pair is $(3, -4)$. This matches option A.

The correct answer is A.

Dot Plots

Data can be represented graphically, or visually, in many ways. We have seen data represented using a coordinate plane. Data may also be represented through dot plots, stem-and-leaf plots, histograms, and box plots.

A **dot plot** is a type of graph where values are lined up vertically, like a number line, and dots or x's are used to show the frequency of each value, or how many times that value appears in the data. Dot plots are used to show how often something happens. Dot plots are mostly used when gathering data from multiple trials or surveys. Using a dot plot is a way to represent these types of results in an organized way.

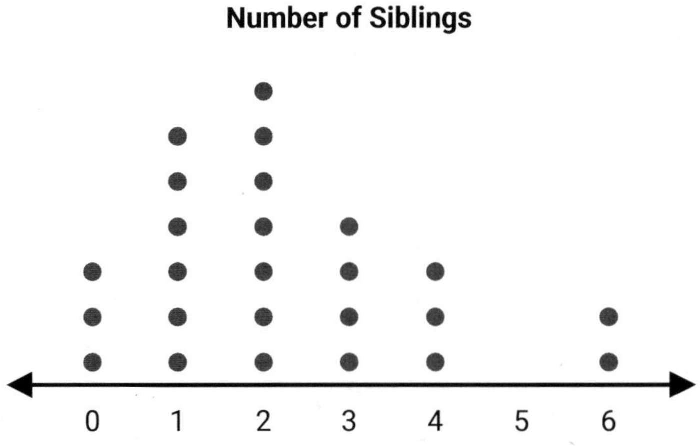

This dot plot shows the data from a survey of the 6th graders in a classroom. The survey gathered data about the number of siblings each 6th grader has in their family. The numbers along the bottom represent the number of siblings and the dots represent the number of students. Each dot is equal to one student. Based on this dot plot, you can tell that 7 people said that they have 2 siblings because there are 7 dots above 2.

The data from this dot plot can also be written in list form.

6, 6, 4, 4, 4, 3, 3, 3, 3, 2, 2, 2, 2, 2, 2, 2, 1, 1, 1, 1, 1, 1, 0, 0, 0

0, 0, 0, 1, 1, 1, 1, 1, 1, 2, 2, 2, 2, 2, 2, 2, 3, 3, 3, 3, 4, 4, 4, 6, 6

3, 2, 2, 3, 0, 1, 2, 1, 1, 6, 2, 4, 2, 3, 6, 0, 0, 1, 1, 2, 4, 2, 4, 3, 1

As you can see, each value is represented on the dot plot. Regardless, there are 2 people who have 6 siblings, 0 people with 5 siblings, 3 people with 4 siblings, 4 people with 3 siblings, 7 people with 2 siblings, 6 people with 1 sibling, and 3 people with 0 siblings.

Review Video: Line Plot
Visit mometrix.com/academy and enter code: 754610

EXAMPLE

The dot plot shows the scores of a middle school basketball season.

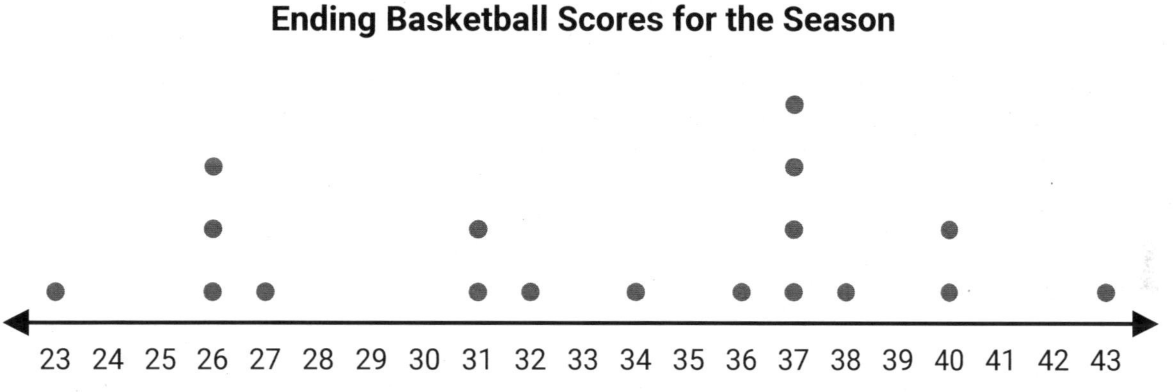

Which statement is true about the data represented by the dot plot?

a. Less than half of the scores were between 30 and 39 points.
b. The range of the scores is 18.
c. There were more games that ended with a score of 31 than there were that ended with a score of 40.
d. Half of the games ended with fewer than 35 points.

Read each answer choice and compare the statements to the data provided in the graph.

Choice A states that less than half of the scores were between 30 and 39 points. To decide if that statement is true or not, we need to compare the number of values between 30 and 39, to the total number of values.

Based on the graph, we can see that 10 scores are between 30 and 39, and there are 18 total scores. 10 is more than half of 18, since 9 is half of 18, so this statement is not true. The answer is not A.

Choice B states that the range of the scores is 18. We know that the range of a data set is the distance between the lowest value and the highest values. The lowest value on this graph is 23 and the highest value is 43. To calculate the distance between 23 and 43, we can use subtraction. $43 - 23 = 20$. So, the range of the data set is 20. The range is NOT 18, so this statement is not true. The answer is not B.

Choice C states that there were more games that ended with a score of 31 than there were that ended with a score of 40. Based on the graph, we can see that 2 games had a score of 31 and 2 games had a score of 40. There were NOT more games that ended with a score of 31 than with a score of 40, there were an equal number of games that ended in these scores. This is not a true statement, so the answer is not C.

Choice D states that half of the games ended with less than 35 points. To decide if this statement is true or not, we need to identify how many games ended with fewer than 35 points and compare that value to the total number of values.

Based on the graph, we can see that 9 games ended with less than 35 points, and the total number of games was 18. We know that 9 is half of 18 because $18 \div 2 = 9$, so this statement is true.

The correct answer is D.

Stem-and-Leaf Plots

A **stem-and-leaf plot** is a way to illustrate data with multi-digit values. This type of data representation is best used with a large number of data points that vary in value, say values from 0 to 100. Two common cases where stem-and-leaf plots are used are plotting the ages of a population and plotting temperature values.

In a stem-and-left plot, values are separated by place value. There is a list of numbers listed vertically along the left side; these are the stems. There is a list of numbers to the right of each stem; these are the leaves. There is a line dividing the stems from the leaves.

The stem-and-leaf plot below describes the ages of people at a family reunion.

Stem	Leaf
0	2, 2, 4, 5, 8, 8, 9
1	1, 2, 3, 3, 3, 4, 4, 5, 7, 9
2	0, 2, 8
3	2, 4, 6, 6, 7
4	3, 4, 9
5	0, 4, 5, 5, 6
6	4, 5, 5
7	0, 1
8	2
9	0, 4
10	2

Key:

$9|4 = 94$

$10|2 = 102$

You can see that there are values 0 to 9 on the left, a dividing line, and numbers to the right. The numbers on the left describe the tens place. The numbers to the right describe the ones place.

So, let's look at the second to last row, the 9's row. All these values have 9 in the tens place, and the listed value in the ones place. So, the values represented by this row are 90 and 94. This means that there are two people at the reunion in their 90s and their ages are 90 and 94.

Now let's look at the first row, the zero row. All these values have a zero in the ten's place. This means these are one-digit numbers. So, the ages represented in this row are 2, 2, 4, 5, 8, 8, 9. That means there are 7 people at the reunion under 10 years old. There are two 2-year-olds, a 4-year-old, a 5-year-old, two 8-year-olds, and a 9-year-old.

Now, sometimes your values will increase, like with our last row. We can see that 10 cannot technically be in the tens place, but this row gives the value 102. It is possible to see two digits in the stem part of the list.

Review Video: Stem-and-Leaf Plots
Visit mometrix.com/academy and enter code: 302339

EXAMPLE

The stem-and-leaf plot shows temperature readings in degrees Celsius.

Temperature Readings

Stem	Leaf
1	8, 9, 9, 9
2	2, 2, 3, 5, 6, 6, 6, 6, 7, 9
3	0, 1, 1, 1, 2, 3

Which statement best describes the data represented by the stem-and-leaf plot?

a. The number of readings between 10 and 20 degrees is greater than the number of readings 30 or above.
b. More than half of the readings were over 26 degrees Celsius.
c. The most common temperature reading was 9 degrees Celsius.
d. 50% of the temperature readings were in the 20s.

In this problem we are given a stem-and-leaf plot that has a series of temperatures. We need to select the statement that is true about the data represented by the plot.

To approach this type of problem, we should examine the statements and determine if they are true or not based on the data on the plot.

Choice A states that the number of readings between 10 and 20 degrees is greater than the number of readings over 30. To decide if this statement is true or not, we need to identify the number of readings that are between 10 and 20 and compare this to the number of readings over 30.

By reviewing the stem-and-leaf plot, we can see that there are 4 readings between 10 and 20: 18, 19, 19, and 19. We can also identify that there are 5 readings that are over 30: 31, 31, 31, 32, and 33. Because there are 5 readings above 30 degrees and 4 readings between 10 and 20, the number of readings between 10 and 20 is not greater than the number of readings 30 or above. This statement is not true, so A is not our answer.

Choice B states that more than half of the readings were over 26 degrees Celsius. To decide if this statement is true, we need to identify the number of readings over 26 degrees and compare this to the total number of readings.

By reviewing the stem-and-leaf plot, we can see that there are 8 readings that were over 26: 27, 29, 30, 31, 31, 31, 32, and 33. The total number of readings is 20. 8 is not more than half of 20 because half of 20 is 10, and 8 is less than 10. This statement is not true, so B is not our answer.

Choice C states that the most common temperature reading was 9 degrees Celsius. To decide if this statement is true, we need to review the data on the table. We can see that there are four 9s on the stem-and-leaf plot, but this does not mean the readings are 9 degrees. Instead, the readings with 9's are 19, 19, 19, and 29. Because there are no readings that read 9 degrees, this statement is not true, so C is not our answer.

While we have eliminated the untrue statements, we need to review the last choice to be sure.

Choice D states that 50% of the temperature readings were in the 20s. To decide if this statement is true, we need to identify the number of readings in the 20s and compare that to the total number of readings.

By reviewing the stem-and-leaf plot, we can see that there are 10 readings in the 20s: 22, 22, 23, 25, 26, 26, 26, 26, 27, and 29. We also know that the total number of readings is 20. 10 is half, or 50%, of 20, so this is a true statement.

The correct answer is D.

HISTOGRAMS

Data can be represented visually in many ways including bar graphs, histograms, dot plots, and circle graphs.

A **histogram** organizes data by showing the frequency of data in certain ranges. A histogram contains a vertical and horizontal axis. Typically, the frequency is listed vertically. Histograms can illustrate many types of data sets.

Review Video: Data Interpretation of Graphs
Visit mometrix.com/academy and enter code: 200439

EXAMPLE

The table shows the number of likes some promotional videos each received on a social media platform.

953	1,634	1,348	450	2,349	879
1,334	2,145	587	994	1,045	950
2,231	1,287	1,898	1,934	2,150	2,476

Which histogram displays the data in the table accurately?

a. 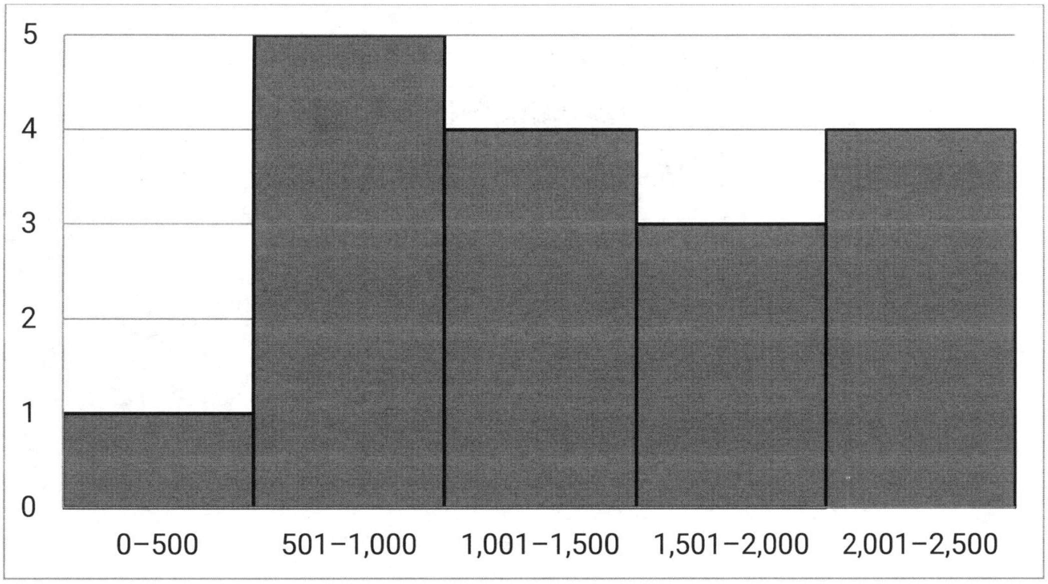

b. 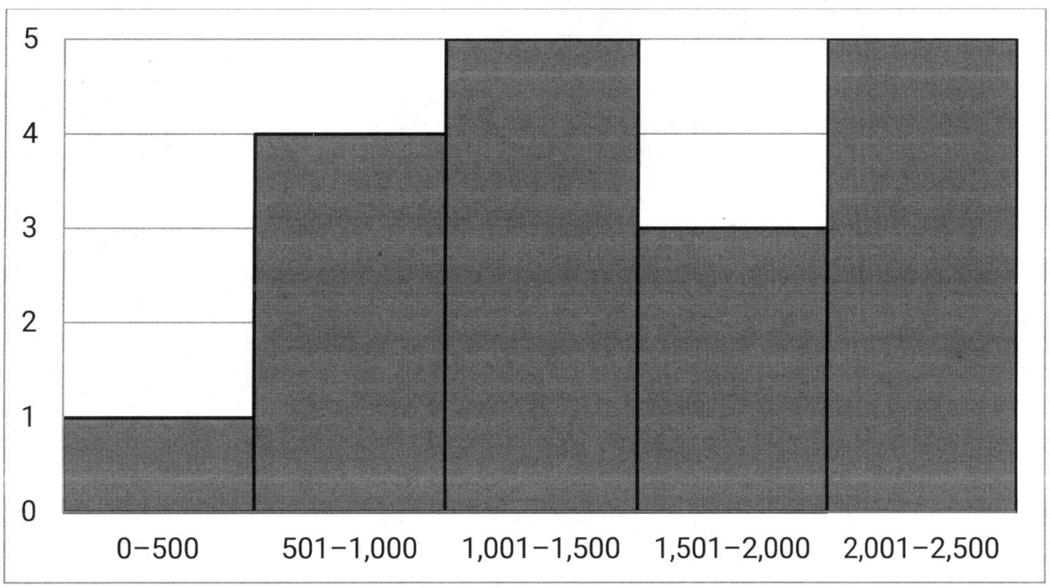

c.

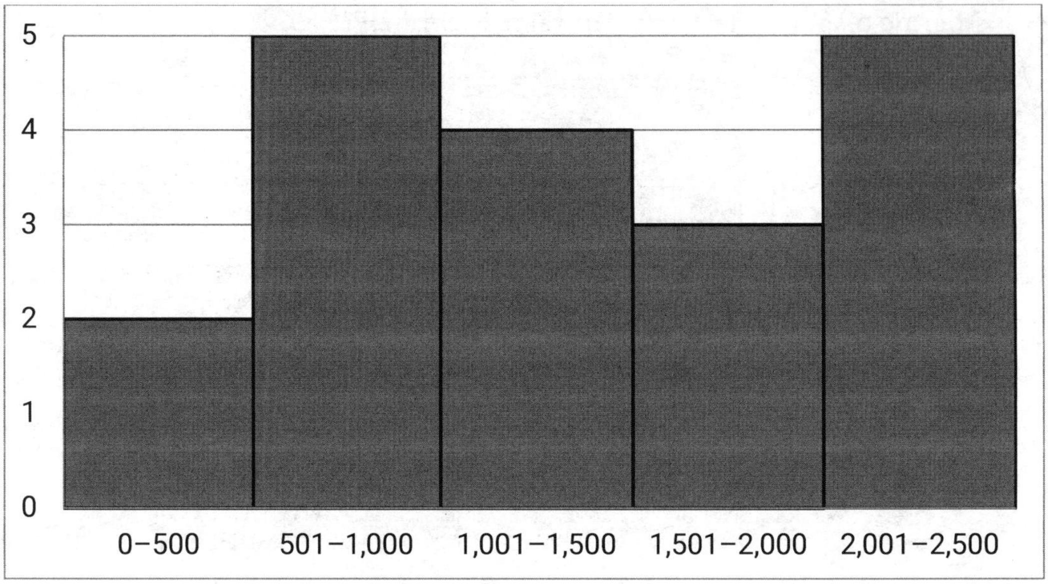

d.

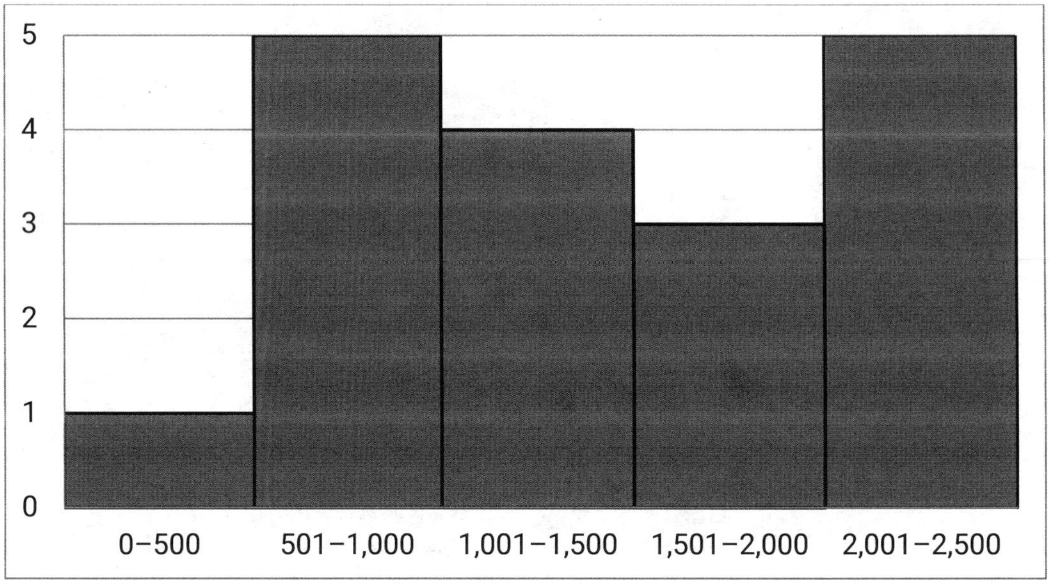

In this problem, we are given a table of values. Each value represents the number of likes a promotional video got. We need to choose the histogram that accurately displays the data.

To solve this problem, we need to first understand the data in the table, and the data on the graphs. As you can see, each graph option has the same horizontal and vertical values. Each number along the left of the histogram represents the number of videos, or the frequency, and increases by 1. Along the bottom, the values are divided by 500s. We have five categories: 0-500, 500-1,000, 1,000-1,500, 1,500-2,000, and 2,000-2,500. Each bar on the graph will show how many videos got a number of likes within these ranges.

First, we need to identify how many videos got the number of likes in each category.

By going through the list, we can see that 1 video got between 0 and 500 likes. It got 450.

5 videos had between 500 and 1,000 likes.

4 videos had between 1,000 and 1,500 likes.

3 videos had between 1,500 and 2,000 likes.

5 videos had between 2,000 and 2,500 likes.

Now that we have this information, we can compare the given choices.

Choice A shows accurate data in every column except the last one. Instead of 5 videos between 2,000 and 2,500 likes, it shows only 4. This is not the correct graph.

Choice B switches the data in the second and third columns. Instead of 5 videos between 500 and 1,000 likes and 4 videos between 1,000 and 1,500 likes, it shows 4 videos and 5 videos. This is not the correct graph.

Choice C shows accurate information in every column except the first column. Instead of showing 1 video with 0-500 likes, this graph shows that 2 videos had between 0 and 500 likes. This is not the correct graph.

Choice D shows all accurate information.

The correct answer is D.

Comparing Data

To compare data, we need to understand measures of center, the spread of data distribution, the shape of data, and how to interpret data from dot plots and box plots.

Measures of Center

The **measures of center** are different methods for estimating or measuring the center of a data set. The center of a data set can be described by the most frequent value in a data set, the value appearing in the middle of a data set arranged from least to greatest, or the value that is the average of that data set. The terms used to describe the center of a data set are mode, median, and mean.

Mode

The **mode** of a data set is the number that shows up most frequently.

Let's say we are given this data set.

$$\{0, 0, 1, 1, 1, 1, 1, 1, 1, 1, 1, 1, 2, 2, 2, 2, 3, 4, 5\}$$

The mode in a data set is the number that repeats the most frequently. If we look at this list of values, we can see that 1 shows up the most often, so the mode of this data set is 1.

Median

The **median** of a data set is the literal middle value in a set of values. If you have a list of values, the median is going to be the value directly in the middle of a list of these values when the values are listed from least to greatest.

Let's say we have a set of data in a list.

$$\{3, 2, 2, 3, 0, 1, 2, 1, 1, 6, 2, 4, 2, 3, 6, 0, 0, 1, 1, 2, 4, 2, 4, 3, 1\}$$

This is a list of values, and we can determine the center, or median value in the data set by lining the values up from least to greatest and finding the middle value.

$$\{0, 0, 0, 1, 1, 1, 1, 1, 1, 2, 2, 2, 2, 2, 2, 2, 3, 3, 3, 3, 4, 4, 4, 6, 6\}$$

Now that we have our data set listed from least to greatest, the median will be the middle number in the set.

12 12

0 0 0 1 1 1 1 1 1 2 2 2 (2) 2 2 2 3 3 3 3 4 4 4 6 6

The center, or median value in this data set is 2, because when you list the values from least to greatest, 2 is the middle number. It is in the middle because it is the same distance from the smallest value to the greatest value and there are the same number of values, 12, on each side.

Finding the median of a data set that has even number of values requires a slightly different approach.

Let's say we are given this data set.

$$\{15, 16, 18, 20, 22, 12, 13, 14, 19, 21, 21, 11, 12, 14\}$$

First, we need to list the values from least to greatest to find the middle.

$$\{11, 12, 12, 13, 14, 14, 15, 16, 18, 19, 20, 21, 21, 22\}$$

Now, we can count to find the middle.

11 12 12 13 14 14 15|16 18 19 20 21 21 22

In this data set, there is not a middle number. Instead, the middle position lies between 15 and 16. So, to find the median value, we will have to find the mean of the two middle numbers, 15 and 16.

To find the mean of these middle values, we will add them together and divide by 2.

$$15 + 16 = 31$$
$$31 \div 2 = 15.5$$

So, the median of this data set is 15.5.

Mean

The **mean** of a data set is often called the **average**. To find the mean of a data set, add the values in the data set together, and divide the sum by the total number of values.

In school, we are familiar with the mean of data sets because this is the way average grades are calculated. To get a final grade, often teachers will add the grade on each assignment or test together and divide by the total number of assignments or tests.

Let's say you are in a math class and your scores are listed in a data set.

$$\{76, 82, 82, 84, 87, 90, 85, 100, 94, 90\}$$

To find the mean, or average, of your scores, add the values and divide by the number of values. In this data set, if we add all the given grades together, we will get a total of 870. Now, if we divide 870 by the total number of grades, 10, we will get 87. That means that the final grade, the average grade, or the mean of the data set is 87.

Review Video: Mean, Median, and Mode
Visit mometrix.com/academy and enter code: 286207

Example

The graph shows the number of students in each 6th grade homeroom class.

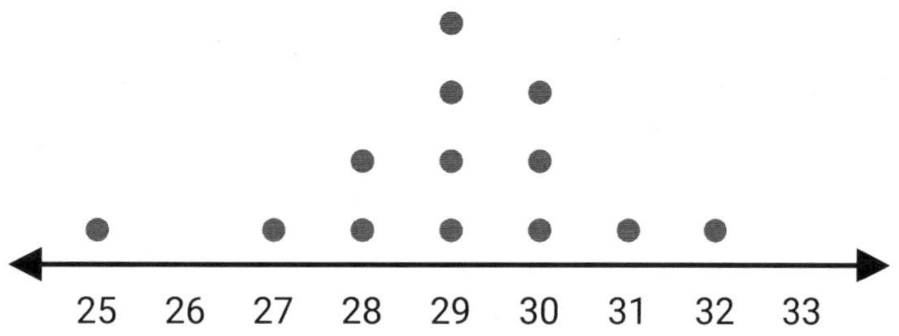

What is the mean number of students in each 6th grade homeroom class?

In this problem, we are given a dot plot that shows the number of students in each 6th grade homeroom class. We need to find the mean number of students in each class.

The mean is the average, and this is found by adding all values and dividing by the number of values.

To approach this problem, we need to start by decoding the graph. Let's list the values on the graph. The order that we write the values does not matter, but let's order them from least to greatest.

25, 27, 28, 28, 29, 29, 29, 29, 30, 30, 30, 31, 32

There are a total of 13 dots, so there are 13 homeroom classes. Now we need to add the number of students in all 13 classes.

$$25 + 27 + 28 + 28 + 29 + 29 + 29 + 29 + 30 + 30 + 30 + 31 + 32 = 377$$

So, there are 377 6th grade students. Now, to find the mean, we need to take the total value and divide by the number of values. In other words, divide the number of students by the number of classes.

There are 13 classes, or 13 values, so we need to divide 377 by 13.

377 divided by 13 is 29, so the mean number of students in each class is 29.

EXAMPLE

The table shows the amount of rainfall each day in inches during the rainiest 2 weeks in April.

Rainfall April 1-14

April 1-7	4.0 in	1.2 in	3.5 in	3.8 in	0.0 in	2.4 in	0.0 in
April 8-14	3.1 in	3.5 in	3.4 in	1.0 in	4.5 in	6.0 in	0.2 in

What is the median amount of daily rainfall during these weeks?

In this problem, we are given a table showing the rainfall over 14 days and need to find the median amount of daily rainfall during this time.

The median value is the middle value in a data set. To approach this problem, we need to start by listing the values from least to greatest.

0.0, 0.0, 0.2, 1.0, 1.2, 2.4, 3.1, 3.4, 3.5, 3.5, 3.8, 4.0, 4.5, 6.0

Now that the values are listed from least to greatest, we can find the middle of the data set.

0.0 0.0 0.2 1.0 1.2 2.4 3.1|3.4 3.5 3.5 3.8 4.0 4.5 6.0

The middle of this data set falls in the middle of two numbers. So, to find the median amount of rainfall, we need to find the mean of these two middle values, 3.1 inches and 3.4 inches. To find the mean of these amounts, we need to add the two values and divide by 2.

$$3.1 + 3.4 = 6.5$$
$$6.5 \div 2 = 3.25$$

The median amount of rainfall during these two weeks is 3.25 inches.

SPREAD OF A DATA DISTRIBUTION

The **spread** of a data distribution is a way to describe the range, or how spread out or close together the data is. Data with a large spread means that there is a large variety of values, or the values are far away from each other. Data with a small spread means that there is not very much variety of values, or the values are close to each other. There are two ways we describe the spread of data. One way to describe the spread is through **range**. The range of data is the difference between the smallest value and the largest value.

Let's say you are given two sets of data.

Data Set 1

953	1,634	1,348	450	2,349	879
1,334	2,145	587	994	1,045	950
2,231	1,287	1,898	1,934	2,150	2,476

Data Set 2

3	6	1
2	3	2
2	0	7
4	4	3
5	2	3

Let's compare the range of these data sets. To compare the ranges, we need to identify the difference between smallest and largest values in each data set.

In data set 1, the smallest value is 450 and the largest value is 2,476. The rage in this data set is the difference between these two values, so we will use subtraction to identify the range.

$$2{,}476 - 450 = 2{,}026$$

So, the range of data set 1 is 2,026.

In data set 2, the smallest value is 0 and the largest value is 7. So, the range is the difference between these values.

$$7 - 0 = 7$$

So, the range of data set 2 is 7.

Now, we can compare. Data set 1 has a large range compared to data set 2 because 2,026 is greater than 7.

INTERQUARTILE RANGE

Another way to describe the spread is by identifying the **interquartile range**, or IQR. The interquartile range is a way to describe the middle 50% of a data set. The interquartile range is the distance between the first quartile and the third quartile.

To identify the interquartile range of a data set, you need to identify the first quartile and the third quartile. The interquartile range is the "box part" of a box plot.

Let's say you are given a list of values: 44, 41, 40, 43, 41, 45, 43, 42, 45.

To find the interquartile range, we need to identify the first and third quartiles. To find the first and third quartiles, we will start with finding the median.

The median in this data set is 43.

40 41 41 42 (43) 43 44 45 45

The next step is identifying the first quartile. The first quartile is the median of the values to the left of the median. In this case, the first quartile lies between 41 and 41, or is the mean of 41 and 41, which is 41.

40 41 41 42 (43) 43 44 45 45

↑

First Quartile

The next step is identifying the third quartile. The third quartile is the median of the values to the right of the median. In this case, the third quartile lies between 44 and 45, or is the mean of 44 and 45, which is 44.5.

40 41 41 42 (43) 43 44 45 45

↑

Third Quartile

So, now that we have identified the first quartile value, 41, and the third quartile value, 44.5, we can identify the interquartile range. The interquartile range is the distance between the first and third quartiles, so we subtract.

$$44.5 - 41 = 3.5$$

The interquartile range, or IQR, of this data set is 3.5.

EXAMPLE

The stem-and-leaf plot below shows the temperatures of patients at a doctor's office.

	Patient Temperatures
9	6.2, 8.5, 8.6, 8.6, 8.8, 9.0, 9.2, 9.7
10	0.2, 0.5, 1.5, 2.0, 4.1

What is the range of these temperatures in degrees Fahrenheit?

In this problem, we are given a stem-and-leaf plot with the temperatures of patients, and we need to find the range of these temperatures.

We know that the range of a data set is the difference between the smallest and the largest value in a data set. So, first, we need to identify the smallest and greatest value.

In a stem-and-leaf plot, the values are already organized from least to greatest. The first value listed is the smallest value and the last value listed is the largest value. The first value on the stem -and-leaf plot has a 9 in the tens place and 6.2 following the 9. The smallest value is 96.2.

The last value has a 10 in the tens place and 4.1 following the 10. The largest value is 104.1.

Now, to find the range, we need to find the difference of these two values using subtraction, $104.1 - 96.2 = 7.9$.

The range of the temperatures is 7.9 degrees Fahrenheit.

Example

A graph represents the number of paintings sold by 10 artists.

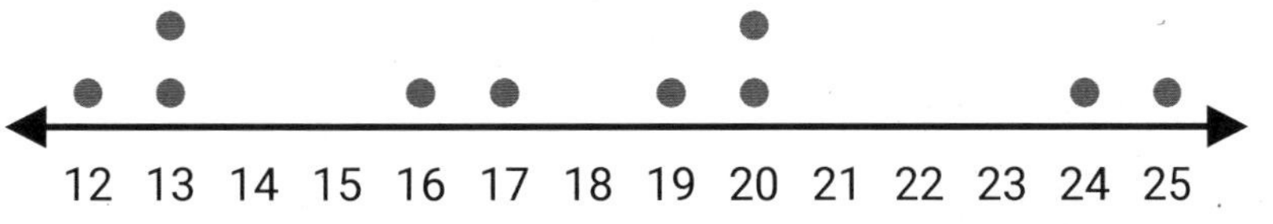

What is the interquartile range of the data set?

In this problem, we are given a dot plot that represents the number of paintings sold and we need to identify the interquartile range of the data represented by the graph.

The IQR is the difference between the first quartile and the third quartile.

The first step to solving this problem is to list the values from the graph from least to greatest.

12, 13, 13, 16, 17, 19, 20, 20, 24, 25

Once we have a list of values, we can identify the median, first quartile, third quartile, and finally the interquartile range.

Let's start with identifying the median.

12 13 13 16 17 | 19 20 20 24 25

$$17 + 19 = 36$$
$$36 \div 2 = 18$$

The median value in this data set is the mean of 17 and 19, which is 18.

Now, we can identify the first quartile by finding the median of the values to the left of the median.

12 13 (13) 16 17 | 19 20 20 24 25

The first quartile is 13.

Now, we can identify the third quartile by finding the median of the values to the right of the median.

12 13 13 16 17 | 19 20 (20) 24 25

The third quartile is 20.

To find the interquartile range, we calculate the difference between the first quartile and third quartile using subtraction.

$$20 - 13 = 7$$

The interquartile range of the data set is 7.

The correct answer is A.

Shape of a Data Distribution

The **shape** of data distribution describes the way that a set of data looks when it is represented visually. Graphs are visual illustrations of data, and we can observe the way data is displayed to make judgements. We can describe the shape of data based on symmetry, uniformity, peaks, gaps, clusters, and if it is skewed to one side or another.

Symmetry

A graph with **symmetry** is a graph that has a symmetrical shape, or it is the same shape on both sides. A symmetrical graph can be folded in half and look the same on both sides. Each side is a mirror image. The bar graph, dot plot, and box plot below show symmetrical sets of data.

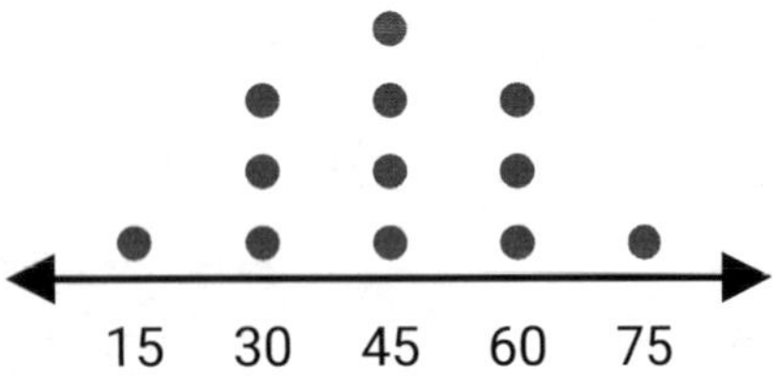

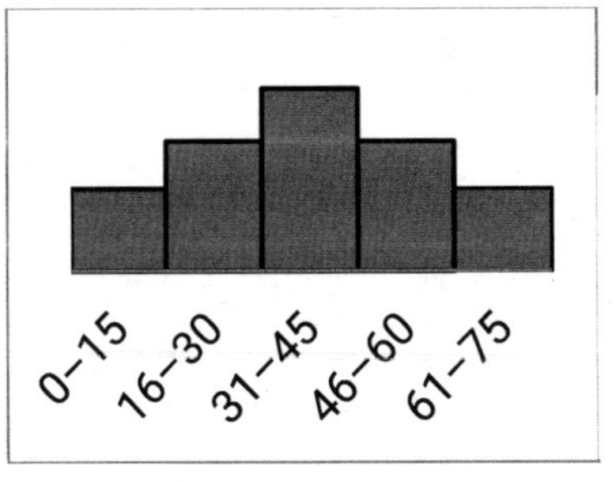

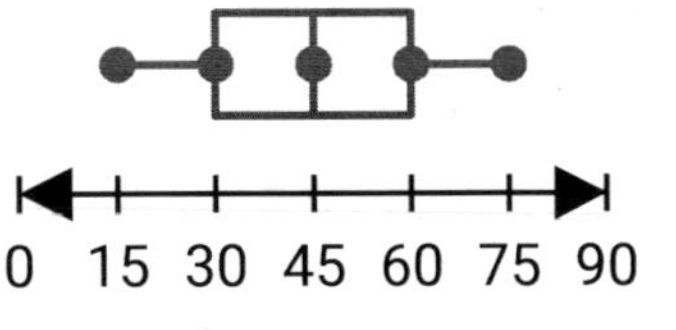

Peaks

A **peak** on a graph is an area where there are more data points. A peak will be a tall part of a graph, where there is one area with the most data. The bar graph below shows a graph with two peaks. There is a peak at 16–30 and another peak at 46–60.

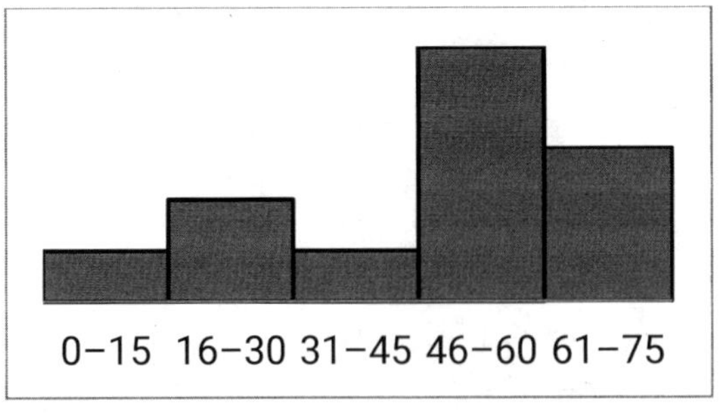

A **uniform** graph does not have any peaks.

GAPS

A **gap** on a graph is an area on the graph where there is no data and there is a blank area, or gap, in the graph. The dot plot below shows a graph with a gap at 60 because there is no data at 60, but there is data surrounding 60.

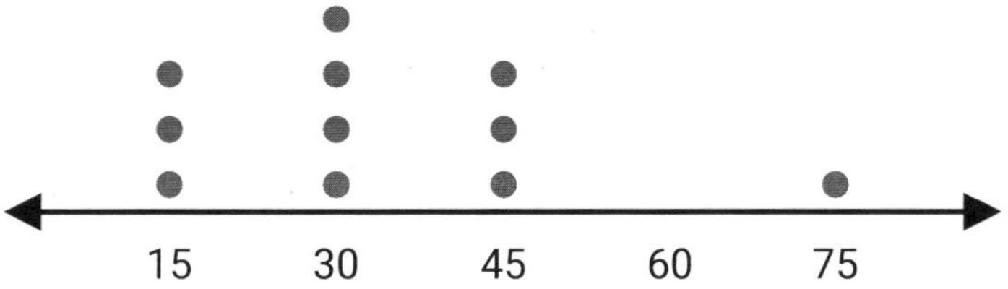

CLUSTERS

A **cluster** on a graph is an area where the majority of the data lies. The bar graph below shows a graph with a cluster from 0 to 45 because the majority of the data is at 0–15, 15–30, and 30–45.

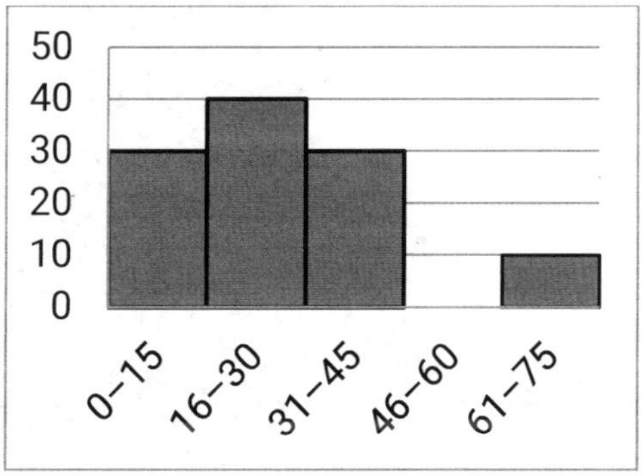

SKEWS

A **skewed** graph shows more data on one side of a graph than another. In a skewed graph, there is a peak and a tail. The peak in a graph is an area with the most data. The **tail** in a graph is an area with the least data. A graph with the tail to the right is described as "skewed to the right". A graph with the tail to the left is described as "skewed to the left".

Skewed to the right:

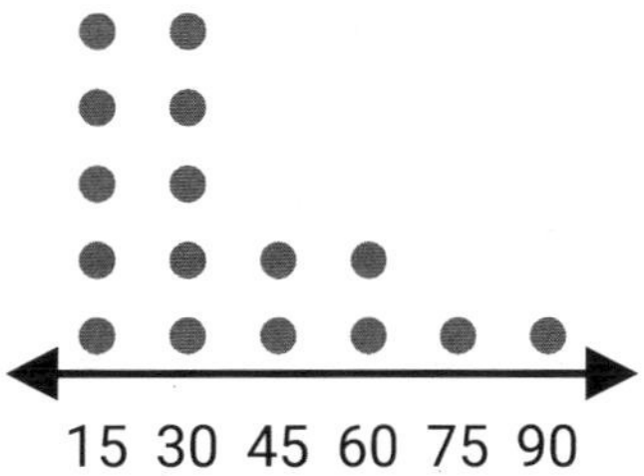

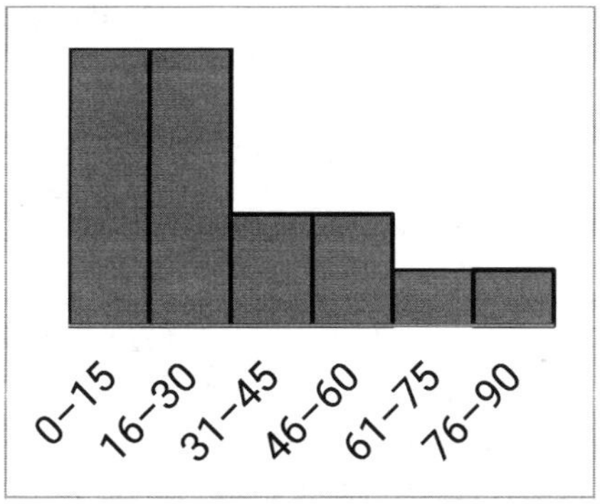

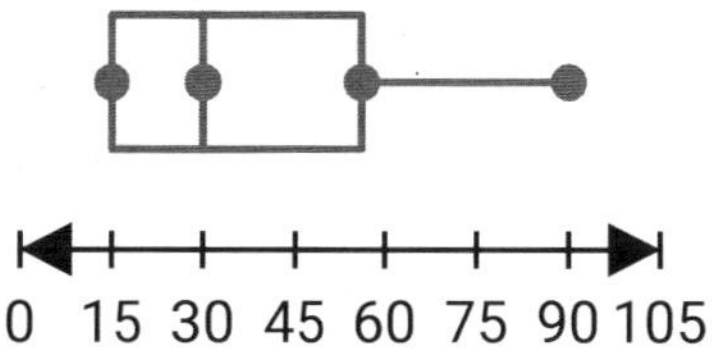

Skewed to the left:

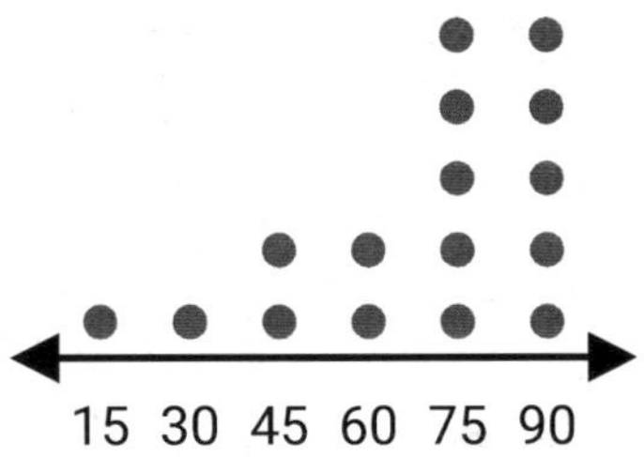

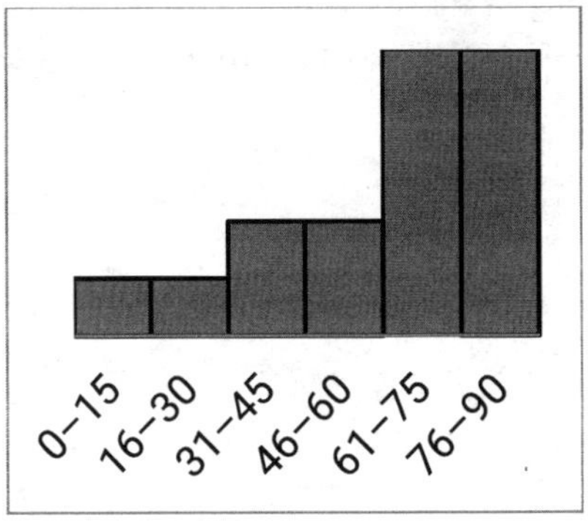

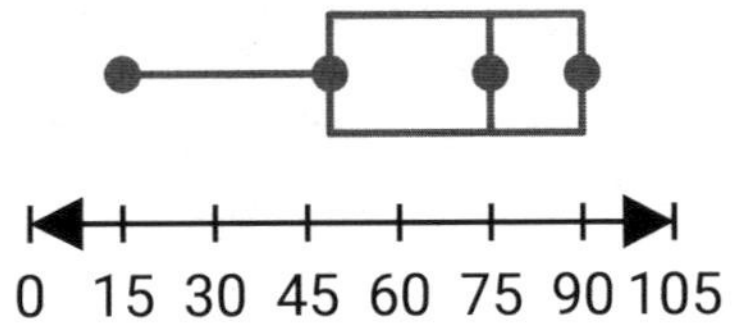

EXAMPLE

A histogram is shown below.

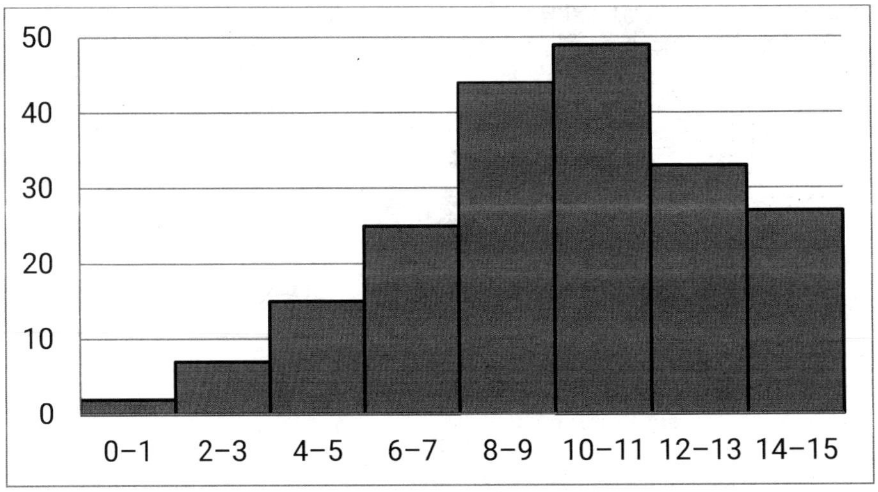

Which statement is NOT true about the data shown in the histogram?

a. The data distribution is skewed.
b. The data distribution has no gaps.
c. The data distribution is symmetrical.
d. The peak of the data is at 10-11.

In this problem we are given a histogram and four statements about the data on the histogram. We need to determine which statement does not describe the data.

To approach this problem, we should observe the graph and review the statements that describe the graph.

- Choice A states that the data distribution is skewed. We know that a skewed graph means there is a peak on one side and a tail on the other. In this graph, the majority of data is on the right and there is less data on the left. The peak is on the right, and there is a tail on the left, so this graph is skewed to the left. This statement is true.
- Choice B states that the data distribution has no gaps. We know that a gap in data means that there is a blank space on the graph. In this graph, there are no gaps because there are no blank spaces. This statement is true.

- Choice C states that the data distribution is symmetrical. We know that a symmetrical graph looks the same on both sides, often with a U shape or bell shape. This graph is not symmetrical because there is more data on one side than the other. This statement does not describe the graph. This is the correct answer.
- Choice D states that the peak of the data is at 10–11. We know that the peak is the area of the graph that has the most data. On the graph, the bar above 10–11 is the tallest, which means that there is more data at 10–11. This statement is true.

Since the question asks us to select the statement that is not true, the correct answer is C.

Box Plots

Box plots show the minimum value, the maximum value, the median value, the first quartile, and the third quartile of a data set. The minimum value is the smallest value and the maximum value is the largest value. The median is the exact center of a data set.

The **first quartile** is the median of the lower half of the data set, or the median of the values to the left of the median. The **third quartile** is the median of the upper half of the data set, or the median of the values to the right of the median.

This list gives the heights in inches of students in a 6th grade math class.

$$\{52, 52, 53, 55, 56, 56, 57, 57, 57, 57, 58, 58, 59, 59, 59, 59, 60, 60, 62, 62, 64, 64, 65, 65\}$$

This box plot represents the data in this list.

Minimum Value First Quartile Median Third Quartile Maximum Value

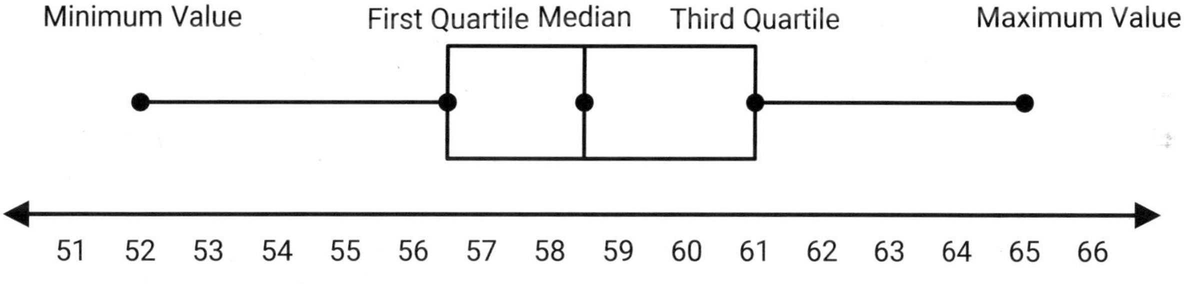

The point farthest to the left represents the minimum value in the data set, 52 inches.

The point farthest to the right represents the maximum value in the data set, 65 inches.

The point inside the box represents the median value in the data set, 58.5 inches, the mean of 58 and 59.

The first quartile is represented by the edge of the box to the left of the median. This value is the median of the values to the left of the median, 56 inches.

The third quartile is represented by the edge of the box to the right of the median. This value is the median of the values to the right of the median, 62 inches.

A box plot represents the four quarters of a data set.

The first 25% of a data set lies between the minimum and first quartile.

The next 25% of the data lies between the first quartile and the median.

The next 25% of the data lies between the median and the third quartile.

And the last 25% of a data set lies between the third quartile and the maximum.

Review Video: Box and Whisker Plots
Visit mometrix.com/academy and enter code: 810817

EXAMPLE

The box plots represent the data collected from measuring the daily temperatures during the months of July and December in degrees Fahrenheit.

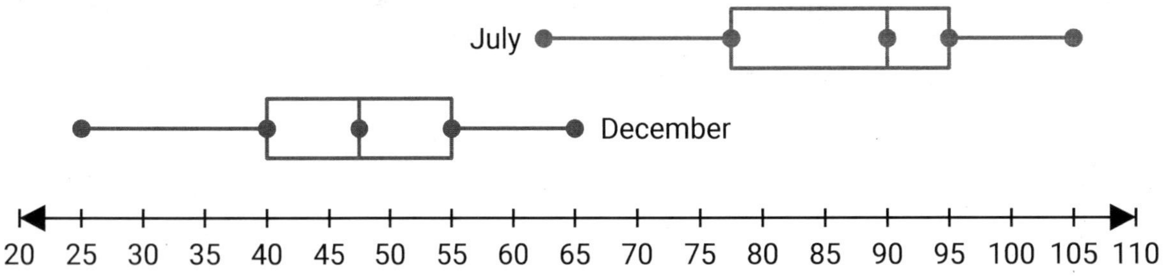

Which statement is NOT true about the data represented by the box plots?

a. The range in temperatures for December is 80.
b. Half of the temperatures in July were equal to or above 90 degrees.
c. The interquartile range for December is 15.
d. More than half of the temperatures in December were less than or equal to 55 degrees.

In this problem we are given two box plots that represent the temperature data collected during July and December. We need to select the statement that does NOT describe the data in the provided graph.

To approach this problem, we need to examine the options and compare the statements with the data represented by the box plots.

Choice A states that the range in temperatures for December is 80. We know that the range is the difference between the highest and the lowest values. The lowest temperature recorded for December is 25 and the highest is 65. To find the range, we subtract., $65 - 25 = 40$. The range for December is not 80, so this statement is untrue. Choice A is the correct answer.

Choice B states that half of the temperatures in July were equal to or above 90 degrees. As we observe the July box plot, we can see that the median value is at 90, and we know that the median is the middle value, or the halfway point. This means that half of the temperatures in July are equal to or above 90 degrees, so this statement is true.

Choice C states that the interquartile range for December is 15. We know that the interquartile range is the range between the first quartile and the third quartile. This means it is the range of the lowest and highest values that make the "box" in the box plot. We can see that the first quartile, or lower "box" value, is 40 and the third quartile, or higher "box" value, is 55. The range is the distance between these numbers. We can subtract to find that. $55 - 40 = 15$. The interquartile range is 15, so this statement is true.

Choice D states that more than half of the temperatures in December were less than 55 degrees. Based on the graph, we can see that the median value in the December box plot is halfway between 45 and 50, and the third quartile is at 55. This means three-fourths of the data is less than or equal to 55 degrees, which is more than half of the temperatures recorded in December. This statement is true.

The only statement that is NOT true is that the range in temperatures recorded in December is 80.

The correct answer is A.

EXAMPLE

A group of 6th graders have decided to volunteer at an animal shelter. The list represents the number of hours each person spent at the animal shelter last week.

2, 3, 4, 4, 5, 5, 5, 6, 6, 6, 7, 8, 8, 8

Which box plot best summarizes the hours spent at the animal shelter last week?

a.

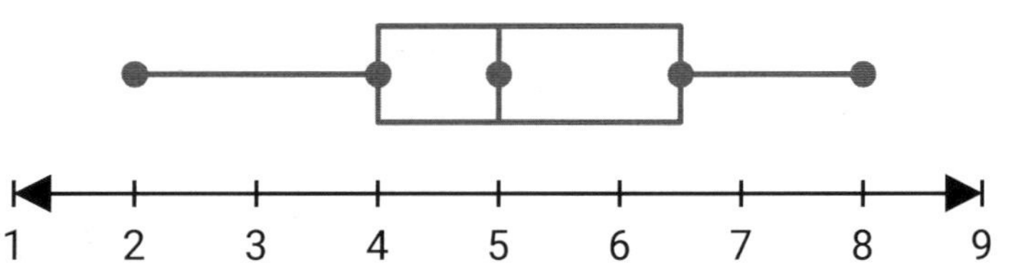

b.

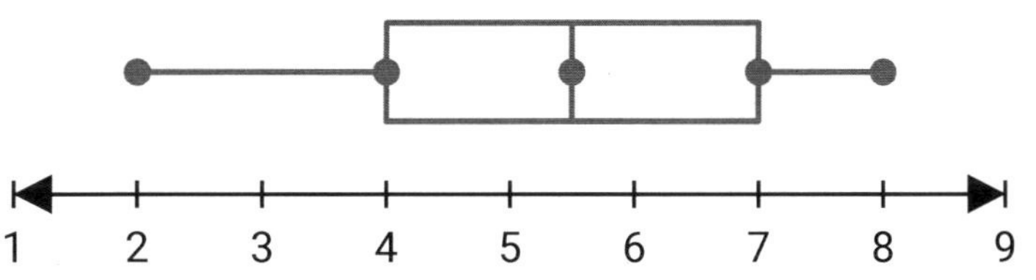

c. 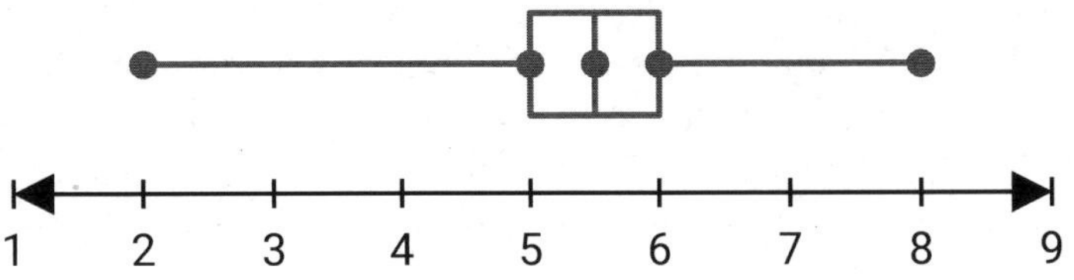

d. 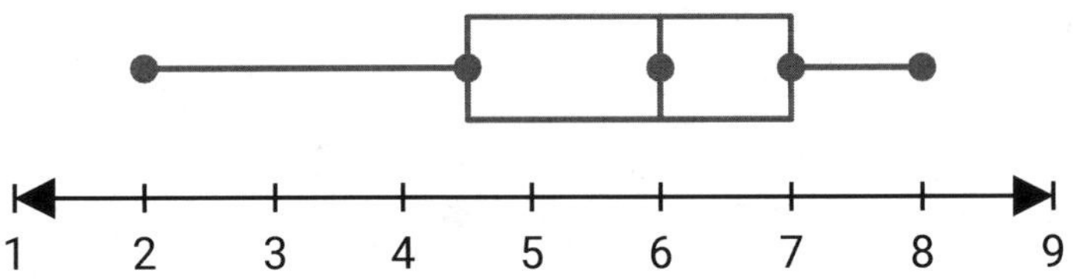

In this problem, we are given a list of values and we need to select the box plot that best represents the data.

To approach this problem, we need to consider the five points that are displayed on a box plot. On a box plot, we have a minimum, a first quartile, a median, a third quartile, and a maximum value shown.

First, let's identify the minimum and maximum values. The list provided is organized from least to greatest, so we can identify the minimum as 2, and the maximum as 8.

If we review our choices, all choices give a minimum and maximum of 2 and 8. We will build our box plot starting with these values.

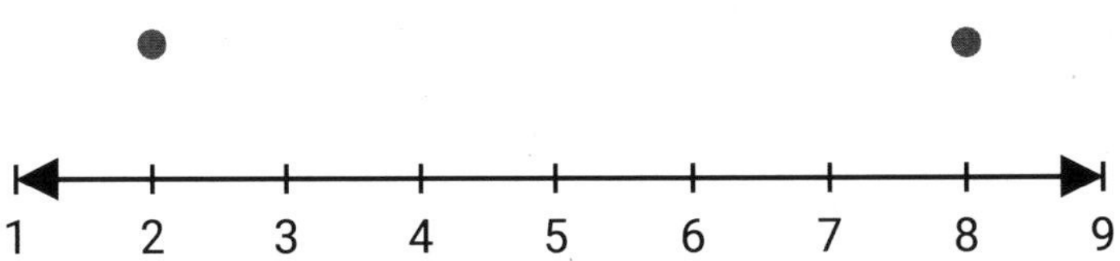

Now, we need to identify the median value. To find the median value, we need to count to the middle of our list.

2 3 4 4 5 5 (5 6) 6 6 7 8 8 8

The middle of the list is in between the values 5 and 6, so the median is the mean of 5 and 6. To find the mean, we will add these values together and divide by two.

$$5 + 6 = 11$$
$$11 \div 2 = 5.5$$

If 5.5 is the median, we can eliminate two choices. Choice A gives the median value of 5, and choice D gives a median value of 6. Choices A and D can be eliminated.

Add the median value to our box plot.

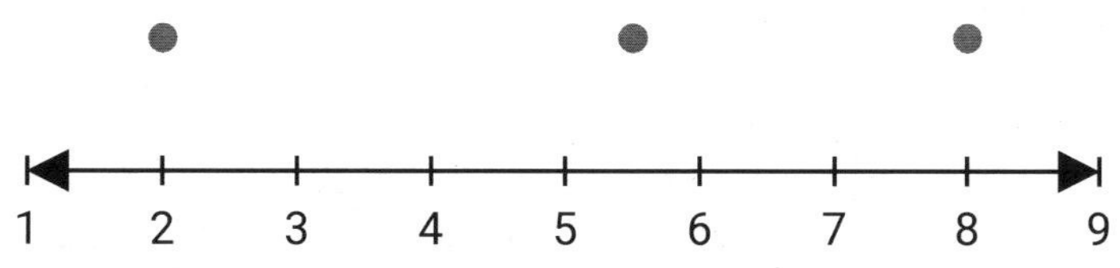

Now, we need to find the first quartile and third quartile. We know that the first quartile is the median of the left values. The median of the left values is 4.

2 3 4 4 5 5 5 6 6 6 7 8 8 8

We also know that the third quartile is the median of the right values. The median of the right values is 7.

2 3 4 4 5 5 5 6 6 6 7 8 8 8

Now, we know all the data points that belong on our box plot.

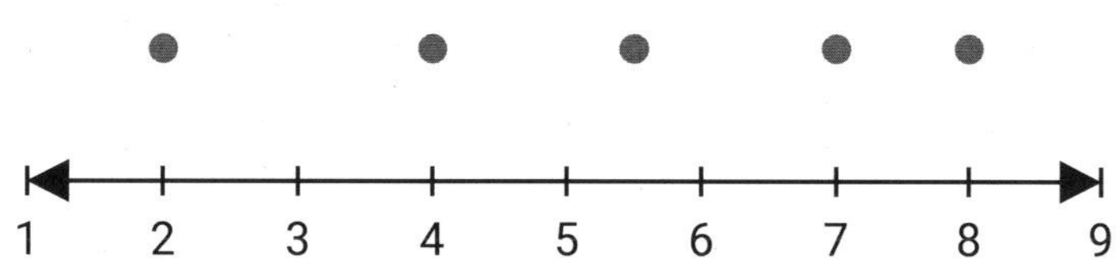

We can add a line to connect the first quarter of values, draw a box connecting the second quarter, a box connecting the third quarter, and a line to connect the last quarter of values.

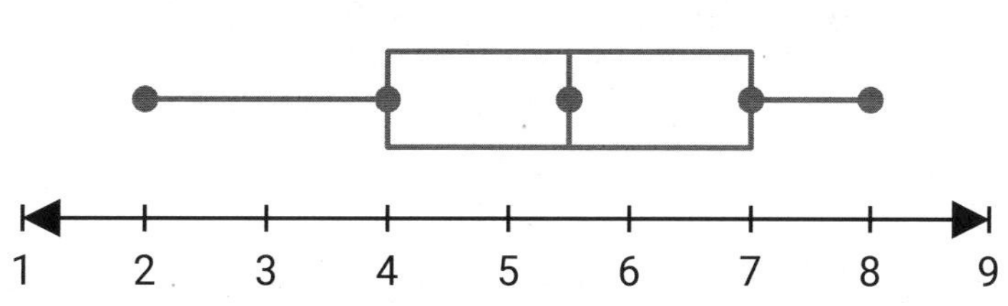

Lastly, we can compare choices. Choice B matches our graph and includes all the appropriate data points. Choice C gives the first quartile value as 5 and the third quartile value as 6.

The correct answer is B.

Frequency Tables

Categorical data is data that is divided into qualitative categories. You get categorical data if you are taking a survey of favorite foods, or when a company collects data about the sizes of t-shirts they sold. This type of data is categorical data because the data can be divided into categories. One way to describe categorical data is through frequency tables. A **frequency table** is a table that visually divides this categorical data into categories and shows how frequently a category shows up in the data. For example, let's say a food truck is keeping track of how often each menu item is ordered to see which is their most popular item. The food truck sells tacos, sandwiches, salads, and burgers. A frequency table can be created to keep track of this data throughout the day.

Menu Item	Number Sold
Tacos	
Sandwiches	
Salads	
Burgers	

As items are sold, tallies or marks can be made on the frequency table to keep track of information. Let's say the food truck sold 13 taco plates, 10 sandwiches, 9 salads, and 18 burgers. These frequency tables display the data from the food truck.

Menu Item	Number Sold
Tacos	𝍸 𝍸 |||
Sandwiches	𝍸 𝍸
Salads	𝍸 ||||
Burgers	𝍸 𝍸 𝍸 |||

Menu Item	Number Sold
Tacos	13
Sandwiches	10
Salads	9
Burgers	18

Relative Frequency Tables

A **relative frequency table** gives the same data as a frequency table, but also includes the percentages to show what percentage of the data goes with each category. For example, with the food truck, we can use a relative frequency table to identify the percentage of customers that ordered tacos.

To find the relative frequency of a category, we write the relationship between the category and the total as a fraction. Once we have a fraction, we can use division or equivalent fractions to find the percentage. In this example, we would write a fraction to represent the relationship between the number of tacos ordered and the total number of items ordered.

We can find the total number of items ordered by adding up the total number of data items: in this example, the food truck sold a total of 50 items because $13 + 10 + 9 + 18 = 50$.

There are 13 tacos sold and 50 total items, so the relationship can be written as the fraction $\frac{13}{50}$.

Now, to find the percentage of customers that bought tacos, or any menu item, we can use equivalent fractions and convert $\frac{13}{50}$ to a fraction over 100, and then a percentage.

We can also use division and divide 13 by 50 and multiply the quotient by 100% to get a percentage.

In this case, the most efficient process will be using equivalent fractions.

We can complete the relative frequency table to find the percentage of customers that bought each menu item.

Menu Item	Number Sold	Fraction	Percent
Tacos	13	$\frac{13}{50} = \frac{26}{100}$	26%
Sandwiches	10	$\frac{10}{50} = \frac{20}{100}$	20%
Salads	9	$\frac{9}{50} = \frac{18}{100}$	18%
Burgers	18	$\frac{18}{50} = \frac{36}{100}$	36%

There are many ways to interpret data from a frequency table. We know that 26% of customers bought tacos. We know that burgers are the most popular item because 36% of customers bought a burger.

Remember, when converting frequency to a percentage, the total of all percentages will be 100%. 100% of customers recorded purchased an item, so $26\% + 20\% + 18\% + 36\% = 100\%$. It is a good idea to double check your percentages by adding them up to see if they add up to 100%. If they do not add up to 100%, you may need to double check your calculations.

Percent Bar Graphs

The information on a relative frequency table can also be illustrated by a percent bar graph. A **percent bar graph** is a graph that shows percent frequencies of each category in a bar labeled by percentages from 0% to 100%.

We can convert the data from the relative frequency table to a percent bar graph.

26% of customers bought tacos. 20% of customers bought sandwiches. 18% of customers bought salads. 36% of customers bought burgers. Which means that 100% of customers bought something off the food truck menu.

This information can be shown using a percent bar graph. A percent bar graph can be horizontal or vertical.

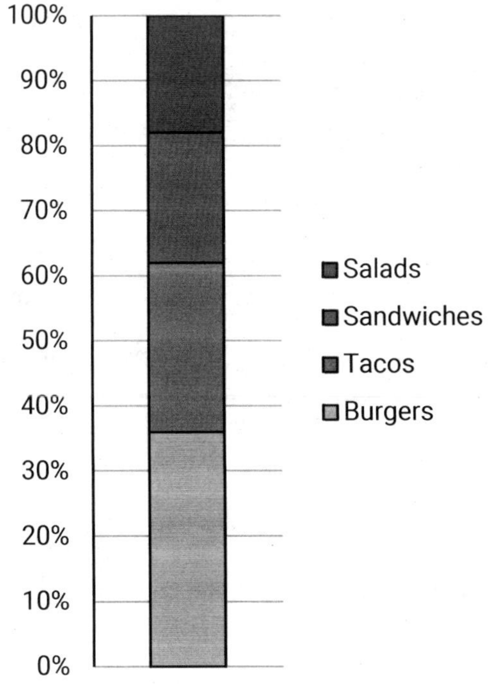

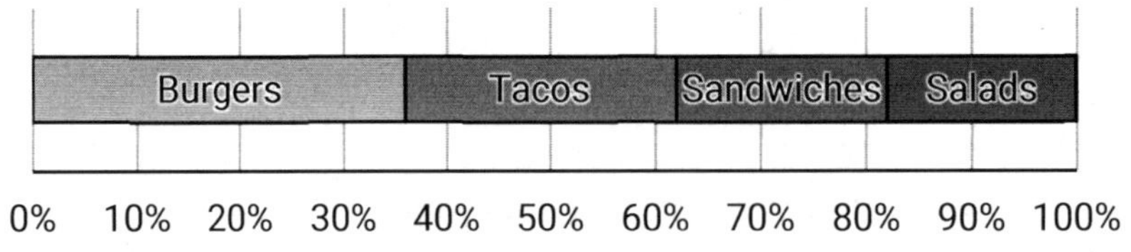

A percent bar graph will be labeled from 0 to 100, sometimes with whole number values and sometimes with percentages. Each part of the bar represents a different data category. In this example, there are four: burgers, tacos, sandwiches, and salads.

Typically, a percent bar graph will show data from greatest to least, where the category with the highest frequency starts at 0% and the category with the least frequency ends the 100%. In this example, burgers is the highest frequency category with 36%, so the burger section goes from 0% to 36%. Salads is the lowest frequency category with 18%, so the salads section goes from 82% to 100%.

Sometimes each category will be labeled with words; other times it will be labeled by color with a key. Each category will show the percent frequency, and the total percent frequency will add up to 100%.

Example

A middle school is changing their mascot and asked students to vote for their choice. The table shows the number of votes each mascot received.

Mascot	Votes	Key for Bar Graph
Lion	58	
Tiger	120	
Bear	22	

Which percent bar graph best represents the data?

a.
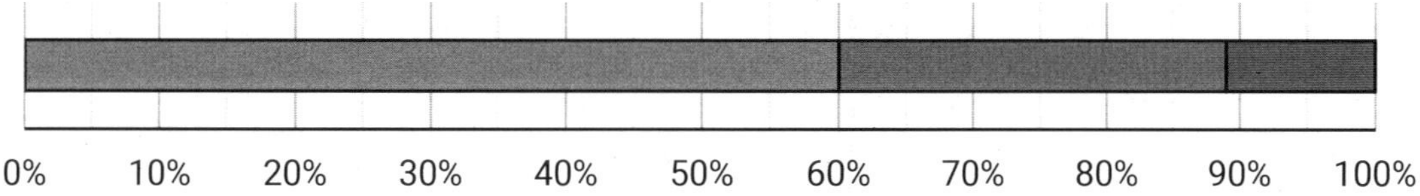

b.
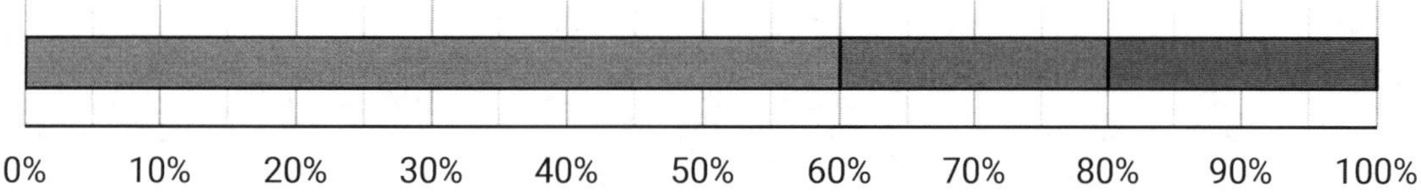

c.
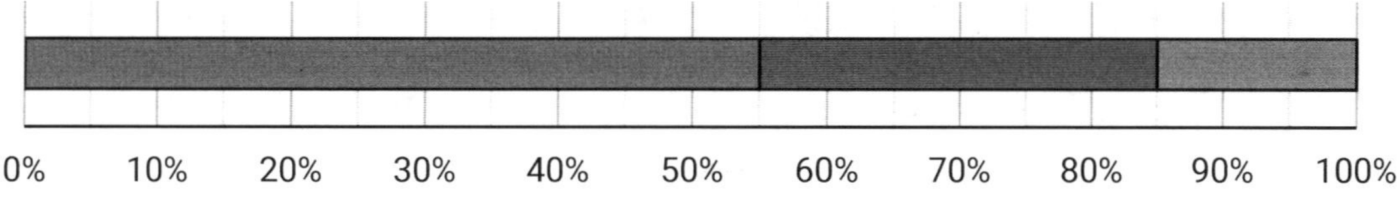

d.
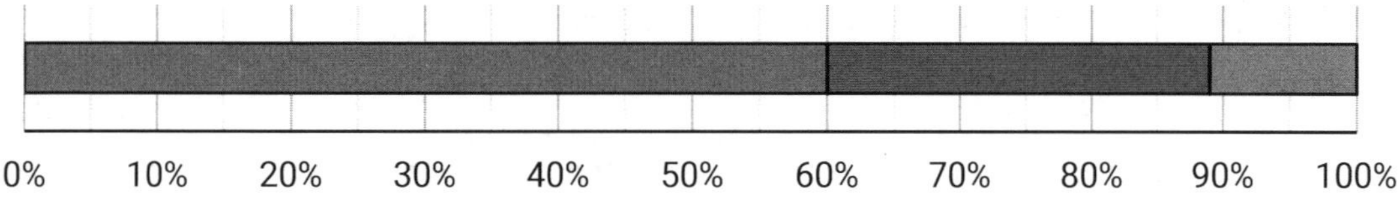

In this problem, we are given a frequency table that shows the number of votes each mascot received and we need to choose the percent bar graph that best represents the data.

To approach this problem, we need to first identify the percentage of the votes each mascot received. To find the percentage, we need to divide the number of votes for each mascot by the total number of votes.

We can find the total number of votes by adding the number of votes for each mascot.

$$58 + 120 + 22 = 200$$

The total number of votes cast was 200.

Now, we can find the percentages for each mascot.

The lion mascot got 58 votes, or $\frac{58}{200}$ of the votes. We can convert this to a percentage by using division or equivalent fractions.

Using division:

$$\begin{array}{r} 0.29 \\ 200\overline{)\,58.00} \\ \underline{40\,0} \\ 18\,00 \end{array}$$

$$0.29 \times 100 = 29\%$$

Using equivalent fractions:

$$\frac{58}{200} \div \frac{2}{2} = \frac{29}{100} = 29\%$$

Lion got 29% of the votes.

The tiger mascot got 120 votes, or $\frac{120}{200}$ of the votes. We can find the percentage by using division or equivalent fractions. Using equivalent fractions is a little faster because it is simple to convert fractions out of 200 to fractions out of 100.

$$\frac{120}{200} \div \frac{2}{2} = \frac{60}{100} = 60\%$$

Tiger got 60% of the votes.

The bear mascot got 22 votes, or $\frac{22}{200}$ of the votes.

$$\frac{22}{200} \div \frac{2}{2} = \frac{11}{100} = 11\%$$

Bear got 11% of the votes.

Now that we know the percentage of the total votes each mascot received, we can compare these values to our choices.

Choice A matches the percentages we found and matches the given key for the data.

Variability

Situations used to gather data can give data with high variability and low variability. **Variability** of data is a way to describe the type of data that can be collected from a situation. A situation with **low variability** would give a low variety of data. A situation with **high variability** would give a high variety of data.

Let's say you are collecting data about peoples' favorite animals. If you surveyed people and asked them, "What is your favorite animal?", there is a huge variety of possible answers you could be given. In fact, you could have a different answer from every person you surveyed. This is an example of high variability. There is a high chance of variety, meaning there are a lot of possible answers that could be given from that question. A lot of possible answers means high variability.

Now, if you are looking for a situation with low variability, you could ask people, "Out of these four choices, which is your favorite animal?". In this case, the answers are limited to four choices. Instead of thinking of any animal that is their favorite, they are given just a few choices. There are only a few possible answers you could be given in this situation, so there is low variability. A limited number of answers means low variability.

Personal Financial Literacy

Personal Financing Options

A bank account is used to store and keep track of money. Instead of keeping cash under a bed or in a piggy bank, a person may choose to keep their money in a bank account. When someone opens a **bank account**, they give their money to a bank, and the bank keeps that money safe. Bank accounts are insured by the federal government. That means that if something happens to the bank, the government is guaranteeing that you will not lose your money. In modern times, most banks do not keep your money physically in the bank. Instead, the money that is shown in your account is digital, and each transaction you make is a digital transaction. A **transaction** is a term used to describe any exchange of money. If you buy something from a store, you exchanged money for something at the store. This is an example of a transaction. The bank will keep track of these exchanges digitally. However, banks keep cash on hand, so if you need physical money, you can go to a bank and take cash from your account.

Types of Bank Accounts

Banks offer many types of accounts. The main types of accounts are checking accounts and savings accounts. A **checking account** is an account where you are holding money that you will use regularly. A **savings account** is an account where you are holding money that you do not plan to use right away. Instead, you plan to keep it there for an extended period. Some checking accounts and savings accounts have fees and features.

A checking account can have fees to open the account, monthly fees, debit card fees, ATM fees, and overdraft fees. Some banks have free accounts without these fees. Checking account fees are not very common anymore, but it is important to understand them and be able to compare the fees different banks charge.

Account Fees and Minimums

A fee to open an account is exactly as it sounds. You may have to pay a **fee** upfront to open the account. A monthly fee is a small fee for the bank to hold your money and let you use it, but this is not very common anymore. A debit card fee is a fee someone pays to get a debit card. A **debit card** is a small plastic card that is connected to a checking account. This card can be used to make purchases in a store or online. An ATM fee is a fee a bank will charge to use an ATM. An **ATM** is a machine where someone can use a debit card to withdraw, or remove, money from their account and get physical cash. Some banks will charge a fee to get cash from an ATM. An **overdraft fee** is a fee a bank will charge if someone spends more than is in their account. Some checking accounts will not allow someone to spend more than they have, but some checking accounts will, and they charge large fees when an overdraft occurs.

A savings account can also have fees to open the account, monthly fees, and withdrawal fees. A **withdrawal fee** is common with a savings account because the account is designed to keep money saved for a long time. A withdrawal fee means that when someone uses the money, or takes money out, they are charged a small fee.

Checking and savings accounts can also have **account minimums**. This means that to open and keep the account, you must have at least a certain amount of money in the account. If an account has a \$100 account minimum, that means you must have at least \$100 to open the account, and you have to keep at least \$100 in the account to avoid fees.

Check Registers

A **check register** is a way to track what happens to money in an account and how it affects the balance. The **balance** of an account is the total number of dollars in the account. In a check register, you will see and use different types of transactions: deposits, withdrawals, and transfers. Each transaction will include a name for the transaction and an amount. A **deposit** is money coming into an account and adds money to the balance. Examples of deposits are refunds from a store, a paycheck, or a cash deposit where you have physical cash and take it to the bank to put in your account. Either way, a deposit is an increase in a total balance and is either labeled "deposit" or shown using a positive, or +, before the number.

Date	Description	Type	Amount
2/25	Paycheck	Deposit	+$253.50

A **withdrawal** is money coming out of the account and subtracts money from the balance. A withdrawal may come in the form of a purchase, a payment, or a cash withdrawal from an ATM. A withdrawal is a decrease in the total balance and is labeled either "withdrawal" or shown using a negative, or −, before the number.

Date	Description	Type	Amount
2/31	Car Payment	Withdrawal	−$120.25

A **transfer** is money either coming into or out of an account. When you have multiple accounts or you have an account that is connected to other accounts, you may use account transfers. You can transfer your money between accounts, and other people can send money to your account through their accounts. If you receive a bank transfer, you will get money as a deposit. If you transfer money out of an account, you will lose that money from the balance like a withdrawal.

Balancing a check register means interpreting types of transactions and being able to keep track of a balance based on transactions.

Credit Cards and Debit Cards

There are two main types of bank cards that people use. A **debit card** is a plastic card with a series of numbers or a chip that is directly connected to your checking account. A debit card is similar to cash. If you have money in your account, then you can use it, but if you do not have money in your account, you cannot use a debit card. A **credit card** is another plastic card with a series of numbers or a chip that is connected to a borrowing account. A credit card is used to make purchases while borrowing money from a bank. The bank can give people a limit they can borrow, and then that person is allowed to spend up to that amount of money using a credit card. Borrowing is not free, since credit cards sometimes have fees, and if you do not pay the money back every month, the bank will charge interest along with the money you owe. So, a debit card is connected to a checking account with your money and a credit card is connected to a borrowing account with a bank's money that you can borrow.

Credit

Credit Reports and Scores

A **credit report** is a report that includes the borrowing history of a person. Credit reports are used to measure how likely it is that someone is trustworthy to lend money to. Usually banks, credit card companies, mortgage companies, car lenders, and other types of lending services will check a person's credit report before choosing to lend money to a person. A credit report can include things like how many accounts someone has, what types of accounts they have, how long they have had any accounts, and if they have ever missed a payment. All these things are put into an algorithm to give a **credit score**.

Credit History

To have a positive credit history, you must have some accounts open, it helps to have money that you borrowed, and to make all payments on time. The longer you have positive credit history, the better your credit history will look.

There are many items that can negatively affect credit history. Missed and late payments is the number one reason for poor credit history. These are often referred to as **delinquent payments**. Making a late payment or missing a payment completely can drastically lower a credit score and negatively impact credit history. When there are multiple delinquent payments, or someone stops paying on an account, the account becomes a **delinquent account**. If someone has a delinquent account, the lender will take action. The lender may close the account. A **closed delinquent account** means that you did not pay your bill, and this will stay on your credit history for years.

A lender may also choose to repossess the item for which the money was borrowed. A **repossession** is when there are too many missed payments and the lender takes the item the person owes money on.

Bankruptcy

When a person opens too many accounts or loses all of their money and cannot pay any of their bills, they may enter bankruptcy. **Bankruptcy** is a legal process where someone borrowed too much money and cannot pay any of their debts. This person can go to court. The court may decide to declare that the person is no longer responsible for the debt. This is one of the worst things that can happen to a person's credit history.

Only one missed payment can lower a credit score by up to 180 points, and negative items can stay on a credit report for 7 to 10 years, depending on the type. That means even a missed payment can stay on a credit report for 7 to 10 years.

The Impact of Positive Credit History

Good credit history and high credit scores are important to borrowers and lending agencies. Borrowers want to have a high credit score because it shows that they have a good credit history and can handle borrowing money and pay back the money they borrowed on time. Credit history will also affect how much interest a company will charge someone. If you have a negative credit history and a low credit score, a company will think you are not very trustworthy with money and will charge you higher penalties if you do not pay your bill and charge higher borrowing fees. If you have a high credit score, they will think you are trustworthy and might charge you less for borrowing money from them.

Interest

One borrowing fee that is very common is interest. When a person borrows money from a lender, the lender makes money on interest. **Interest** is a percentage of the total money borrowed that the person must pay in addition to the original amount borrowed. When a borrower has a positive credit history, they will pay less in interest, or have a **lower interest rate**. This means they will pay a lower percentage of the total amount. When a borrower has a negative credit history, they will pay more in interest, or have a **higher interest rate**. This means they will pay a higher percentage of the total amount.

Let's say you need to buy a car, but you do not have enough cash to buy the car. You may go to a lending company to borrow the money and make payments. Suppose you need to borrow $10,000 for the car. If you have a high credit score, or a positive credit history, you may only have a 2.5% interest rate, which means you will pay $250 in extra interest. Now, if you have a low credit score, or a negative credit history, you may end up having a 15% interest rate, meaning you will have to pay $1,500 in extra interest! It pays to have good credit history.

Paying for College

When you plan to go to college, the cost of college can be a factor in choosing where to go to school or choosing whether to go at all. College is an expensive option, but there are many ways that a student can pay for college.

- One way someone can pay for college is through **savings**. Parents and students can use savings accounts to save money that can be used to pay for college. Saving a little each month or year can be an option for some families. When it is time to pay for college, the money can be withdrawn.
- **Grants** are another way someone may pay for college. A grant is an amount of money someone is awarded, and they do not have to pay the money back. There are school, personal, and government grants. Grants are usually reserved for people who require assistance due to either financial situations or other challenges. Students must fill out forms and meet requirements for a grant, but once awarded, the student does not have to pay the money back. A grant is like a gift.
- **Scholarships** are another way someone may pay for college. A scholarship is an amount of money someone is awarded that they do not have to pay back. Scholarships usually come from schools, governments, community, or private institutions and are there to award students with high achievements. To be awarded a scholarship, students need to show high achievement, fill out forms, and sometimes write an essay to explain their circumstances and why they deserve a scholarship. This can include anything at which the student excels: math, arts, sports, community service, writing, etc. Scholarships can pay for all of college or a small part. This is money that does not need to be paid back. A scholarship is a reward for achievement.
- **Student loans** are another way someone may pay for college. A student loan is a loan from the government or a lending company where a student borrows money to pay for college and the student pays the money back after they graduate. Student loans are very expensive, and if you have trouble getting a job after graduation, they can put you in a difficult position when you try to pay the money back. Student loans also include interest, so there is a percentage that is paid in addition to the original amount of money. Student loans must be paid back to the lender. Student loans are a type of debt.
- **Work-study** is another way someone may pay for college. A work-study program is a program through the government or a school where students are offered part-time jobs to help them pay for school. This usually will not pay for all the schooling but can help. Students can request that their paychecks come to them or go directly to lower their college bills.

Impact of Education Level on Salary

A **salary** is an amount of money paid for a certain job. Some jobs have annual salaries, an amount paid yearly, and some have hourly salaries, an amount paid per hour of work. Different jobs require different levels of education. Some jobs only require a **high school diploma**, which is a certificate awarded after graduating high school. Some jobs require a **bachelor's degree**, which is a certificate awarded upon completing an undergraduate program, or graduating college. Some jobs require a **master's degree**, which is a certificate awarded after completing a postgraduate program, an education program someone can begin after graduating college. And some jobs require a **doctorate degree**, which is awarded after completing another postgraduate program after a master's program. Typically, the higher the degree or certificate, the higher the salary. On average, jobs that require higher degrees will pay more money.

EXAMPLE

The table shows an average salary for two levels of education.

Average Yearly Salary	
High school diploma	Master's degree
\$43,000	\$72,000

Based on the table, how much more money would a person with a master's degree earn than a person with a high school diploma after 5 years?

In this problem, we are given the average salaries for two levels of education: high school diploma and master's degree. We need to calculate how much more money someone with a master's degree will make after 5 years.

We can approach this problem in a few ways. We could approach this problem by finding the salaries of each degree after 5 years and then subtracting. We could also approach this problem by finding the difference in salaries after one year and multiplying this value by 5.

Let's approach this problem by finding how much each salary will add up to after 5 years and compare.

To find what each salary is after 5 years, we need to multiply each salary by 5.

So, for a high school diploma, we need to multiply \$43,000 by 5 years.

$$43{,}000 \times 5 = (43 \times 5)(1{,}000)$$
$$215 \times 1{,}000 = 215{,}000$$

The salary after 5 years is \$215,000 with a high school diploma.

For a master's degree, we need to multiply \$72,000 by 5 years.

$$72{,}000 \times 5 = (72 \times 5)(1{,}000)$$
$$360 \times 1{,}000 = 360{,}000$$

The salary after 5 years is \$360,000 with a master's degree.

Now, to find out how much more money a master's degree makes than a high school diploma, we need to subtract.

$$\begin{array}{r} 360{,}000 \\ -\ 215{,}000 \\ \hline 145{,}000 \end{array}$$

On average, after five years, a person with a master's degree earns \$145,000 more than a person with only a high school diploma.

The answer is $145,000.

Practice Test #1

1. A customer is buying 2.4 pounds of apples. Apples are on sale for $0.85 per pound. How much will the customer pay for the apples?

a. $2.04
b. $3.92
c. $20.40
d. $39.20

2. Kimi is saving to buy a pair of earbuds that cost $195. She makes money mowing lawns and earns $10 for each lawn she mows. Which inequality illustrates how many lawns, *x*, Kimi needs to mow to make at least $195?

a. $195 < 10x$
b. $195 > 10x$
c. $195 \leq 10x$
d. $195 \geq 10x$

3. A business owner calculated the profit for today using the following expression:

$$60(50) + 30(12) + 50(10) - (125 - 73)$$

How much profit did the business make today? Write your answer in the blank below.

4. 148% is equivalent to what fraction?

a. $\frac{148}{1}$
b. $\frac{37}{25}$
c. $\frac{50}{74}$
d. $\frac{1}{148}$

5. A check register is shown below.

Date	Description	Deposit	Withdrawal	Balance
3/15				$354.75
3/17	Paycheck	$250		
3/19	Gas		$32.25	
3/20	Groceries		$162.31	
3/22	Store Refund	$10.20		

What is the account balance after the last transaction in dollars? Write your answer in the blank below.

6. Ashley is doing research to help her make a choice about going to college. The table below shows three salaries of professions in the dental field and their education level.

Profession	Education	Yearly Salary
Dental Secretary	High School Diploma	$24,000
Dental Assistant	Bachelor's Degree	$52,000
Dentist	Doctorate Degree	$175,000

How much more money does a dental assistant make than a dental secretary after 5 years?

a. $28,000
b. $140,000
c. $175,000
d. $260,000

7. What expression is NOT equal to 5?

a. The absolute value of –5
b. The reciprocal of –5
c. The absolute value of 5
d. The opposite of –5

8. Jordan owns a jewelry business and listed the wire options for their customers below using fraction measurements.

$$\frac{1}{8}, \frac{1}{4}, \frac{3}{8}, \frac{1}{2}$$

Which list correctly lists the wire options in decimal form?

a. 0.12, 0.25, 0.266, 0.5
b. 1.8, 1.4, 3.8, 1.2
c. 0.8, 0.4, 0.38, 0.2
d. 0.125, 0.25, 0.375, 0.5

9. Complete the prime factorization of 168 by finding the missing factor. Write your answer in the blank below.

$$2^3 \cdot 7 \cdot ?$$

10. Tavik bought a fish tank and needs to know the volume of the tank to appropriately choose fish. The measurements are labeled below.

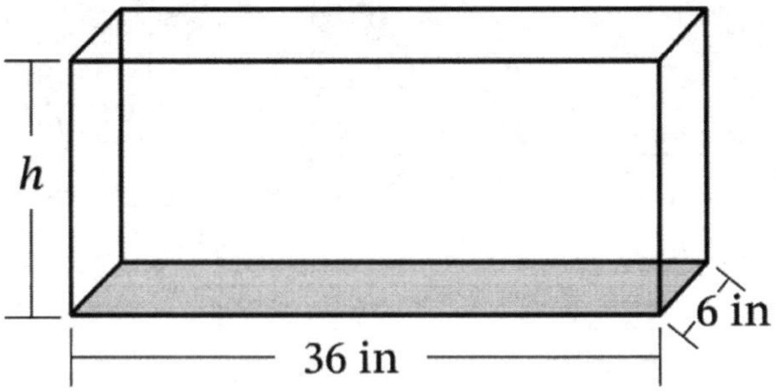

Which equation can be used to find the volume, V, of the fish tank? Write your answer in the blank below.

11. A survey of the sixth grade found that 65% of students played sports after school. If 195 students play sports after school, how many students were surveyed?

a. 585
b. 390
c. 265
d. 300

12. Which expression is equivalent to $3 - (x + 4)$?

a. $3 + 4x$
b. $-3 + 4x$
c. $-x + 4 + 3$
d. $3 - x - 4$

13. The following list represents the grades of students in a middle school math class.

73, 75, 75, 80, 83, 83, 83, 83, 85, 85, 88, 88, 90, 93, 93, 93, 95, 95, 98, 100, 100

Which box plot best represents the data from the list?

a.

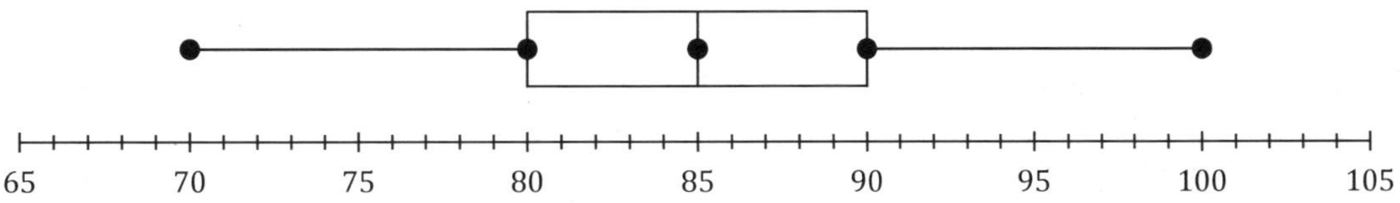

b.

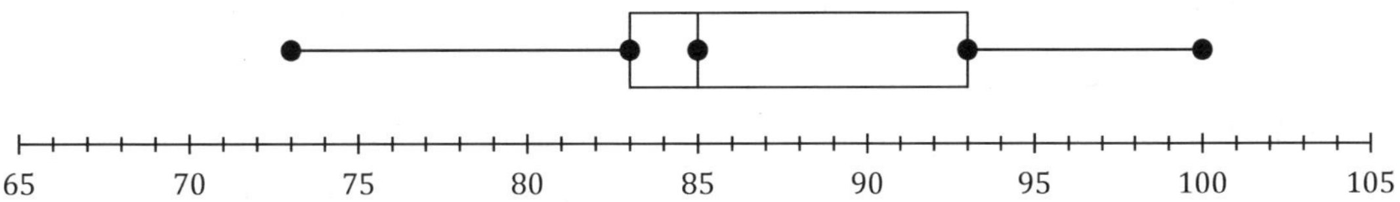

c.

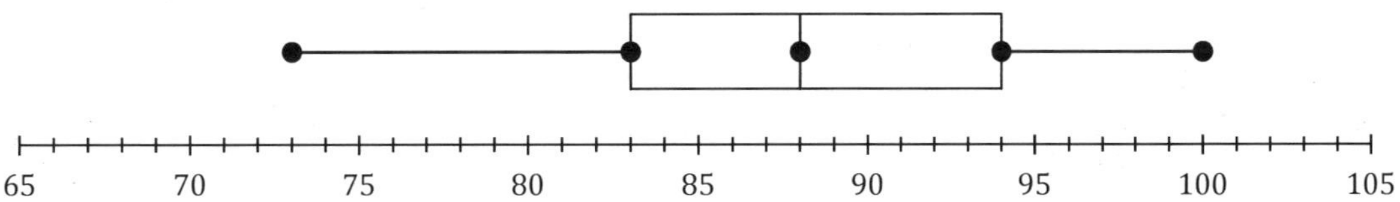

d.

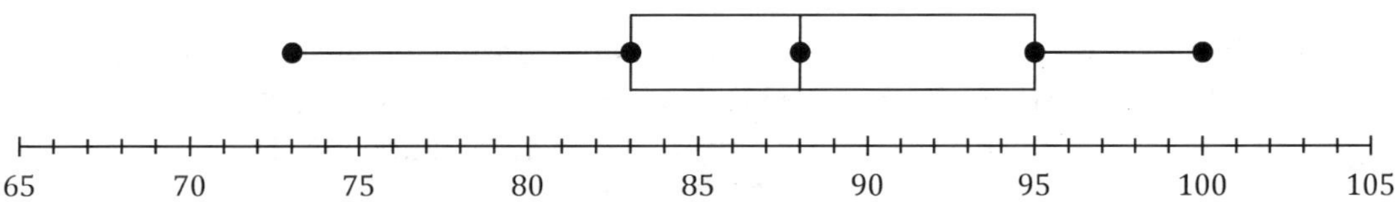

14. The following list represents the heights in inches of tomato plants grown in a garden.

12.0, 12.4, 12.4, 12.4, 12.6, 12.6, 12.8, 13.1, 13.2, 13.5

What is the mean value of the data set?

a. 12.4
b. 12.5
c. 12.6
d. 12.7

15. Choose the correct answer for each blank below. The side lengths of three-sided figures are listed. Which two of side lengths CANNOT be used with the provided side length to make a triangle?

___ units, 21 units,	___ units
13	30
10	9
15	16

16. The average weight of a newborn baby is 120 ounces. What is this weight in pounds?

a. 16
b. 7.8
c. 7.5
d. 12

17. Daryl is explaining to his friend the difference between a credit card and a debit card. Are his statements about the two cards correct or incorrect? Mark your answer for each statement in the table below:

Statement	Correct	Incorrect
A debit card can be used like cash.		
Money spent on a credit card must be paid back with interest.		
A debit card is a way to borrow money from a financial institution.		
A credit card can be used when someone doesn't have money to pay for something.		
A debit card must be paid back each year.		

18. Jocelyn is planning a cruise for herself and her friends. She wrote an expression to find the total cost per person. Which expression is equivalent to the expression Jocelyn wrote?

$$(352.83 - 85.63) + \frac{(399.25 + 260.75)}{4}$$

a. $267.20 + \frac{165}{4}$
b. $333.20 + 660$
c. $267.20 + 165$
d. $333.20 + \frac{660}{4}$

19. Charlie wrote the following scenario:

Damien is 3 years older than Jackson.

Plot 4 points on the graph that represent the story that Charlie wrote.

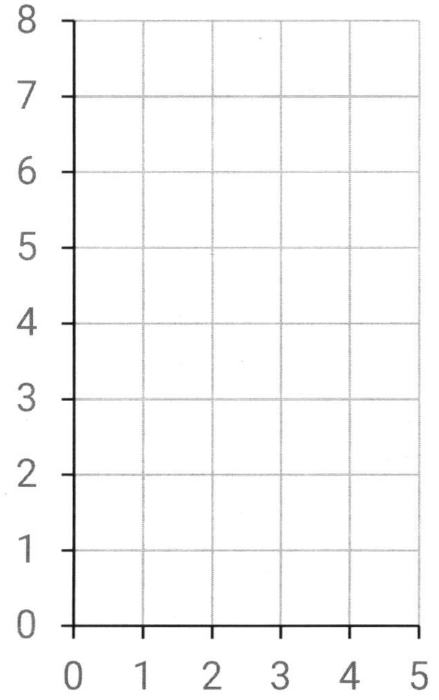

20. Which inequality is true if $b = 3.5$?

a. $17b > 60$
b. $-12.5 + b \geq -10$
c. $15 - b \geq 12$
d. $4.5b < 15$

21. Use the graph below to plot the following ordered pairs:

$$W = (-2,5)$$
$$X = (-2,-5)$$
$$Y = (5,-2)$$
$$Z = (-5,2)$$

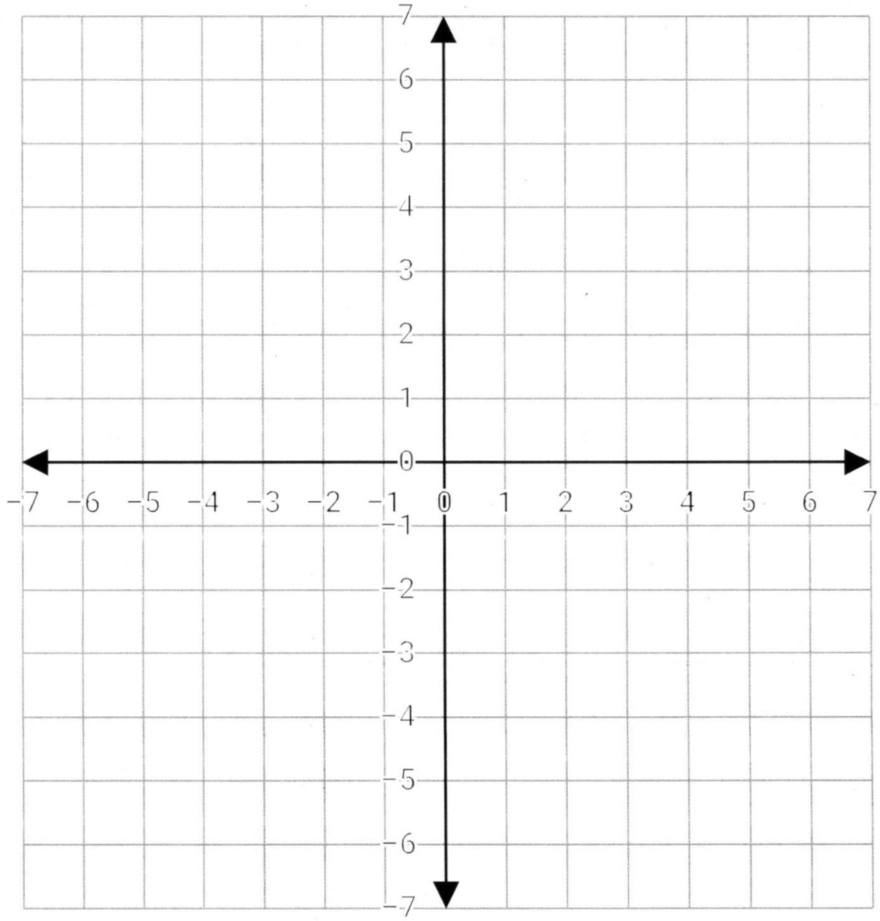

22. Choose the correct answer for each blank below. Caroline put 3 drops of blue food coloring in 2 cups of water. Devon put 5 drops of blue food coloring in 4 cups of water. If more blue food coloring makes a darker shade of blue, what is true about Caroline 's and Devon's water?

__________ water is a darker blue than __________ because ____________________.

Devon's	Devon's	3 : 2 is greater than 5 : 4
Caroline's	Caroline's	5 drops is greater than 3 drops
		5 : 4 is greater than 3 : 2

23. The table shows the number of t-shirts sold in each color.

Color	Number Sold	Key
Black	60	
Blue	30	
Red	15	
White	45	

Which percent bar graph best represents the data?

a.

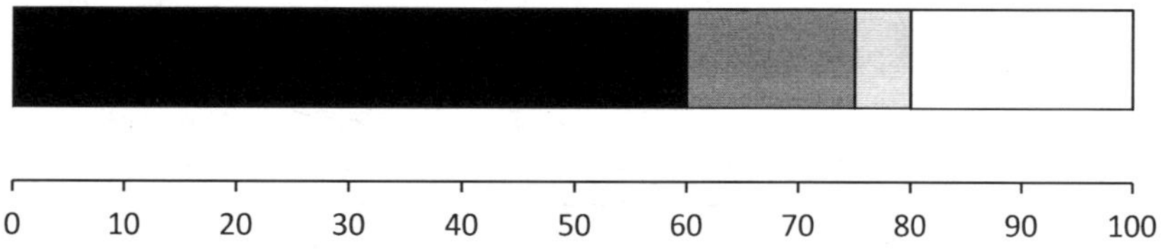

b.

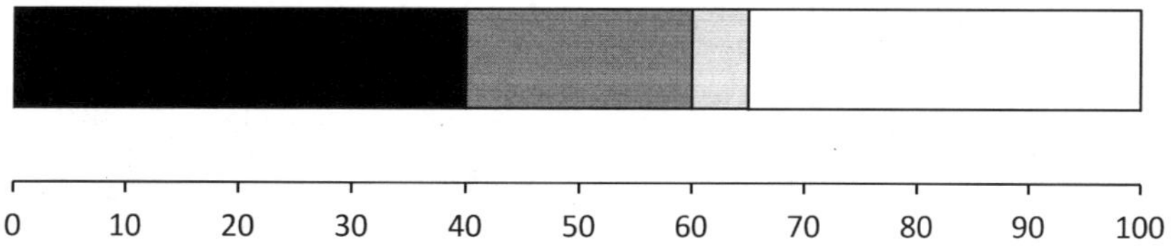

c.

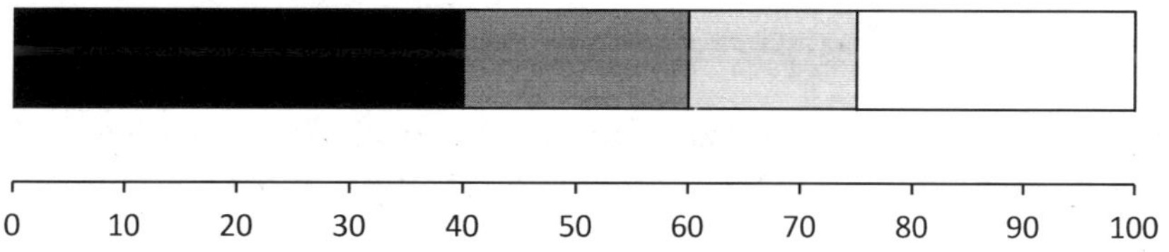

d.

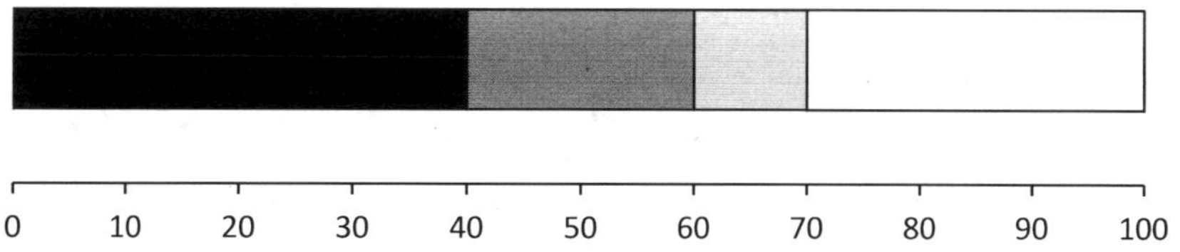

24. Choose the correct answer for each blank below. The table shows a relationship between *s* and *t*, where *s* is the independent value. What equation represents the relationship between *s* and *t*?

s	*t*
1	4
2	8
7	28
9	36

______ = ______

s	$t + 4$
t	$4t$
	$4s$
	$s + 4$

25. Which list includes values that are all equivalent?

a. $20\%, \frac{1}{20}, 0.2$
b. $1.5, 15\%, \frac{15}{100}$
c. $\frac{7}{20}, 35\%, 0.35$
d. $10\%, \frac{1}{10}, 0.01$

26. Which situation best represents the inequality $\frac{n}{4} > 36$?

a. Theresa packaged more than 36 packages when she packaged n cupcakes into packages of 4.
b. Tyler has more than 36 pages to read and reads 4 pages each day for n days.
c. Tamar practiced for n hours on the piano. She practiced the piano for more than 36 hours each day for 4 days.
d. Tamika ran n miles over 4 days, which is less than 36 miles.

27. Simplify the expression.

$$\frac{(-9+3)}{2}$$

a. 6
b. −6
c. 3
d. −3

28. André drew a data table that represents the relationship between x and y where $y = 3x$. Which two tables could NOT be the data tables that André drew? Select all that apply.

a.

x	1	3	5
y	3	6	8

b.

x	3	6	9
y	1	2	3

c.

x	2	4	6
y	6	12	18

d.

x	1.5	2	2.5
y	4.5	6	7.5

e.

x	1	10	50
y	3	30	150

29. The bar graph shows the number of views a viral video has on four different platforms.

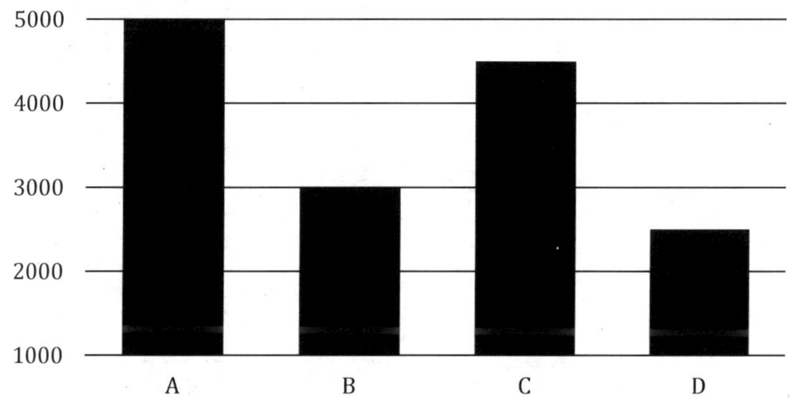

Which statement is supported by the data?

a. The number of views on platform B is twice the number of views on platform C.
b. The number of views on platform A is greater than the number of views on platform B and D combined.
c. The number of views on platform D is half the number of views on platform C
d. The number of views on platform A is double the number of views on platform D

30. Choose the correct answer for each blank below. A scientist tracked the population of cicadas in an area over 5 years. The table shows the population of cicadas each year in millions. How did the population of cicadas change over time?

Year 1	Year 2	Year 3	Year 4	Year 5
4	12	36	108	324

The population of cicadas __________ by a scale factor of __ each year.

decreased
increased

4
8
3
6

31. Write the correct answers in the blanks below. The list gives the heights in inches of plants grown in a science class. Put the plant heights in order.

$2\frac{3}{5}$	$2\frac{2}{5}$	2.23

______, ______, 2.53, ______

greatest	least

These heights are listed from __________ to __________.

32. Bella is limiting her social media time to no more than 420 minutes per week. If she spends the same amount of time on social media each day, which inequality describes all possible numbers of *m* minutes Bella could spend each day of the week on social media?

a. $60 \geq m$
b. $60 \leq m$
c. $60 < m$
d. $60 > m$

33. Triangle *XYZ* is pictured below.

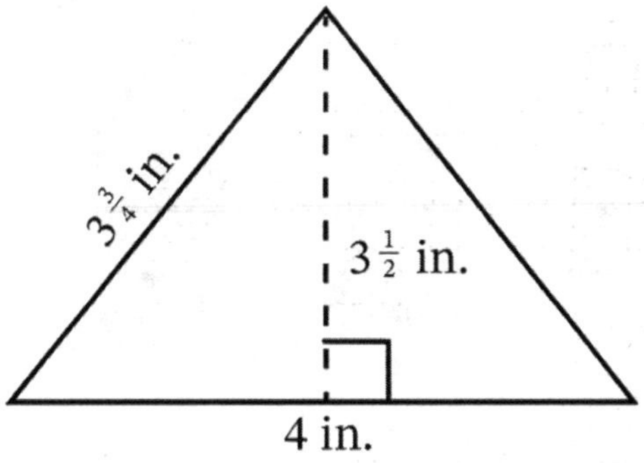

What is the area of triangle *XYZ* in square inches? Write your answer in the blank below.

34. Garcelle is an artist selling art prints. She sells each print for $5.50. Which table represents the relationship between prints sold and money made?

a.

Number of Prints Sold	25	35	45	55
Money Made	$30.50	$40.50	$50.50	$60.50

b.

Number of Prints Sold	20	30	40	50
Money Made	$110	$165	$220	$275

c.

Number of Prints Sold	25	30	35	40
Money Made	$125	$150	$175	$200

d.

Number of Prints Sold	20	25	30	35
Money Made	$110	$115.50	$121	$126.50

35. The area of a rectangle is 364.5 square centimeters, and its height is 27 centimeters. What is *b*, the base of the rectangle, in centimeters?

a. 13.4
b. 13.8
c. 14.18
d. 13.5

36. Nova is redecorating her bedroom and spent $\frac{7}{25}$ of her time painting. What percentage of her time did Nova spend painting?

a. 28%
b. 7%
c. 25%
d. 48%

Answer Key and Explanations for Test #1

1. A: TEKS Standard (6.3)(E)

This problem focuses on multiplying decimals. To find the amount of money the customer will pay for the apples, 2.4 will be multiplied by 0.85. $2.4 \times 0.85 = 2.040$, so the customer will pay $2.04 for 2.4 pounds of apples.

2. C: TEKS Standard (6.9)(A)

If Kimi makes $10 for each lawn, where x is the number of lawns, then the expression $10x$ describes the number of dollars Kimi makes. If the earbuds Kimi wants cost $195, she needs at least $195 to buy the earbuds. If Kimi needs at least $195, that means that she can make more than $195 to get the earbuds but cannot make less than $195. This means that the number of dollars made, $10x$, must be more than or equal to $195. The expression that represents this is $10x \geq 195$, or $195 \leq 10x$.

3. 3,808: TEKS Standard (6.3)(D)

To find the profit for the day, the expression must be simplified. Using PEMDAS as a guide to the order of operations, the first step is to remove the parentheses. $60 \cdot 50 = 3{,}000$, $30 \cdot 12 = 360$, $50 \cdot 10 = 500$, and $125 - 73 = 52$. The simplified expression now reads $3{,}000 + 360 + 500 - 52$, which equals 3,808.

4. B: TEKS Standard (6.4)(G)

This problem focuses on equivalent fractions and percentages. A percentage is a part out of 100, so 148% is equivalent to $\frac{148}{100}$. This fraction can be simplified by dividing the numerator and denominator by the greatest common factor.

$$\frac{148}{100} = \frac{148 \div 4}{100 \div 4} = \frac{37}{25}$$

5. 420.39: TEKS Standard (6.14)(C)

This problem focuses on balancing a check register. The first row shows the account balance on 3/15. The next line shows a deposit of $250 from a paycheck; when this is added to the previous balance, the new balance is $\$354.75 + \$250 = \$604.75$. The next line shows a withdrawal for $32.25, so the new balance is $\$604.75 - \$32.25 = \$572.50$. The next line shows a withdrawal for $162.31, so the new balance is $\$572.50 - \$162.31 = \$410.19$. The last line shows a deposit of $10.20, so the final balance is $\$410.19 + 10.20 = \$420.39$.

6. B: TEKS Standard (6.14)(H)

This problem focuses on comparing salaries. Based on the table, a dental secretary makes $24,000 per year and a dental assistant makes $52,000 per year. This is a difference of $\$52{,}000 - \$24{,}000 = \$28{,}000$ per year. After 5 years, a dental assistant will make $\$28{,}000 \cdot 5 = \$140{,}000$ more dollars than a dental secretary.

7. B: TEKS Standard (6.2)(B)

The absolute value of –5 is 5 because the absolute value represents a number's distance from zero on a number line. The reciprocal of –5 is $-\frac{1}{5}$. The absolute value of 5 is 5. The opposite of –5 is also 5.

8. D: TEKS Standard (6.4)(F)

This problem focuses on converting fractions to decimals. There are a couple strategies that can be used to convert fractions to decimals. One way would be through using division. $\frac{1}{8}$ is equivalent to 0.125, $\frac{1}{4} = 0.25$, $\frac{3}{8} = 0.375$, and $\frac{1}{2} = 0.5$.

9. 3: TEKS Standard (6.7)(A)

The prime factors of a value are the prime numbers that when multiplied together equal the value. There are two ways to solve this problem. One way would be to find the prime factorization of 168 using a factor tree to find the missing value. Another way would be to find the missing value by multiplying the known factors and using division to find the final number. $2^3 = 2 \cdot 2 \cdot 2 = 8$ and $8 \cdot 7 = 56$. That means that 56 times something equals 168. Using division, $168 \div 56 = 3$ and 3 is a prime number. The prime factorization of 168 is $2^3 \cdot 7 \cdot 3$.

10. $V = 36 \cdot 6 \cdot h$: TEKS Standard (6.8)(C)

This problem focuses on the formula for the volume of a rectangular prism. The reference sheet can be used to find the formula for the volume of a rectangular prism: $V = Bh$, where $B = l \cdot w$. Another formula for the volume is $V = lwh$. This means that to find the volume of the rectangular prism fish tank, Tavik could use the formula $V = 36 \cdot 6 \cdot h$.

11. D: TEKS Standard (6.5)(B)

There is more than one way to solve this problem. One strategy is to use proportions. 65% is equivalent to $\frac{65}{100}$. If 195 students represent 65%, this problem involves finding what number of students would represent 100%. This means that $\frac{65}{100} = \frac{195}{x}$ where x represents the total number of students surveyed. Cross multiplication can be used to find that $65x = 19{,}500$. Each expression is divided by 65; $\frac{65x}{65} = x$ and $\frac{19{,}500}{65} = 300$, so $x = 300$. There were 300 total students surveyed.

12. D: TEKS Standard (6.7)(D)

This problem focuses on equivalent expressions using the associative and distributive properties. There are many ways to approach this problem. One place to start would be to use the distributive property and distribute the negative sign, or –1. This can be done because $3 - (x + 4)$ can also be written as $3 - 1(x + 4)$ and because we can distribute the –1 in this problem. This means that $3 - (x + 4)$ is equivalent to $3 - x - 4$ because $-1 \cdot x = -x$ and $-1 \cdot 4 = -4$.

13. C: TEKS Standard (6.12)(A)

This problem focuses on representing data through box plots. To represent the data using a box plot, first the smallest value, 73, the greatest value, 100, and the median value, 88, each need to be identified with a circle. Next, the median value of the lowest half, or first quartile, 83, and the median value of the greater half, or third quartile, 94, each need to be identified with a circle. Lines connect the lowest and first quartile, and the third quartile and greatest value. Next a box connects the first quartile and median value, and a second box connects the median value and third quartile.

14. D: TEKS Standard (6.12)(C)

This problem focuses on finding the mean of a data set. The mean is another word to describe the average. The mean of a data set is found by finding the sum of all values and dividing the sum by the total number of values. In this case, $12.0 + 12.4 + 12.4 + 12.4 + 12.6 + 12.6 + 12.8 + 13.1 + 13.2 + 13.5 = 127 \div 10 = 12.7$.

15. 10, 9: TEKS Standard (6.8)(A)

This problem focuses on triangle side lengths. For a set of side lengths to form a triangle, the sum of any two side lengths must be greater than the third side length. This question asks for the side lengths that will not create a triangle. One of the side lengths must be 21 units, so the other two side lengths must add up to a value that is less than 21. Each pair of side lengths can be added together to find the correct pair. However, a quicker way to approach the problem is to start with the smallest option under each blank and see if they add up to less than 21. $10 + 9 = 19$, and $19 < 21$. All of the other options add up to more than 21, so 10 and 9 are the correct answers.

16. C: TEKS Standard (6.4)(H)

This problem focuses on converting measurements. The conversion sheet can be used to find that 1 pound is equivalent to 16 ounces. To find how many pounds is equivalent to 120 ounces, a proportion can be used. $\frac{1\text{ lb}}{16\text{ oz}} = \frac{x}{120\text{ oz}}$ is equivalent to $16x = 120$, or $x = \frac{120}{16}$, or $x = 7.5$.

17. TEKS Standard (6.14)(B)

Statement	Correct	Incorrect
A debit card can be used like cash.	X	
Money spent on a credit card must be paid back with interest.	X	
A debit card is a way to borrow money from a financial institution.		X
A credit card can be used when someone doesn't have money to pay for something.	X	
A debit card must be paid back each year.		X

This problem focuses on identifying the difference between credit and debit cards. A debit card is connected to a bank account and can be used like cash. A credit card is a way to borrow money from a financial institution to pay for an item if someone doesn't have the money to pay for it now, but the money must be paid back with interest. A debit card can only be used to pay for things that the user has enough money to buy. Debit cards do not need to be paid back.

18. C: TEKS Standard (6.7) (A)

The problem focuses on equivalent expressions. To find the equivalent expression to the one Jocelyn wrote, the best approach would be to simplify the given expression. Order of operations is important to remember when simplifying expressions. The first step would be to solve the first expression in parentheses; $352.83 - 85.63 = 267.20$. The next step would be to solve the following expression in parentheses; $399.25 + 260.75 = 600$. The last step is to simplify the fraction; $\frac{660}{4} = 165$. The given options do not show a completely simplified expression, and one can see that an equivalent expression to the one Jocelyn wrote is $267.20 + 165$.

19. TEKS Standard (6.6)(C)

Correct points may be any four of the following:

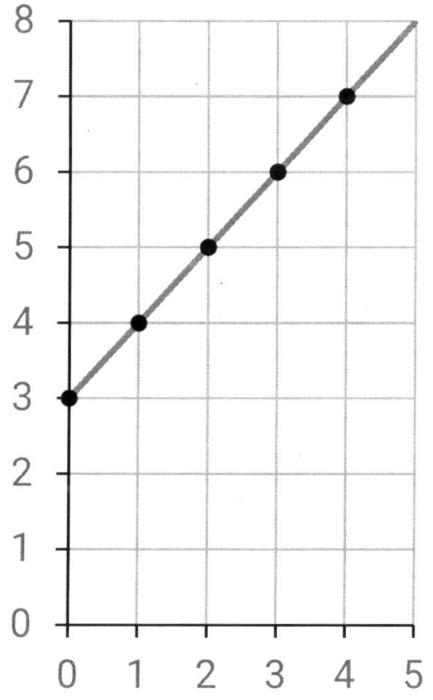

This problem focuses on plotting points on a graph to represent a scenario. There are many strategies that can be used to solve this problem. One strategy is to identify an equation that represents the scenario. The scenario says that Damien is 3 years older than Jackson, so Damien's age is 3 more than Jackson's age. This is an addition problem. Damien's age is the dependent variable, y, and Jackson's age is the independent variable, x. This is because Jackson's age is used to find Damien's age. This means that the equation that represents the scenario is $y = x + 3$. The points on the graph that show this will have a y value that is 3 more than the x value. Since the scenario involves ages, the ordered pairs will include whole numbers. Points that represent the scenario include (0,3), (1,4), (2,5), (3,6), and (4,7).

20. B: TEKS Standard (6.10)(B)

This problem involves testing inequalities with a known variable. To find which inequality is true if $b = 3.5$, each inequality will be tested by replacing b with 3.5 and identifying if the statement is true. In the first choice, $17 \cdot 3.5 = 59.5$, which is less than 60, not greater than 60. In the second choice, $-12.5 + 3.5 = -9$, which is greater than or equal to -10. In the third choice, $15 - 3.5 =$

11.5, which is less than 12, not greater than or equal to 12. In the fourth choice, $4.5 \cdot 3.5 = 15.75$, which is greater than 15, not less than 15.

21. TEKS Standard (6.11)(A)

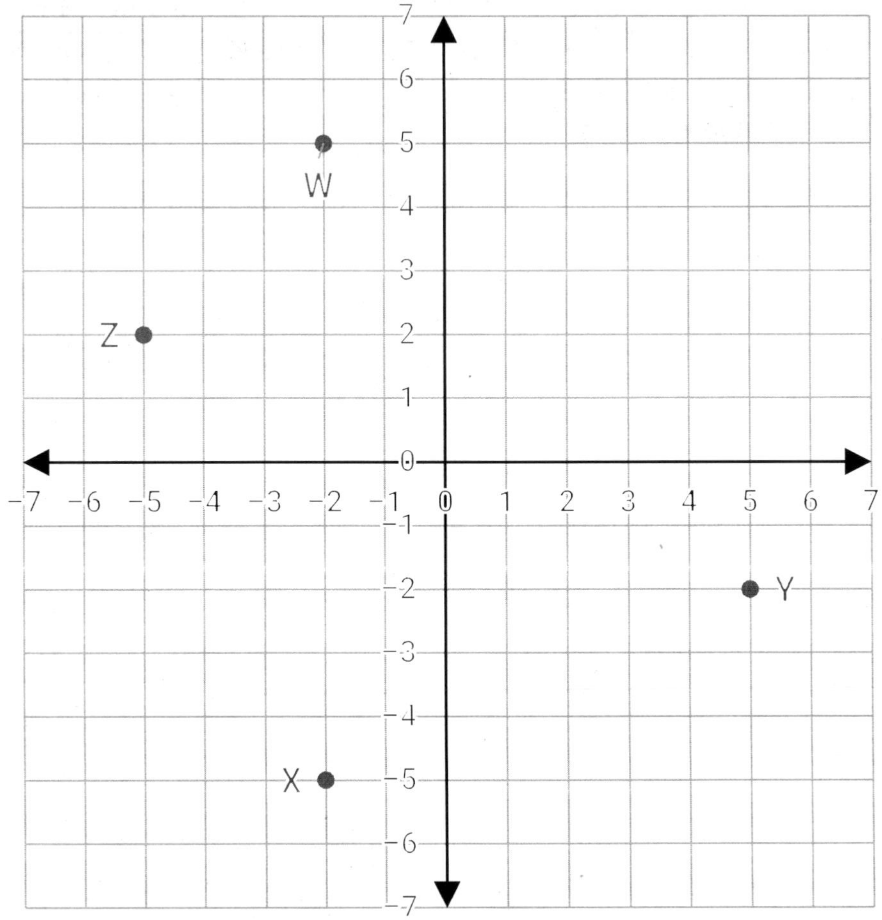

This problem focuses on identifying parts and coordinate points on a graph. The given coordinates are $(-2,5)$, $(-5,2)$, $(-2,-5)$, and $(5,-2)$. When using coordinates to plot points, the x value shows how far to the left or right the point will be from 0. If the x value is positive, the point will be to the right of the y axis. If the x value is negative, the point will be to the left of the y axis. The y value shows how far above or below 0 the point will be. If the y value is positive, the point will be above the x axis. If the y value is negative, the point will be below the x axis.

22. Caroline's, Devon's, 3 : 2 is greater than 5 : 4: TEKS Standard (6.4)(B)

This problem focuses on comparing ratios. There are many ways to compare 3 : 2 and 5 : 4. One way would be by finding the unit ratio of coloring to cups using division. Caroline uses a ratio of 3 : 2 drops to cups, which is equivalent to 1.5 drops to 1 cup because $3 \div 2 = 1.5$. Devon uses a ratio of 5 : 4 drops to cups, which is equivalent to 1.25 drops to 1 cup because $5 \div 4 = 1.25$. If Caroline uses more drops per cup of water, her water is darker because 3 : 2 is greater than 5 : 4. The number of drops alone does not show whose water is darker.

23. D: TEKS Standard (6.12)(D)

This problem focuses on representing data using percent bar graphs. To represent this data in a percent bar graph, first the total number of shirts sold should be found; $60 + 25 + 15 + 50 = 150$. Next, the percentage of each color sold should be found. The percentage of black shirts sold is $\frac{60}{150} = 0.4 \cdot 100 = 40\%$. The percentage of blue shirts sold is $\frac{30}{150} = 0.2 \cdot 100 = 20\%$. The percentage of red shirts sold is $\frac{15}{150} = 0.10 \cdot 100 = 10\%$. The percentage of white shirts sold is $\frac{45}{150} = 0.3 = 30\%$.

24. t, $4s$: TEKS Standard (6.6)(B)

This problem focuses on writing equations from a table. In this table, s is the independent value, which means that an operation is being performed on s to get t. In this example, each s value is multiplied by 4 to get the t value, which is expressed by the equation $t = 4s$.

25. C: TEKS Standard (6.5)(C)

This problem involves finding equivalent fractions, decimals, and percentages. To solve this problem, each value in the list should be compared to identify if they are equivalent. 20% is equivalent to 0.2, but is not equivalent to $\frac{1}{20}$, which is equivalent to 5%. 15% is equivalent to $\frac{15}{100}$, but is not equivalent to 1.5, which is equivalent to 150%. $\frac{7}{20}$ is equivalent to $\frac{35}{100}$ which is equivalent to 35% and 0.35. 10% is equivalent to $\frac{1}{10}$ and 0.1, but it is not equivalent to 0.01.

26. A: TEKS Standard (6.9)(C)

This problem focuses on writing situations that represent inequalities. In this example, 36 is less than n divided by 4. This means that a number n is being divided by 4, and this value is greater than 36. The only situation that describes a total, n divided by 4, being greater than 36 is Theresa packaging n number of cupcakes into packages of 4, which makes more than 36 packages.

27. D: TEKS Standard (6.3)(D)

This problem focuses on solving problems with integers and using the order of operations. The first step is to solve the addition problem in the parentheses, so $-9 + 3 = -6$. The next step is to simplify the fraction $\frac{-6}{2}$ using division, so $-6 \div 2 = -3$.

28. A, B: TEKS Standard (6.4)(A)

To solve this problem, the relationship between x and y needs to be identified for each data table. The relationship in data table A is that y is 3 more than x: $y = x + 3$. The relationship in data table B is that y is one third of x: $y = \frac{1}{3}x$. The relationship in data table C is that y is 3 times as much as x: $y = 3x$. The relationship in data table D is that y is 3 times as much as x: $y = 3x$. The relationship in data table E is that y is 3 times as much as x: $y = 3x$. Data table C, D, and E could be the table that André drew, and neither A nor B could be the table that he drew.

29. D: TEKS Standard (6.13)(A)

This problem focuses on interpreting data from a bar graph. Based on the bar graph, the number of views on platform A is 5,000, platform B is 3,000, platform C is 4,500, and platform D is 2,500. These values should be compared to the statements to find the statement that is supported by the data. 3,000 is not twice the value of 4,500. 5,000 is not greater than $3{,}000 + 2{,}500 = 5{,}500$. 2,500 is not half of 4,500. 5,000 is double 2,500.

30. increased, 3: TEKS Standard (6.5)(A)

This problem focuses on scale factors. According to the table, the population of cicadas increased each year. From year 1 to year 2, the population increased from 4 to 12 million. The population increased by a factor of 3 because $4 \cdot 3 = 12$. From year 2 to year 3, the population increased from 12 to 36 million; $12 \cdot 3 = 36$. From year 3 to year 4, $36 \cdot 3 = 108$. From year 4 to year 5, $108 \cdot 3 = 324$. Each year the population increases by a scale factor of 3.

31. 2.23, $2\frac{2}{5}$, $2\frac{3}{5}$, least, greatest: TEKS Standard (6.2)(D)

To put the given values in order, the first step would be to convert all values to one representation. In this example, there is a mix of fractions and decimals. One way to proceed would be to convert all values to decimals. Two values are already in decimal form: 2.23 and 2.53. There are many ways to convert $2\frac{2}{5}$ and $2\frac{3}{5}$ to decimals; the fractions can be converted to fractional tenths and then to decimals, or division can be used to find the decimal form of the fraction. In either case, $2\frac{2}{5}$ is equivalent to 2.4, and $2\frac{3}{5}$ is equivalent to 2.6. Now, all values can be compared and ordered from least to greatest: 2.23, 2.4, 2.53, 2.6. 2.53 is given as the third value in the list, and it is the third value when these are ordered from least to greatest. This confirms that the list must be ordered from least to greatest.

32. A: TEKS Standard (6.10)(A)

This problem focuses on solutions to inequalities. The story expresses the inequality $420 \geq 7m$ because Bella doesn't want to spend more than 420 minutes on social media during each week, which means that she could spend 420 minutes but cannot go over 420 minutes. This inequality can be simplified by using division. $420 \geq 7m$ is equivalent to $\frac{420}{7} \geq \frac{7m}{7}$, which can be simplified to $60 \geq m$.

33. 7: TEKS Standard (6.8)(D)

This problem focuses on finding the area of a triangle. The reference sheet can be used to find the formula for the area of a triangle, $A = \frac{1}{2}bh$. For triangle XYZ, the base of the triangle measures 4 inches and the height of the triangle measures $3\frac{1}{2}$ inches. The area can be found by using the equation $A = \frac{1}{2} \cdot 4 \cdot 3\frac{1}{2} = 2 \cdot 3\frac{1}{2} = 7$.

34. B: TEKS Standard (6.6)(C)

Garcelle sells art prints for $5.50 per print. This means that the number of dollars made is 5.5 times the number of prints sold. The equation that matches this story is $y = 5.5x$ because each y value, money made, is 5.5 times the x value, number of prints sold. $25 \cdot 5.5 = 137.5$, so options A and C cannot be correct. $20 \cdot 5.5 = 110$ and $30 \cdot 5.5 = 165$, so the table in option B is the only table that appropriately represents this equation.

35. D: TEKS Standard (6.10)(A)

There are many ways to solve this problem. The formula for area is $A = bh$, so one way to solve this problem is to solve the equation $364.5 = b \cdot 27$, which can be simplified to $b = 364.5 \div 27$, and $b = 13.5$.

36. A: TEKS Standard (6.4)(G)

This problem focuses on converting a fraction $\frac{7}{25}$ to a percentage. Converting fractions to percentages can be performed by converting the fraction to a value out of 100, or converting the fraction to a decimal. $\frac{7}{25}$ can be converted to a fraction out of 100 by multiplying the numerator and denominator by 4: $\frac{7}{25} = \frac{28}{100}$, which is equivalent to 28%

Practice Test #2

1. Which statement is true about the product of 5 and $\frac{1}{2}$?

a. The product is less than 5.
b. The product is greater than 5.
c. The product is less than 1.
d. The product is less than $\frac{1}{2}$.

2. A food truck sold 250 meals today. 85 of those meals were kids' meals. What percentage of meals sold were kids' meals?

a. 34%
b. 0.34%
c. 29.4%
d. 0.29%

3. Jamie drew a triangle. The angle measures are listed below.

23° 95° ______

What is the missing angle measurement to complete the triangle in degrees? Write your answer in the blank below.

4. Which model shows a true equation when $x = 2$?

a. 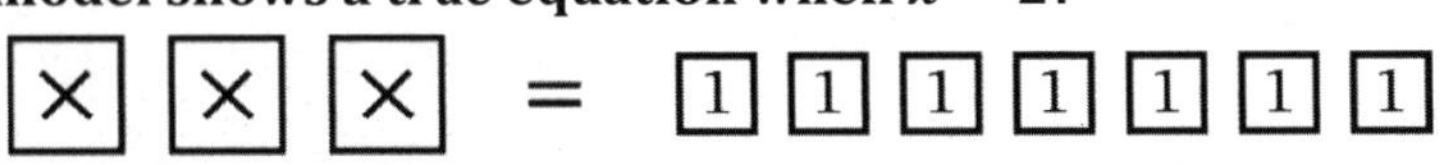

b. 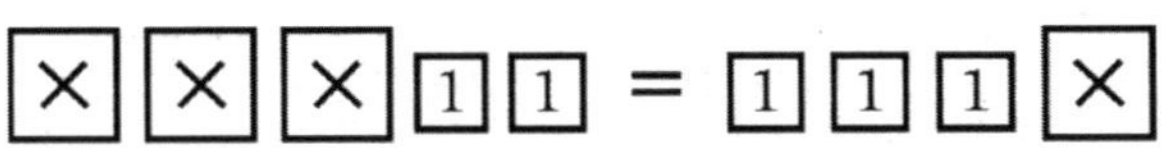

c. 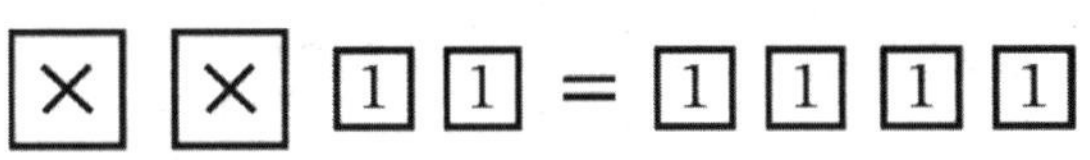

d. 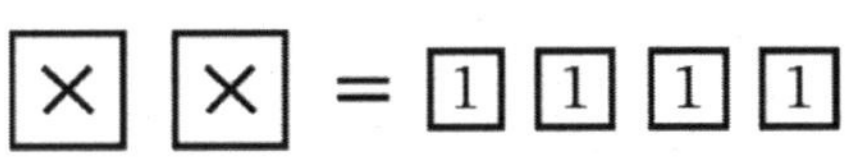

5. The data tables show the relationship between x and y.

Data Set 1

x	y
1	2.5
2	5
5	12.5
10	25

Data Set 2

x	y
1	3.5
2	4.5
5	7.5
10	12.5

Which statement describes the relationship between x and y?

a. Both data sets are additive relationships. In data set 1, y is 1.5 more than x, and in data set 2, y is 2.5 more than x.
b. Both data sets are multiplicative relationships. In data set 1, y is 2.5 times as much as x, and in data set 2, y is 3.5 times as much as x.
c. Data set 1 is a multiplicative relationship and data set 2 is an additive relationship. In data set 1, y is 2.5 times as much as x, and in data set 2, y is 2.5 more than x.
d. Data set 1 is an additive relationship and data set 2 is a multiplicative relationship. In data set 1, y is 1.5 more than x, and in data set 2, y is 2.5 times as much as x.

6. A blueprint of a trapezoidal backyard is pictured below.

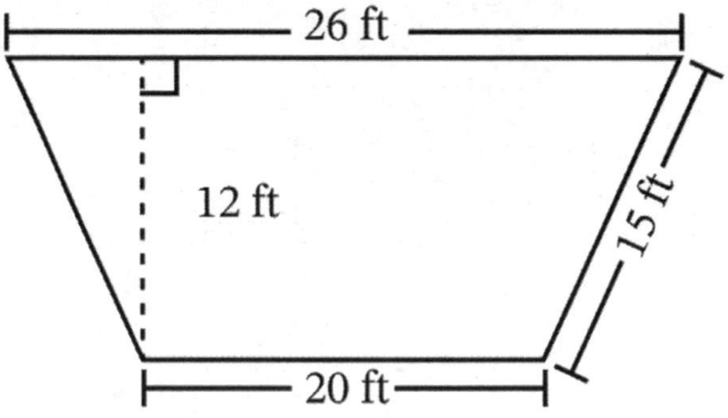

What is the area of the backyard in square feet?

a. $552\ ft^2$
b. $276\ ft^2$
c. $690\ ft^2$
d. $345\ ft^2$

7. 5 out of 8 animals at the shelter are dogs. What is $\frac{5}{8}$ as a decimal? Write your answer in the blank below.

8. The table lists the average temperatures in Dallas, Texas over 2 weeks.

Week 1	87	89	87	92	95	98	95
Week 2	96	102	100	98	96	90	92

What is the range of temperatures listed?

9. Select the correct answer for each blank below. The bar graph below describes a set of data.

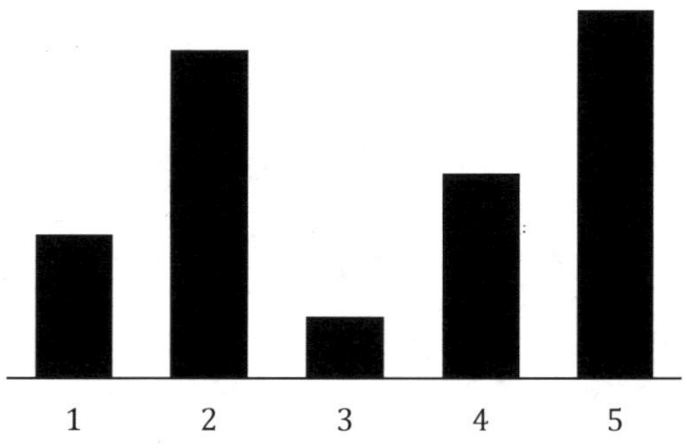

What is true about the data distribution?

The data has __________ at _______.

a gap	2 and 5
peaks	3
symmetry	1 and 4

10. Use the graph below to plot the following ordered pairs:

$$R = (-3,2)$$
$$S = (-1,3)$$
$$T = (3,-6)$$
$$U = (-5,-5)$$

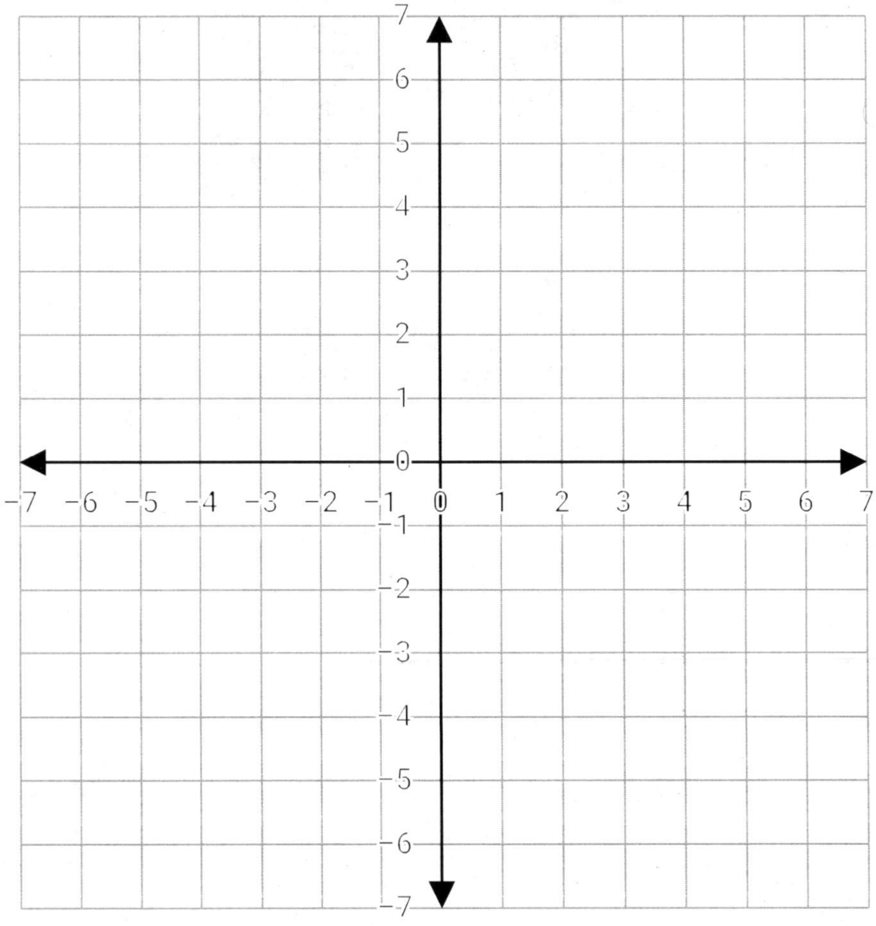

11. Choose the correct answer for each blank below. What is true of the examples below?

Example 1	Example 2
$2x + 4 - x$	$2x - x = -4$

Example 1 is an __________ and Example 2 is an ___________.

equation / expression — equation / expression

12. Add a point and arrow to the number line to represent the solution to $25x \leq 150$?

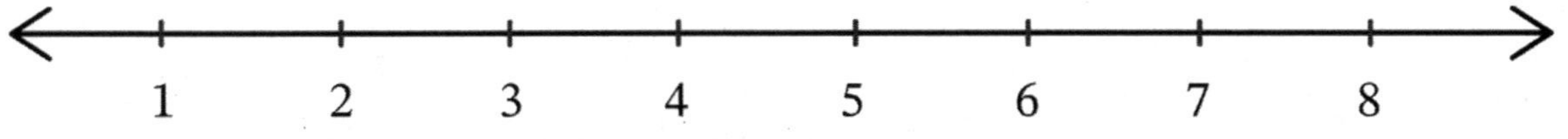

13. The stem-and-leaf plot describes the class sizes in a middle school.

Stem	Leaf
2	2 4 4 4 6 7 8 8
3	0 1 1 3 5

Which statement is true about the data on the stem-and-leaf plot?

a. Exactly half of the classrooms have fewer than 30 students.
b. 4 classrooms have a total of 24 students.
c. No classrooms have the same number of students.
d. 5 classrooms have 30 or more students.

14. Akita is thinking of a number. The number is the opposite of 7. What must be true about Akita's number?

I. The number is 7.
II. The number is −7.
III. The number has an absolute value of 7.
IV. The number has an absolute value of −7.

a. II and III
b. I and III
c. II and IV
d. I and IV

15. Which situation best represents the inequality $12.5x \geq 375$?

a. Dustin can ride his bike 12.5 miles per hour and rides 375 miles in x hours.
b. Darla needs to drive at least 375 minutes to get her driver's permit and has driven 12.5 minutes so far and has x number of minutes remaining.
c. Desiree makes $12.5 per hour and made more than $375 over x hours.
d. Desmond has a goal of making at least 375 bracelets and makes 12.5 bracelets each day for x days.

16. Quing is planning to go to college and has applied for some payment assistance programs. Quing was awarded payment assistance by submitting a high-quality essay and demonstrating high achievement in math and science. Quing does not need to pay the money back. What type of payment assistance did Quing receive?

a. Student Loan
b. Grant
c. Scholarship
d. Work-study

17. Elyse wrote a list of values.

$0.23, \frac{20}{100}, 45\%, 0.6, \frac{2}{5}$

Which list correctly orders the values from greatest to least?

a. $45\%, \frac{2}{5}, \frac{20}{100}, 0.6, 0.23$
b. $0.6, 45\%, \frac{2}{5}, 0.23, \frac{20}{100}$
c. $0.6, 45\%, 0.23, \frac{2}{5}, \frac{20}{100}$
d. $45\%, 0.6, \frac{2}{5}, 0.23, \frac{20}{100}$

18. Which two expressions are equivalent to $5^3 + 4 \cdot 7 + 6$? Select all that apply.

a. $(125 + 4) \cdot 13$
b. $125 + 28 + 6$
c. $(25 \cdot 5) + (4 \cdot 13)$
d. $(5 \cdot 5 \cdot 5) + (4 \cdot 7 \cdot 6)$
e. $25 \cdot 5 + 34$

19. The table shows the rate a babysitter charges for babysitting services.

Hours	Dollars
3	30
5	50
6	60
8	80

Which best represents the dependent variable in the table?

a. Hours
b. Dollars
c. Dollars per hour
d. $10 per hour

20. Point J, K, L, and M are labeled on a number line.

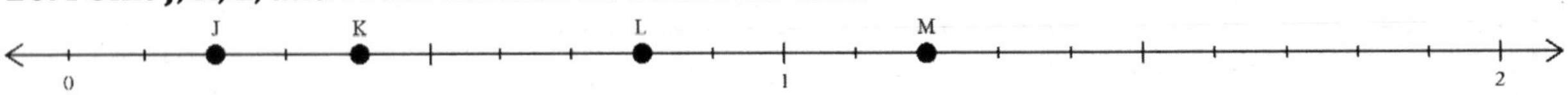

Which point best represents the placement of $\frac{2}{5}$ on the number line?

a. Point J
b. Point K
c. Point L
d. Point M

21. Which percentage is equivalent to $\frac{5}{8}$?

a. 16%
b. 58%
c. 62.5%
d. 60%

22. Which is NOT an impact of having negative items on a credit report?

a. A financial institution may charge more money on interest on a loan if there are negative items.
b. A financial institution may not choose to lend money if there are negative items.
c. A negative item will stay on the credit report for 7-10 years.
d. A negative item may cause someone to go bankrupt.

23. The table shows the number of rare cards in sets of card collector packs.

Number of Rare Cards	Number of Packs
5	8
15	24
45	72
25	40

How many rare cards will be in a box with 136 packs?

a. 85
b. 90
c. 125
d. 75

24. A recipe calls for 5 cups of flour for every 2 cups of sugar. Azah wrote a proportion to find the amount of sugar needed with 8 cups of flour. Which proportion could Azah have written?

a. $\frac{2}{5} = \frac{8}{x}$
b. $\frac{2}{8} = \frac{x}{5}$
c. $\frac{5}{8} = \frac{2}{x}$
d. $\frac{5}{2} = \frac{8}{x}$

25. Allison is making lemonade. She uses 3 cups of sugar for every 2 gallons of water. Which ratio of sugar to water would make a lemonade with the same sweetness?

a. 10 : 6
b. 2 : 3
c. 12 : 8
d. 27 : 16

26. Which expression is represented on the number line?

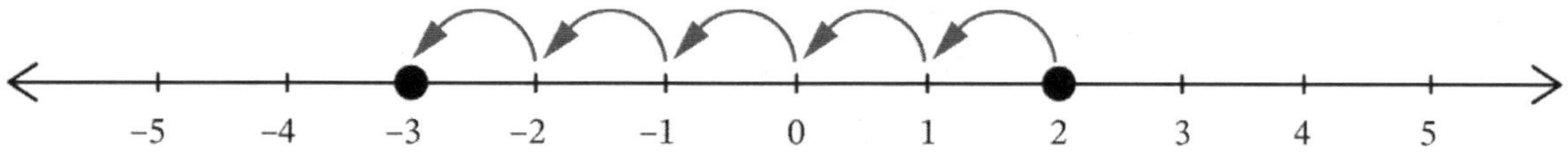

Write your answer in the blank below.

27. What is the solution for the equation $\frac{x}{24} = -6$?

a. 4
b. −4
c. 144
d. −144

28. A social media company creates 75 posts per hour. Add four points to the graph that represent the relationship between the number of posts, y, and hours worked, x.

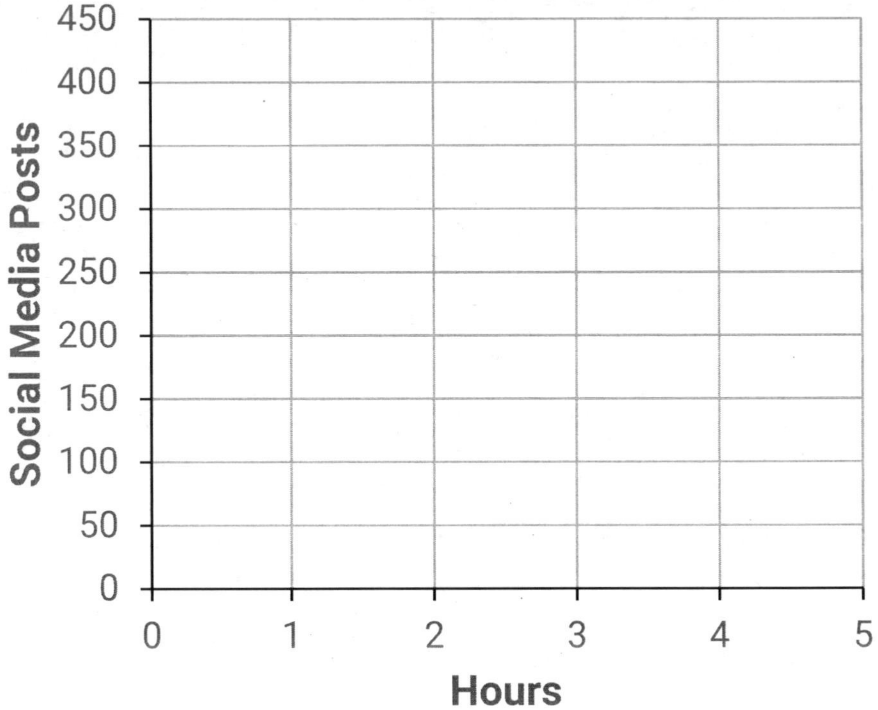

29. Are the following expressions equivalent to 7,536? Mark your answer for each expression in the table below:

Expression	Equal to 7,536	NOT Equal to 7,536
$(3 \cdot 2{,}000) + (3 \cdot 500) + (3 \cdot 12)$		
$(25 \cdot 300) + (18 \cdot 2)$		
$(7 \cdot 1{,}000) + (53 \cdot 100) + 6$		
$(5 \cdot 500) + (5 \cdot 1{,}000) + (9 \cdot 4)$		
$(2 \cdot 3{,}500) + (5 \cdot 200) + (4 \cdot 9)$		

30. A rectangular prism is pictured below.

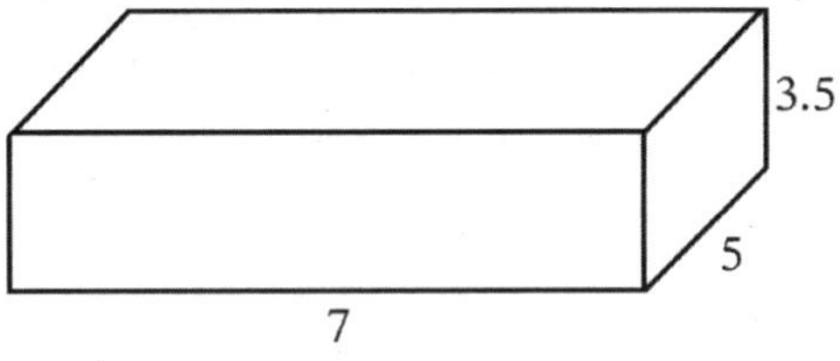

What is the volume of the rectangular prism in cubed units?

a. 122.5 un^3
b. 105.5 un^3
c. 35 un^3
d. 15.5 un^3

31. The length of a classroom is 7.3 meters. Which length is equivalent to 7.3 meters?

a. 0.0073 kilometers
b. 7,300 centimeters
c. 0.073 kilometers
d. 73 millimeters

32. Mr. Chavez took a poll of students' favorite book genres. The results of the survey are represented by the percent bar graph.

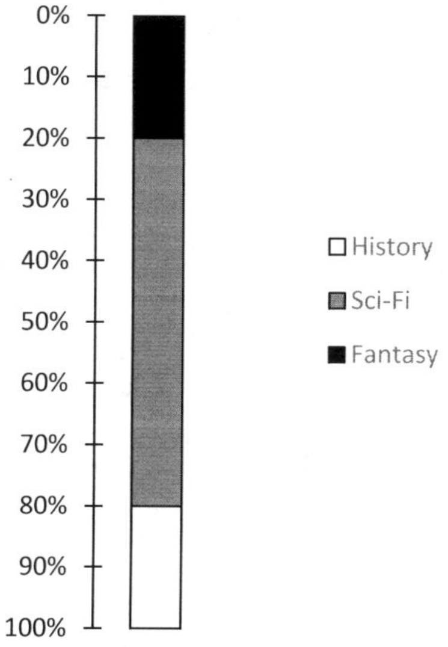

Which table could NOT be the data taken from the survey?

a.

Genre	Votes
Fantasy	7
Sci-Fi	21
History	7

b.

Genre	Votes
Fantasy	5
Sci-Fi	15
History	5

c.

Genre	Votes
Fantasy	12
Sci-Fi	36
History	12

d.

Genre	Votes
Fantasy	15
Sci-Fi	30
History	15

33. The diagram represents the relationship between whole numbers, integers, and rational numbers.

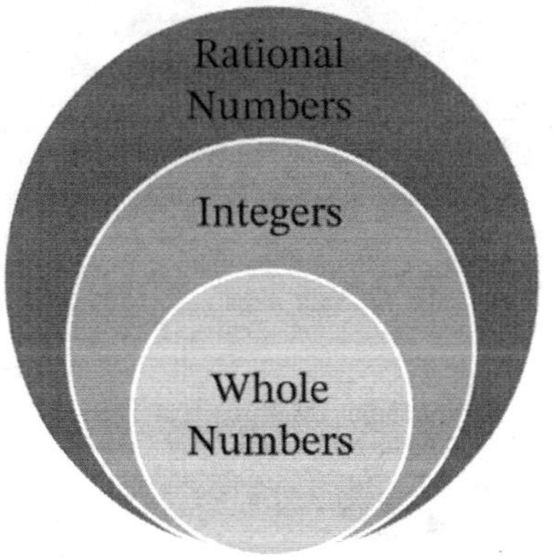

Write the following values in the correct categories on the diagram above.

$-\sqrt{64}$	$\frac{33}{2}$	32.4	467

34. An illustrated recipe is shown below.

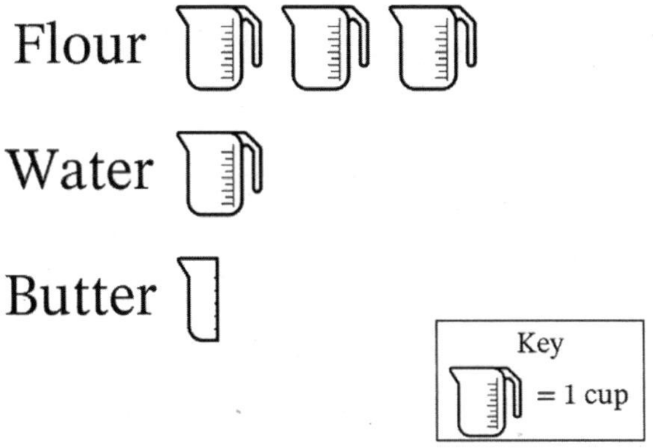

What is the ratio of flour to water?

a. 1 : 3
b. 1 : 2
c. 3 : 1
d. 2 : 1

35. Choose the correct answer for each blank below. Tommy is 4 years older than Gianna. Which equation represents the relationship between Tommy's age, *t*, and Gianna's age, *g*?

_______	=	_______
$4 + t$		g
$4 + g$		4
$4 - t$		t
$g - t$		

36. A waiter was paid a 23% tip on a dinner that cost $56. How much was the waiter's tip in dollars? Write your answer in the blank below:

Answer Key and Explanations for Test #2

1. A: TEKS Standard (6.3)(B)

The product of 5 and $\frac{1}{2}$ is the same as the value of $5 \cdot \frac{1}{2}$. The product of a whole number multiplied by a fraction is less than the whole number. 5 times $\frac{1}{2}$ must be less than 5. The product cannot be greater than 5, and the product must be greater than 1 and $\frac{1}{2}$ because $5 \cdot \frac{1}{2} = \frac{5}{2}$ which is greater than 1 and $\frac{1}{2}$.

2. A: TEKS Standard (6.5)(B)

There is more than one way to solve this problem. One strategy would be to use division. There were 85 kids' meals sold out of 250 total, which can be represented by the division problem $\frac{\text{85 kids' meals}}{\text{250 total meals}}$. $85 \div 250 = 0.34$. A percentage is a value out of 100, and 0.34 can be converted to a percentage by multiplying by 100. $0.34 \cdot 100 = 34$, so 34% of the meals sold were kids' meals.

3. 62: TEKS Standard (6.8)(A)

This problem focuses on triangle angle measurements. The sum of all angles of a triangle is 180°. This means that Jamie's triangle angle measurements could be described using the equation $23 + 95 + x = 180$ where $x = 180 - 23 - 95 = 62$.

tens place as the "stem" and the digit in the ones place as the "leaf", where the first row will include 1: 4, 4, 4, 7, 8, 9, 9 and the next row will include 2: 0, 1, 1, 2, 5.

4. D: TEKS Standard (6.10)(B)

This problem focuses on modeling equations. If $x = 2$, the first model represents the equation $3x = 7$, or $3 \cdot 2 = 7$, which is not true because $6 \neq 7$. The second model represents the equation $3x + 2 = 3 + x$, or $6 + 2 = 3 + 2$, which is not true because $8 \neq 5$. The third model represents the equation $2x + 2 = 4$, or $4 + 2 = 4$, which is not true because $6 \neq 4$. The fourth model represents the equation $2x = 4$, or $2 \cdot 2 = 4$, which is a true statement because $4 = 4$.

5. C: TEKS Standard (6.4)(A)

This question includes two data tables that describe the relationships between x and y. In data set 1, the y values are 2.5 times x, which is a multiplicative relationship, $y = 2.5x$. In data set 2, the y values are 2.5 more than x, which is an additive relationship, $y = x + 2.5$.

6. B: TEKS Standard (6.8)(D)

This problem focuses on using the area formula of a trapezoid. The reference sheet can be used to find the area formula for a trapezoid: $A = \frac{1}{2}(b_1 + b_2) \cdot h$. Using the diagram and the formula, $A = \frac{1}{2}(20 + 26) \cdot 12 = \frac{1}{2}(46) \cdot 12 = 23 \cdot 12 = 276\ \text{ft}^2$.

7. 0.625: TEKS Standard (6.4)(G)

This problem focuses on converting a fraction to a decimal. One way to convert a fraction to a decimal is using division. The decimal form of $\frac{5}{8}$ can be found by solving 5 divided by 8. By using long division, $\frac{5}{8} = 0.625$.

8. 15: TEKS Standard (6.12)(C)

This problem focuses on finding the range in a data set. The range of a data set is the difference between the least and greatest values. In this table, the lowest temperature is 87° and the highest temperature is 102°. $102 - 87 = 15$, so the range of the data set is 15.

9. peaks, 2 and 5: TEKS Standard (6.12)(B)

This problem focuses on interpreting a data distribution. Based on the bar graph, the data does peak at 2 and 5. This is visible on the graph because the bar for 2 is much taller than the bars for 1 and 3, and the bar for 5 is much taller than the bar for 4. The data is not symmetrical because when split down the middle, in this case, at the category labeled 3, the shape of the data is not the same on both sides. There is no gap at all because there are no items with the value of zero. The data does not peak at 3, as the bar for 3 is the shortest of all the bars on the graph.

10. D: TEKS Standard (6.11)(A)

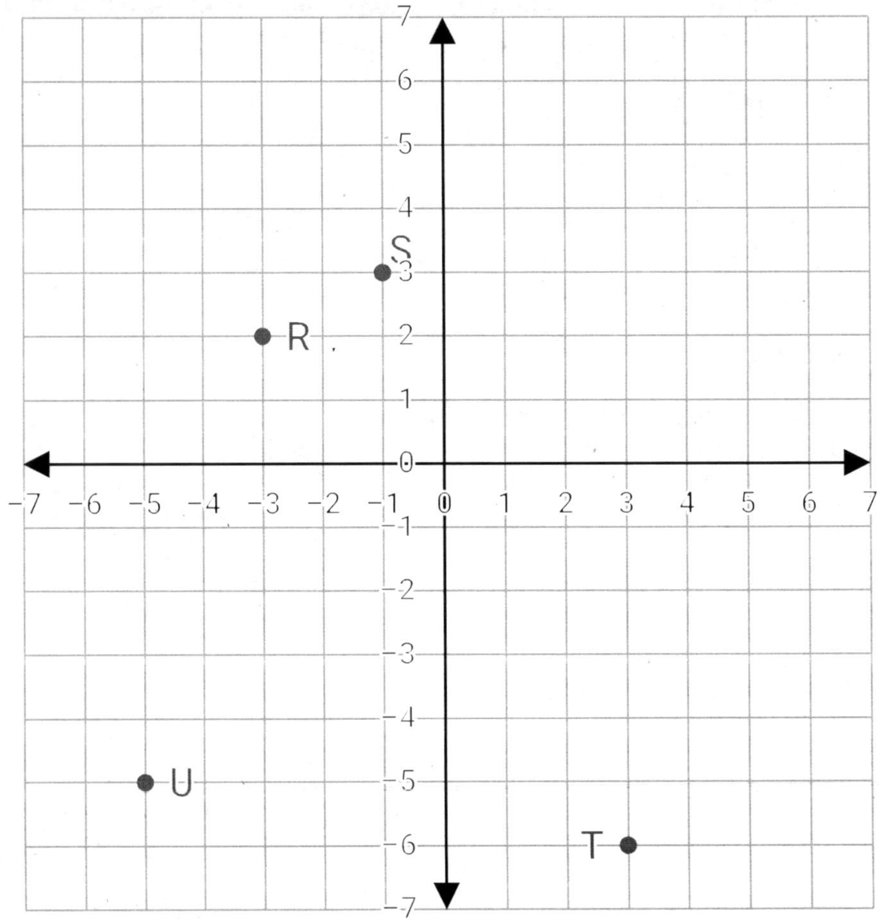

This problem focuses on identifying coordinate points, or ordered pairs, on a coordinate plane. The given ordered pairs are $(-1,3)$, $(-3,2)$, $(-5,-5)$, and $(3,-6)$. Remember that the x value in an ordered pair shows how far to the left or right the point is from 0. If the x value is negative, the point will be to the left of 0, and if it is positive, the point will be to the right of 0. The y value shows how far above or below the point is from 0. If the y value is negative, the point will be below 0, and if it is positive, the point will be above zero.

11. expression, equation: TEKS Standard (6.7)(B)

This problem focuses on the difference between an equation and an expression. An expression is a number, variable, or group of numbers, variables, and operations. Expressions are often meant to be simplified, can stand alone, and can be found on one side of an equal sign. An equation is a group of expressions separated by an equal sign. Equations are often meant to be solved, usually solving for a variable. In this problem, $2x + 4 - x$ is a group of numbers, variables, and operations that does not include an equal sign, so Example 1 is an expression. $2x - x = -4$ is a set of expressions; $2x - x$ and –4 are both expressions. These expressions are separated by an equal sign, so Example 2 is an equation.

12. A: TEKS Standard (6.9)(B)

This problem focuses on graphing the solution to an inequality. If $25x \leq 150$, then $x \leq 6$ because $150 \div 25 = 6$. An inequality is graphed on a number line by notating the solution for x. If $x \leq 6$, 6 will be notated by a closed circle because x could be equal to 6, and the arrow will be pointing to the left of 6 because if x is not 6, it is less than 6.

13. D: TEKS Standard (6.13)(A)

This problem focuses on interpreting data from a stem-and-leaf plot. Based on the stem-and-leaf plot, the number of students in each class could be listed as 22, 24, 24, 24, 26, 27, 28, 28, 30, 31, 31, 33, and 35. It is not true that exactly half of the classrooms have fewer than 30 students because 8 out of 13 classrooms have fewer than 30 students. It is not true that 4 classrooms have 24 students because only 3 classrooms have 24 students. It is not true that no classrooms have the same number of students because 3 classrooms have 24 students and 2 classrooms have 31 students. It is true that 5 classrooms have 30 or more students because there are 5 values that are greater than or equal to 30.

14. A: TEKS Standard (6.2)(B)

The number Akita is thinking of is the opposite of 7. The opposite of a number is the value that is the same distance from zero on the other side of a number line. Akita must be thinking of the number −7. The absolute value of a number is its distance from zero. When looking at a number line, −7 is 7 away from zero, so the absolute value of −7 is 7. The true statements about Akita's number are II: the number is −7, and III: the number has an absolute value of 7.

15. D: TEKS Standard (6.9)(C)

The inequality $12.5x \geq 375$ means that 375 is less than or equal to 12.5 times a value x, or a value x times 12.5 is greater than or equal to 375. Option A describes an equation where $12.5x = 375$. Option B describes the inequality $12.5 + x \geq 375$. Option C describes the inequality $12.5x > 375$. Option D describes the inequality $375 \leq 12.5x$ because Desmond makes 12.5 bracelets each day for x days, $12.5x$, and has a goal of making at least 375 bracelets, which means that $12.5x$ must be greater than or equal to 375.

16. C: TEKS Standard (6.14)(G)

This problem focuses on identifying different methods to pay for college. Quing applied for this assistance by writing an essay and demonstrating high achievement, and this assistance does not need to be paid back. This best describes a scholarship. Student loans must be paid back. Grants are generally based on need rather than scholastic achievement. Work-study gives the student an opportunity to work for money but does not give the student the money outright.

17. B: TEKS Standard (6.2)(D)

There are many ways to order the given values. One way is to convert all values to decimals. 0.23 and 0.6 are already in decimal form. $\frac{20}{100}$ is equivalent to 0.2, 45% is equivalent to 0.45, and $\frac{2}{5}$ is equivalent to 0.4. These decimal values listed from greatest to least are 0.6, 0.45, 0.4, 0.23, 0.2.

18. B, E: TEKS Standard (6.7)(A)

This problem focuses on equivalent expressions using order of operations and exponents. There are many strategies that can be used to solve this problem. One way to solve this problem is to gradually simplify the expression and compare to the options. The first step to simplify the given expression is to simplify the exponents. The expression 5^3 is equivalent to many expressions, including $5 \cdot 5 \cdot 5$, $25 \cdot 5$, and 125. Each option includes an equivalent expression to 5^3. The next step to simplifying the expression is to multiply 4 and 7, which is 28. Option A shows the expression $(125 + 4) \cdot 13$, where addition is performed before multiplication when $7 + 6$ is solved before multiplying 4 and 7. Option B shows the expression $125 + 28 + 6$, which shows that 5 has been cubed and 4 and 7 have been multiplied before any addition has taken place. Option C shows the expression $(25 \cdot 5) + (4 \cdot 13)$, where, again, addition is performed before multiplication when $7 + 6$ is solved before multiplying 4 and 7. Option D shows the expression $(5 \cdot 5 \cdot 5) + (4 \cdot 7 \cdot 6)$ where the addition operation $7 + 6$ is changed to multiplication. Option E shows the expression $25 \cdot 5 + 34$ where each operation is performed in the correct order when the multiplication of 4 and 7 is performed and then 6 is added to the product.

19. B: TEKS Standard (6.6)(A)

In this table, the x values represent the number of hours and the y values represent the number of dollars. The number of hours is the independent value because the number of dollars is dependent on the number of hours.

20. B: TEKS Standard (6.2)(C)

The are many ways to identify $\frac{2}{5}$ on the number line. Two items to note with any number line problem are the first and last value on the number line. This number line starts at 0 and ends at 2. The next item to note is the number of lines. This number line has 20 small lines dividing 0 and 2. This means that each line represents one tenth. One strategy to identify $\frac{2}{5}$ would be to first estimate the placement. $\frac{2}{5}$ is less than 1, so this point will lie between 0 and 1. The next step would be to convert $\frac{2}{5}$ to tenths. This can be done using division to find a decimal or equivalent fractions to find a fraction. Using either method, $\frac{2}{5}$ is equivalent to 0.4, or $\frac{4}{10}$. This can be placed on the number line at 4 tenths to the right of 0, at point K.

21. C: TEKS Standard (6.5)(C)

This problem focuses on equivalent percentages and fractions. To find the equivalent percentage to $\frac{5}{8}$, division can be performed and the decimal quotient can be multiplied by 100.

$$5 \div 8 = 0.625$$
$$0.625 \cdot 100 = 62.5\%.$$

22. D: TEKS Standard (6.14)(E)

This problem focuses on understanding the impact of negative items on a credit report. A credit report is a report that financial institutions use to decide if someone is responsible enough to borrow money. Negative items can stay on a credit report for 7-10 years, may cause a financial institution to charge more money on interest on a loan, or may cause a financial institution to refuse to lend money to someone based on the negative items. Bankruptcy is not caused by negative items, but instead is an example of a negative item.

23. A: TEKS Standard (6.4)(B)

The problem focuses on equivalent rates and ratios. There are many ways to solve this problem. One strategy is to use decimal unit rates. The rate of rare cards to packs is 5 rare cards per 8 packs, or $\frac{5}{8}$ cards per pack, which equals 0.625 cards per pack. This also works with 15 rare cards per 24 packs, $\frac{15}{24}$ cards per pack, which also equals 0.625 cards per pack. If the rate of rare cards to packs is 0.625 cards to packs, and $0.625 \times 136 = 85$, then there are 85 rare cards in a box of 136 packs.

24. D: TEKS Standard (6.5)(A)

This problem focuses on using proportions to solve a problem. If a recipe calls for 5 cups of flour for every 2 cups of sugar, the ratio of flour to sugar is $\frac{5}{2}$. If Azah needs to know the number of cups of sugar used for 8 cups of flour, this ratio of flour to sugar can be expressed by $\frac{8}{x}$, where x represents the number of cups of sugar. The ratio of flour to sugar stays proportional, which means that $\frac{5}{2} = \frac{8}{x}$.

25. C: TEKS Standard (6.4)(C)

In the story, Allison is making lemonade and uses a ratio of 3 cups of sugar to every 2 gallons of water, or $3 : 2$. A lemonade with the same sweetness would have a ratio that is equivalent to $3 : 2$. One way to solve this problem is to find equivalent ratios using multiplication. $3 : 2$ is equivalent to $6 : 4, 9 : 6, 12 : 8, 15 : 10, 18 : 12, 21 : 14, 24 : 16$, and so on. $12 : 8$ is equivalent to $3 : 2$.

26. $2 - 5$: TEKS Standard (6.3)(C)

The number line begins at 2 and jumps 5 spaces to the left and lands on −3. This illustrates the expression $2 - 1 - 1 - 1 - 1 - 1$, which is equivalent to $2 - 5$.

27. D: TEKS Standard (6.10)(A)

This problem focuses on solving equations with one variable. To solve the equation $\frac{x}{24} = -6$, the goal is to isolate x, or have x alone on one side of the equal sign. To isolate x, each side of the equal sign should be multiplied by 24. $\frac{x}{24} = -6$ can be simplified to $24 \cdot \frac{x}{24} = -6 \cdot 24$, which is further simplified to $x = -144$.

28. TEKS Standard (6.6)(C)

Correct points may be any four of the following:

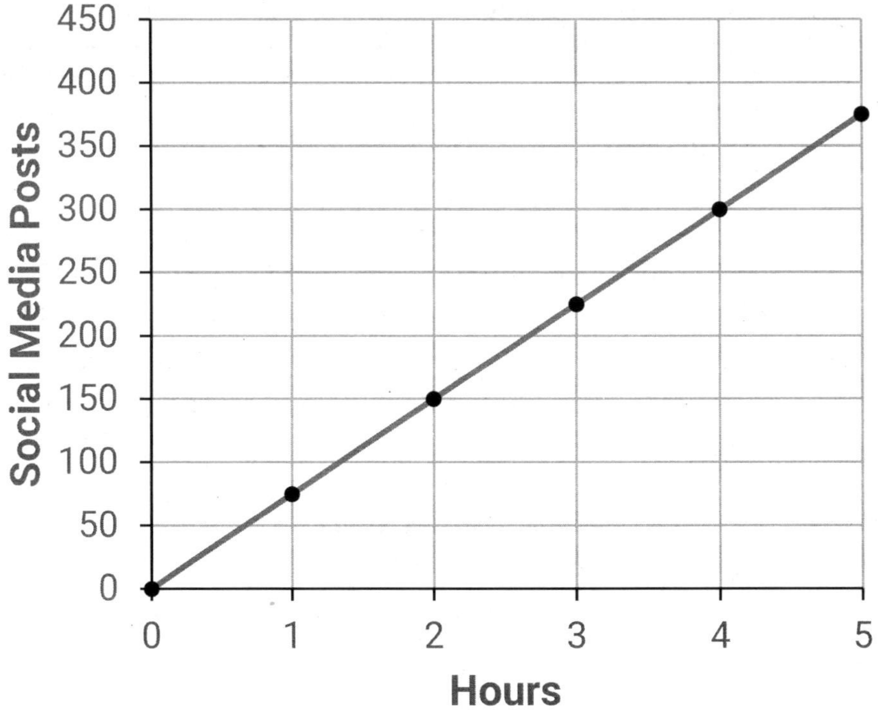

This problem focuses on graphs that represent relationships in a story. If a company creates 75 posts each hour, the equation that represents the story is $y = 75x$, where each y value is 75 times the corresponding x value. This means that after 0 hours, the company would create 0 posts. After 1 hour, the company would create 75 posts. After 2 hours, the company would create 150 posts, and so on. The ordered pairs (0,0), (1,75), (2,150), (3,225), (4,300), (5,375) can be used to represent this relationship on the given coordinate grid.

29. TEKS Standard (6.3)(E)

Expression	Equal to 7,536	NOT Equal to 7,536
$(3 \cdot 2{,}000) + (3 \cdot 500) + (3 \cdot 12)$	X	
$(25 \cdot 300) + (18 \cdot 2)$	X	
$(7 \cdot 1{,}000) + (53 \cdot 100) + 6$		X
$(5 \cdot 500) + (5 \cdot 1{,}000) + (9 \cdot 4)$	X	
$(2 \cdot 3{,}500) + (5 \cdot 200) + (4 \cdot 9)$		X

To solve this problem, each expression should be simplified to see if it is equivalent to 7,536. First, $(3 \cdot 2{,}000) + (3 \cdot 500) + (3 \cdot 12) = 6{,}000 + 1{,}500 + 36 = 7{,}536$. Next, $(25 \cdot 300) + (18 \cdot 2) = 7{,}500 + 36 = 7{,}536$. Then, $(7 \cdot 1{,}000) + (53 \cdot 100) + 6 = 7{,}000 + 5{,}300 + 6 = 12{,}306$. Fourth, $(5 \cdot 500) + (5 \cdot 1{,}000) + (9 \cdot 4) = 2{,}500 + 5{,}000 + 36 = 7{,}536$. And finally, $(2 \cdot 3{,}500) + (5 \cdot 200) + (4 \cdot 9) = 7{,}000 + 1{,}000 + 36 = 8{,}036$.

30. A: TEKS Standard (6.8)(D)

This problem focuses on using the volume formula for a rectangular prism. The reference sheet can be used to find the volume formula of a rectangular prism, $V = Bh$, where B is the area of the base of the rectangular prism. An equivalent formula for the area of a rectangular prism is $V = lwh$. The equation $V = 7 \cdot 3.5 \cdot 5$ can be used to find the volume of the rectangular prism, and $7 \cdot 3.5 \cdot 5 = 122.5$.

31. A: TEKS Standard (6.4)(H)

This problem focuses on converting measurements. The conversion sheet can be used to find that 1 meter is equivalent to 100 centimeters, so 7.3 meters is equivalent to 730 centimeters because $7.3 \cdot 100 = 730$. Also, 1 centimeter is equivalent to 10 millimeters, so 7.3 meters is equivalent to 7,300 millimeters because $7.3 \cdot 1{,}000 = 7{,}300$. Lastly, 1 kilometer is equivalent to 1,000 meters, so 7.3 meters is equivalent to 0.0073 kilometers because $7.3 \div 1{,}000 = 0.0073$.

32. D: TEKS Standard (6.12)(D)

This problem focuses on data from percent bar graphs. To solve this problem, the percentage of each item on each table should be found to compare to the percent bar graph. The first table has a total of 35 votes, where fantasy received 20%, sci-fi received 60%, and history received 20% of the votes. The second table has a total of 25 votes, where fantasy received 20%, sci-fi received 60%, and history received 20% of the votes. The third table has a total of 60 votes, where fantasy received 20%, sci-fi received 60%, and history received 20% of the votes. The fourth table has a total of 60 votes, where fantasy received 25% of the votes, sci fi received 50% of the votes, and history received 25% of the votes.

33.$-\sqrt{64}$:Integers, $\frac{33}{2}$:Rational Numbers, 32. 4: Rational Numbers, 467: Whole Numbers: TEKS Standard (6.2)(A)

This problem focuses on categorizing number values. $-\sqrt{64}$ is equivalent to −8 which is a negative number that can be written without a fraction, so $-\sqrt{64}$ is an integer. $\frac{33}{2}$ is equivalent to 16.5, which can be written as a fraction. However, it cannot be expressed without a fraction or decimal, so it cannot be an integer or a whole number. The same is true of 32.4, which can be written as the fraction $\frac{324}{10}$ or $\frac{162}{5}$. 467 is a positive integer, so it belongs in the "whole number" category.

34. C: TEKS Standard (6.4)(E)

This problem focuses on ratio models. The ratio of flour to water can be found by reviewing the illustration. There are 3 cups of flour and 1 cup of water, which shows that the ratio of flour to water is 3 : 1.

35. $4 + g, t$: TEKS Standard (6.6)(C)

Tommy's age is 4 more than Gianna's age. For example, if Tommy is 13 years old, Gianna is 9 years old. Tommy's age, t, is Gianna's age, g, plus 4. If t is used to represent Tommy's age and g is used to represent Gianna's age, then the equation $t + 4 = g$ can be used to represent the relationship in the story.

36. 12.88: TEKS Standard (6.5)(B)

There are many ways to solve this problem. One strategy to find a percentage of a total is to multiply the total by a decimal form of the percentage. 23% is equivalent to 0.23. To find 23% of \$56, multiply 56 by 23%. $56 \cdot 0.23 = 12.88$, which means the waiter's tip was 12.88 dollars.

Practice Test #3

To take this additional STAAR practice test, visit our online resources page:
mometrix.com/resources719/staarg6math

How to Overcome Test Anxiety

Just the thought of taking a test is enough to make most people a little nervous. A test is an important event that can have a long-term impact on your future, so it's important to take it seriously and it's natural to feel anxious about performing well. But just because anxiety is normal, that doesn't mean that it's helpful in test taking, or that you should simply accept it as part of your life. Anxiety can have a variety of effects. These effects can be mild, like making you feel slightly nervous, or severe, like blocking your ability to focus or remember even a simple detail.

If you experience test anxiety—whether severe or mild—it's important to know how to beat it. To discover this, first you need to understand what causes test anxiety.

Causes of Test Anxiety

While we often think of anxiety as an uncontrollable emotional state, it can actually be caused by simple, practical things. One of the most common causes of test anxiety is that a person does not feel adequately prepared for their test. This feeling can be the result of many different issues such as poor study habits or lack of organization, but the most common culprit is time management. Starting to study too late, failing to organize your study time to cover all of the material, or being distracted while you study will mean that you're not well prepared for the test. This may lead to cramming the night before, which will cause you to be physically and mentally exhausted for the test. Poor time management also contributes to feelings of stress, fear, and hopelessness as you realize you are not well prepared but don't know what to do about it.

Other times, test anxiety is not related to your preparation for the test but comes from unresolved fear. This may be a past failure on a test, or poor performance on tests in general. It may come from comparing yourself to others who seem to be performing better or from the stress of living up to expectations. Anxiety may be driven by fears of the future—how failure on this test would affect your educational and career goals. These fears are often completely irrational, but they can still negatively impact your test performance.

Elements of Test Anxiety

As mentioned earlier, test anxiety is considered to be an emotional state, but it has physical and mental components as well. Sometimes you may not even realize that you are suffering from test anxiety until you notice the physical symptoms. These can include trembling hands, rapid heartbeat, sweating, nausea, and tense muscles. Extreme anxiety may lead to fainting or vomiting. Obviously, any of these symptoms can have a negative impact on testing. It is important to recognize them as soon as they begin to occur so that you can address the problem before it damages your performance.

The mental components of test anxiety include trouble focusing and inability to remember learned information. During a test, your mind is on high alert, which can help you recall information and stay focused for an extended period of time. However, anxiety interferes with your mind's natural processes, causing you to blank out, even on the questions you know well. The strain of testing during anxiety makes it difficult to stay focused, especially on a test that may take several hours. Extreme anxiety can take a huge mental toll, making it difficult not only to recall test information but even to understand the test questions or pull your thoughts together.

Effects of Test Anxiety

Test anxiety is like a disease—if left untreated, it will get progressively worse. Anxiety leads to poor performance, and this reinforces the feelings of fear and failure, which in turn lead to poor performances on subsequent tests. It can grow from a mild nervousness to a crippling condition. If allowed to progress, test anxiety can have a big impact on your schooling, and consequently on your future.

Test anxiety can spread to other parts of your life. Anxiety on tests can become anxiety in any stressful situation, and blanking on a test can turn into panicking in a job situation. But fortunately, you don't have to let anxiety rule your testing and determine your grades. There are a number of relatively simple steps you can take to move past anxiety and function normally on a test and in the rest of life.

Physical Steps for Beating Test Anxiety

While test anxiety is a serious problem, the good news is that it can be overcome. It doesn't have to control your ability to think and remember information. While it may take time, you can begin taking steps today to beat anxiety.

Just as your first hint that you may be struggling with anxiety comes from the physical symptoms, the first step to treating it is also physical. Rest is crucial for having a clear, strong mind. If you are tired, it is much easier to give in to anxiety. But if you establish good sleep habits, your body and mind will be ready to perform optimally, without the strain of exhaustion. Additionally, sleeping well helps you to retain information better, so you're more likely to recall the answers when you see the test questions.

Getting good sleep means more than going to bed on time. It's important to allow your brain time to relax. Take study breaks from time to time so it doesn't get overworked, and don't study right before bed. Take time to rest your mind before trying to rest your body, or you may find it difficult to fall asleep.

Along with sleep, other aspects of physical health are important in preparing for a test. Good nutrition is vital for good brain function. Sugary foods and drinks may give a burst of energy but this burst is followed by a crash, both physically and emotionally. Instead, fuel your body with protein and vitamin-rich foods.

Also, drink plenty of water. Dehydration can lead to headaches and exhaustion, especially if your brain is already under stress from the rigors of the test. Particularly if your test is a long one, drink water during the breaks. And if possible, take an energy-boosting snack to eat between sections.

Along with sleep and diet, a third important part of physical health is exercise. Maintaining a steady workout schedule is helpful, but even taking 5-minute study breaks to walk can help get your blood pumping faster and clear your head. Exercise also releases endorphins, which contribute to a positive feeling and can help combat test anxiety.

When you nurture your physical health, you are also contributing to your mental health. If your body is healthy, your mind is much more likely to be healthy as well. So take time to rest, nourish your body with healthy food and water, and get moving as much as possible. Taking these physical steps will make you stronger and more able to take the mental steps necessary to overcome test anxiety.

Mental Steps for Beating Test Anxiety

Working on the mental side of test anxiety can be more challenging, but as with the physical side, there are clear steps you can take to overcome it. As mentioned earlier, test anxiety often stems from lack of preparation, so the obvious solution is to prepare for the test. Effective studying may be the most important weapon you have for beating test anxiety, but you can and should employ several other mental tools to combat fear.

First, boost your confidence by reminding yourself of past success—tests or projects that you aced. If you're putting as much effort into preparing for this test as you did for those, there's no reason you should expect to fail here. Work hard to prepare; then trust your preparation.

Second, surround yourself with encouraging people. It can be helpful to find a study group, but be sure that the people you're around will encourage a positive attitude. If you spend time with others who are anxious or cynical, this will only contribute to your own anxiety. Look for others who are motivated to study hard from a desire to succeed, not from a fear of failure.

Third, reward yourself. A test is physically and mentally tiring, even without anxiety, and it can be helpful to have something to look forward to. Plan an activity following the test, regardless of the outcome, such as going to a movie or getting ice cream.

When you are taking the test, if you find yourself beginning to feel anxious, remind yourself that you know the material. Visualize successfully completing the test. Then take a few deep, relaxing breaths and return to it. Work through the questions carefully but with confidence, knowing that you are capable of succeeding.

Developing a healthy mental approach to test taking will also aid in other areas of life. Test anxiety affects more than just the actual test—it can be damaging to your mental health and even contribute to depression. It's important to beat test anxiety before it becomes a problem for more than testing.

Study Strategy

Being prepared for the test is necessary to combat anxiety, but what does being prepared look like? You may study for hours on end and still not feel prepared. What you need is a strategy for test prep. The next few pages outline our recommended steps to help you plan out and conquer the challenge of preparation.

Step 1: Scope Out the Test

Learn everything you can about the format (multiple choice, essay, etc.) and what will be on the test. Gather any study materials, course outlines, or sample exams that may be available. Not only will this help you to prepare, but knowing what to expect can help to alleviate test anxiety.

Step 2: Map Out the Material

Look through the textbook or study guide and make note of how many chapters or sections it has. Then divide these over the time you have. For example, if a book has 15 chapters and you have five days to study, you need to cover three chapters each day. Even better, if you have the time, leave an extra day at the end for overall review after you have gone through the material in depth.

If time is limited, you may need to prioritize the material. Look through it and make note of which sections you think you already have a good grasp on, and which need review. While you are studying, skim quickly through the familiar sections and take more time on the challenging parts.

Write out your plan so you don't get lost as you go. Having a written plan also helps you feel more in control of the study, so anxiety is less likely to arise from feeling overwhelmed at the amount to cover.

STEP 3: GATHER YOUR TOOLS

Decide what study method works best for you. Do you prefer to highlight in the book as you study and then go back over the highlighted portions? Or do you type out notes of the important information? Or is it helpful to make flashcards that you can carry with you? Assemble the pens, index cards, highlighters, post-it notes, and any other materials you may need so you won't be distracted by getting up to find things while you study.

If you're having a hard time retaining the information or organizing your notes, experiment with different methods. For example, try color-coding by subject with colored pens, highlighters, or post-it notes. If you learn better by hearing, try recording yourself reading your notes so you can listen while in the car, working out, or simply sitting at your desk. Ask a friend to quiz you from your flashcards, or try teaching someone the material to solidify it in your mind.

STEP 4: CREATE YOUR ENVIRONMENT

It's important to avoid distractions while you study. This includes both the obvious distractions like visitors and the subtle distractions like an uncomfortable chair (or a too-comfortable couch that makes you want to fall asleep). Set up the best study environment possible: good lighting and a comfortable work area. If background music helps you focus, you may want to turn it on, but otherwise keep the room quiet. If you are using a computer to take notes, be sure you don't have any other windows open, especially applications like social media, games, or anything else that could distract you. Silence your phone and turn off notifications. Be sure to keep water close by so you stay hydrated while you study (but avoid unhealthy drinks and snacks).

Also, take into account the best time of day to study. Are you freshest first thing in the morning? Try to set aside some time then to work through the material. Is your mind clearer in the afternoon or evening? Schedule your study session then. Another method is to study at the same time of day that you will take the test, so that your brain gets used to working on the material at that time and will be ready to focus at test time.

STEP 5: STUDY!

Once you have done all the study preparation, it's time to settle into the actual studying. Sit down, take a few moments to settle your mind so you can focus, and begin to follow your study plan. Don't give in to distractions or let yourself procrastinate. This is your time to prepare so you'll be ready to fearlessly approach the test. Make the most of the time and stay focused.

Of course, you don't want to burn out. If you study too long you may find that you're not retaining the information very well. Take regular study breaks. For example, taking five minutes out of every hour to walk briskly, breathing deeply and swinging your arms, can help your mind stay fresh.

As you get to the end of each chapter or section, it's a good idea to do a quick review. Remind yourself of what you learned and work on any difficult parts. When you feel that you've mastered the material, move on to the next part. At the end of your study session, briefly skim through your notes again.

But while review is helpful, cramming last minute is NOT. If at all possible, work ahead so that you won't need to fit all your study into the last day. Cramming overloads your brain with more information than it can process and retain, and your tired mind may struggle to recall even previously learned information when it is overwhelmed with last-minute study. Also, the urgent nature of cramming and the stress placed on your brain contribute to anxiety. You'll be more likely to go to the test feeling unprepared and having trouble thinking clearly.

So don't cram, and don't stay up late before the test, even just to review your notes at a leisurely pace. Your brain needs rest more than it needs to go over the information again. In fact, plan to finish your studies by noon or early afternoon the day before the test. Give your brain the rest of the day to relax or focus on other things, and get a good night's sleep. Then you will be fresh for the test and better able to recall what you've studied.

Step 6: Take a Practice Test

Many courses offer sample tests, either online or in the study materials. This is an excellent resource to check whether you have mastered the material, as well as to prepare for the test format and environment.

Check the test format ahead of time: the number of questions, the type (multiple choice, free response, etc.), and the time limit. Then create a plan for working through them. For example, if you have 30 minutes to take a 60-question test, your limit is 30 seconds per question. Spend less time on the questions you know well so that you can take more time on the difficult ones.

If you have time to take several practice tests, take the first one open book, with no time limit. Work through the questions at your own pace and make sure you fully understand them. Gradually work up to taking a test under test conditions: sit at a desk with all study materials put away and set a timer. Pace yourself to make sure you finish the test with time to spare and go back to check your answers if you have time.

After each test, check your answers. On the questions you missed, be sure you understand why you missed them. Did you misread the question (tests can use tricky wording)? Did you forget the information? Or was it something you hadn't learned? Go back and study any shaky areas that the practice tests reveal.

Taking these tests not only helps with your grade, but also aids in combating test anxiety. If you're already used to the test conditions, you're less likely to worry about it, and working through tests until you're scoring well gives you a confidence boost. Go through the practice tests until you feel comfortable, and then you can go into the test knowing that you're ready for it.

Test Tips

On test day, you should be confident, knowing that you've prepared well and are ready to answer the questions. But aside from preparation, there are several test day strategies you can employ to maximize your performance.

First, as stated before, get a good night's sleep the night before the test (and for several nights before that, if possible). Go into the test with a fresh, alert mind rather than staying up late to study.

Try not to change too much about your normal routine on the day of the test. It's important to eat a nutritious breakfast, but if you normally don't eat breakfast at all, consider eating just a protein bar. If you're a coffee drinker, go ahead and have your normal coffee. Just make sure you time it so that the caffeine doesn't wear off right in the middle of your test. Avoid sugary beverages, and drink enough water to stay hydrated but not so much that you need a restroom break 10 minutes into the test. If your test isn't first thing in the morning, consider going for a walk or doing a light workout before the test to get your blood flowing.

Allow yourself enough time to get ready, and leave for the test with plenty of time to spare so you won't have the anxiety of scrambling to arrive in time. Another reason to be early is to select a good seat. It's helpful to sit away from doors and windows, which can be distracting. Find a good seat, get out your supplies, and settle your mind before the test begins.

When the test begins, start by going over the instructions carefully, even if you already know what to expect. Make sure you avoid any careless mistakes by following the directions.

Then begin working through the questions, pacing yourself as you've practiced. If you're not sure on an answer, don't spend too much time on it, and don't let it shake your confidence. Either skip it and come back later, or eliminate as many wrong answers as possible and guess among the remaining ones. Don't dwell on these questions as you continue—put them out of your mind and focus on what lies ahead.

Be sure to read all of the answer choices, even if you're sure the first one is the right answer. Sometimes you'll find a better one if you keep reading. But don't second-guess yourself if you do immediately know the answer. Your gut instinct is usually right. Don't let test anxiety rob you of the information you know.

If you have time at the end of the test (and if the test format allows), go back and review your answers. Be cautious about changing any, since your first instinct tends to be correct, but make sure you didn't misread any of the questions or accidentally mark the wrong answer choice. Look over any you skipped and make an educated guess.

At the end, leave the test feeling confident. You've done your best, so don't waste time worrying about your performance or wishing you could change anything. Instead, celebrate the successful completion of this test. And finally, use this test to learn how to deal with anxiety even better next time.

Review Video: Test Anxiety
Visit mometrix.com/academy and enter code: 100340

Important Qualification

Not all anxiety is created equal. If your test anxiety is causing major issues in your life beyond the classroom or testing center, or if you are experiencing troubling physical symptoms related to your anxiety, it may be a sign of a serious physiological or psychological condition. If this sounds like your situation, we strongly encourage you to seek professional help.

Online Resources

Due to our efforts to try to keep this book to a manageable length, we've created a link that will give you access to all of your online resources:

mometrix.com/resources719/staarg6math

It's Your Moment, Let's Celebrate It!

Share your story @mometrixtestpreparation